LETTERS FROM A TRAVELLER

During the *Croisière jaune*

PIERRE TEILHARD DE CHARDIN

LETTERS
FROM A
TRAVELLER

HARPER & BROTHERS PUBLISHERS

NEW YORK

GENERAL EDITOR'S NOTE

This, the third of P. Teilhard de Chardin's collected works to appear in English, contains the two French volumes : *Lettres de Voyage, 1923–1939*, and *Nouvelles Lettres de Voyage, 1939–1955*. These collected letters were edited and annotated by Claude Aragonnès (Mlle Teillard-Chambon), the author's cousin. The letters cover and extend beyond the period in which the author was composing *The Phenomenon of Man* and *Le Milieu divin*. By way of special introduction to this volume we have added a translation of *Teilhard de Chardin tel que je l'ai connu* by his colleague and friend, Pierre Leroy (published by Plon), as it throws new light on the author's personality and on his relations with his superiors in religion. We have preserved the introduction to the French edition by Claude Aragonnès, and there is a short note by Sir Julian Huxley, who did much to present Teilhard's scientific work to English-speaking readers at the time of the publication of *The Phenomenon of Man*.

This translation has been achieved after a concerted effort, and readers owe their thanks to the participants : Mr René Hague, Mrs Violet Hammersley, Mrs Barbara Wall, and Mr Nöel Lindsay. A special and additional word of thanks should go to Mr René Hague for the preparation of the volume in the later stages.

BERNARD WALL

Contents

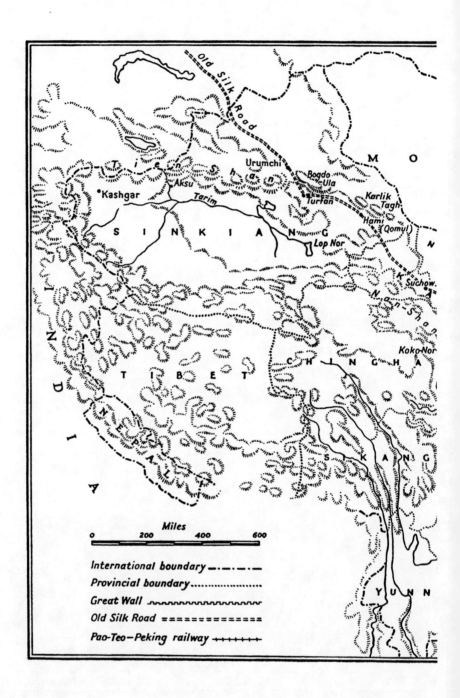

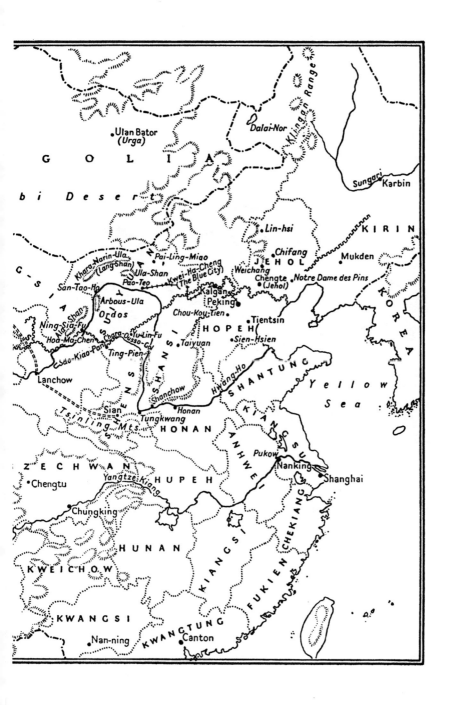

List of Illustrations

THE THINKER *by* SIR JULIAN HUXLEY

Pierre Teilhard de Chardin was a remarkable man. On his mother's side he could claim collateral relationship with Voltaire, on his father's side with Pascal. He was a leading paleontologist, and a wide traveller with an unusual knowledge of the geology of different regions of the world. His paleontological work gave him a consuming interest in the general problem of evolution, while his experience of human societies at different levels and along different directions of cultural advance led him to a new approach to the problem of man and his evolution.

He was forbidden to publish during his lifetime and in consequence his works only appeared after his death. His work is now widely acclaimed and his ideas are exerting a powerful influence on thought, especially in France, and are beginning to bring almost a rapprochement between biologists, theologians and philosophers.

I personally have always been grateful for having known him. We first met soon after I came to Paris as Director-General of Unesco, and immediately established a firm friendship, which lasted until his death. We were both biologists by training, but we both had wide interests outside our specialisms. We had the same broad aim in common—that of exploring the vast process of evolution as fully as possible, of attempting to frame some effective picture of its pattern and of man's place within it, of pursuing its implications into the illimitable future. We both had drawn similar conclusions as to the unique position and role of man in the cosmos, and both were attempting to deduce something as to the probable future trends of human evolution, though Père Teilhard's hypotheses as to the increasing convergence of human variety and the resultant increase of psychosocial pressure—which in turn would increasingly direct the course of man's further evolution—were more radical than mine, and I was quite unable to follow him in his approach to what he believed was the ultimate goal of evolution's march, his so-called Point Omega, in which natural and supernatural are combined in a mystical and to me incomprehensible manner.

However, in spite of wide differences in respect of theology and metaphysics, we found ourselves in agreement and indeed in active co-operation over the subject of the future of mankind, and its transcendent importance for the thought of our times. The important thing, we both agreed, is to study the problem of mankind as a phenomenon and to look at it *sub specie evolutionis*, confident that increasing understanding will gradually bring about a reconciliation of theoretical differences, as well as leading to practical improvements.

Père Teilhard de Chardin's most important contribution to thought is undoubtedly *The Phenomenon of Man*—a notable and I think a seminal work which has now been translated into English. But this collection of letters and diary extracts (which should be read in conjunction with the larger work) gives us many illuminating and sometimes moving glimpses of his unique personality.

THE MAN *by* PIERRE LEROY, S.J.

The look in his eyes when they met your eyes revealed the man's soul : his reassuring sympathy restored your confidence in yourself. Just to speak to him made you feel better ; you knew that he was listening to you and that he understood you. His own faith was in the invincible power of love : men hurt one another by not loving one another. And this was not naïveté but the goodness of the man, for he was good beyond the common measure. In him, this belief was no mere conventional sentiment grafted on a generous nature, but the fruit of long meditation ; it was a certainty that came only with years of reflection. It was this deep-seated spiritual conviction that led Père Pierre Teilhard de Chardin to the practice of self-forgetfulness : self being forgotten in a sympathetic union with all men and with every individual man.

The combination of priest and scientist is nothing new ; but in his case what was really astonishing was his closeness to the earth and his deep feeling for the value of matter. People who were shocked by him never realised how deep lay the roots of this simultaneous love of God and of the world. ' Throughout my whole life,' he wrote ' during every moment I have lived, the world has gradually been taking on light and fire for me, until it has come to envelop me in one mass of luminosity, glowing from within. . . . The purple flush of matter fading imperceptibly into the gold of spirit, to be lost finally in the incandescence of a personal universe. . .

'This is what I have learnt from my contact with the earth—the diaphany of the divine at the heart of a glowing universe, the divine radiating from the depths of matter a-flame.'

There was something paradoxical in a priest who seemed outwardly so little the ecclesiastic, who was at home in even the least religious intellectual circles, who took his place in the advance-guard of thought, and devoted his life to the study of the properties of man as animal. It seemed paradoxical, too, that a specialist in the scientific history of the past should be interested only in the future.

He was all this : but above all he was a priest, deeply attached to the Church and its teaching, faithful to the end in spite of the annoyances and difficulties, the insinuations, too, that assailed him from every side.

Père Pierre Teilhard de Chardin lived during a period of doubt and perplexity. He witnessed the modernist crisis, with the sacrifices it entailed ; he was driven from his own country by the injustice of political strife ; and when he reached manhood he was caught up in the terrible war of 1914. A few years later he saw the collapse in the heat of revolution of social structures to which centuries of history seemed to have given permanence. He was present when forces were let loose which were to lead to a second world war ; he was in Pekin when the atom bombs were dropped on Hiroshima and Nagasaki. It was his own fate to be misunderstood and condemned to silence, and to suffer torments that at times came near to overwhelming him. Like many others, he might well have retreated into his own solitary existence and abandoned his chosen field of activity, but his reaction was the exact opposite. In all that he did, as in all that he taught, there was no bitterness nor disillusioned cynicism, nothing but a constant optimism. Far from railing against the pettiness of men or the chaos of the world, he made it a rule never to assume the presence of evil. And when he was unable to deny the evidence of his eyes, he looked not for the damning but for the saving element in what he saw : a mental attitude that surely, if unexpectedly, provides the only road to truth.

This optimism had much more than a temperamental basis (of which we shall have more to say later) ; it was a conviction rooted deep in thought.

His scientific studies had taught Père Teilhard that the universe has its own history : it has a past, and it must be directed towards some final goal. 'From the smallest individual detail to the vastest aggregations, our living universe (in common with our inorganic universe) has a structure, and this structure can owe its nature only to a phenomenon of growth.' The world with all its riches, life with its astounding achievements, man with the constant prodigy of his inventive powers, all are organically integrated in one single growth and one historical process, and all share the same upward progress towards an era of fulfilment. The inescapable dimension of time is a real function of growth and maturation, essential to our individual and collective becoming.

This growth must have some definite objective ; there must be some term to the process : 'The main stem of the tree of life,' writes Père Teilhard, 'has always climbed in the direction of the largest brain,' towards, that is, greater spontaneity and greater consciousness.

Thus the slow progress of energies must reach a peak 'from which life will never slip back'. To overcome every obstacle, to unite our beings without loss of individual personality, there is a single force which nothing can replace and nothing destroy, a force which urges us forwards and draws us upwards : this is the force of love.

We can thus appreciate the central position in Père Teilhard's whole philosophy, of Christ, prototype of Man-Love; 'God-Love reaching self-fulfilment only in love. Christianity,' he tells us, 'is nothing more nor less than a "phylum of love" within nature.'

Such, in his unshakable optimism and his passionate following of Christ, was Père Pierre Teilhard de Chardin. Today our minds are increasingly and agonisingly dismayed by the richness of matter and our own inability to find some coherent rule of conduct; our souls are perplexed by what we see happening around us and by the threat of what tomorrow may bring; and when, puzzled and terrified, we find a Christian with such confidence in the future both of man and of the world, we may tend to give a shrug of indifference and withdraw further into our shell of scepticism. Some of us will feel that the real, unhappily, can have nothing in common with the ideal; and it is to these disillusioned minds that the life of Père Teilhard provides an answer.

Much has already been written about him; his work as a scientist and his speculations in philosophy are beginning to be better known, but little has been said about what sort of a person he was in the daily business of life. It is not my intention, then, to analyse any particular aspect of his work, to deal with his scientific research or the expression he gave to his thought, nor to say any more about the difficulties he had to face and which in the end drove him into exile. My aim is rather to give a picture of the man I knew, to follow him through the different stages of his career and at the same time to try to read the secret that enabled him, in spite of the complications of his life, to achieve perfect interior unity.

During the years in which it was my good fortune, under unusual conditions, to live close to him and work with him, I was able to some extent to decipher the mystery of his personality. I only hope that I may now succeed in explaining, in all humility, certain aspects of it and so make it easier to understand what lay behind the shining intelligence whose influence we now see to be so far-reaching.

The part of France in which he was born, Sarcenat, is a rugged country in which family life stood for a great deal. The family lived in an eighteenth-century manor-house, and the windows of the principal rooms gave on to a vista of volcanoes and rounded hills. From the top of the terrace, framed in greenery, you can see the capital of Auvergne, the vast plain of Clermont, with the foothills of the Puy mountains in the distance. No sound disturbs the tranquillity of the scene but the murmur of running water flowing with graceful constancy in a stone fountain.

Pierre Teilhard was born on 1 May, 1881, in a room on the first floor that looks out on the mountains. There used to be a very delicate pastel drawing hanging just opposite the left-hand window, which shows him as a curly-headed little boy, with the candid forehead and the thoughtful eyes that were his most striking features.

His childhood was that of an amenable little boy. ' I was an affectionate child,' he said, ' good, and even pious.' The predominating influence was that of his mother—his ' dear, sainted maman '—to whom he owed ' all that was best in his soul.' ' To rouse the fire into a blaze, a spark had to fall upon me ; and the spark by which my own universe—still only halfway to being individually personalised—was to succeed in centring itself on its own fullness, undoubtedly came through my mother to light up and fire my child's soul.'

His father, Emmanuel Teilhard de Chardin, was a man who held strongly to a solid body of tradition, and he demanded from his children (Pierre was the fourth of eleven) active co-operation in a disciplined family life. Pierre owed to his father ' more things than I could count,' he wrote, ' certain well-defined ambitions, no doubt, but even more a certain basic balance on which everything else was built.'

Every day the household gathered in the dining-room after the evening meal to say prayers together. Pierre was to show me later, when I accompanied him to Sarcenat, his favourite place at prayers : he used to kneel by the wall while his parents rested their elbows on the table in the middle of the room.

The countryside is rich in rocks and minerals, in insect life and wild flowers, and M. Teilhard took pleasure in teaching his children how to understand and appreciate natural history. During their walks they would all gather mineral, zoological and botanical specimens and it was this interesting collection of local history that first encouraged Pierre's vocation as a scientist.

There was, however, another dominating interest that was typical of his temperament. He looked always for durability in his possessions and was not greatly attracted by the frail colouring of butterflies or the evanescent beauty of flowers. He has left a description of his feelings for what he calls his ' idols ' : a plough-spanner carefully hidden in a corner of the courtyard, the top of a little metal rod, or some shell splinters picked up on a neighbouring range. ' You should have seen me as in profound secrecy and silence I withdrew into the contemplation of my " God of Iron ", delighting in its possession, gloating over its existence. A God, note, of Iron ; and why iron ? Because in all my childish experience there was nothing in the world harder, tougher, more durable than this wonderful substance. There was about it a feeling of full personality, sharply individualised [. . .] But I can never forget the pathetic depths of a child's despair, when I realised one day that iron can be scratched and can rust [. . .] I had to look elsewhere for substitutes that would console me. Sometimes in the blue flame (at once so material, and yet so pure and intangible) flickering over the logs in the hearth, but more often in a more translucent and more delightfully coloured stone : quartz or amethyst crystals, and most of all glittering fragments of chalcedony such as I could pick up in the neighbourhood.'

So we meet in his early youth the two components from which his whole life, both interior and in his relations with others, was to be built—a feeling for matter and a feeling for the durable.

He was sent to the Jesuit school at Villefranche ; he was a good pupil, often at the top of his class, except in religious instruction. Not, indeed, that he was not ready to accept such teaching —far from it—but his mind seems to have instinctively reacted against the way in which it was taught. At that time the subject was still wrapped up in conventional phraseology and its presentation to children was dry and stodgy. Consider, for example, what Henri Brémond quotes in this respect : ' Nothing is sweeter than to bask in the warmth that comes with the caress of grace. Jesus, my own brother, how well I know that the sweetest hours of my life are those of my monthly retreat, when I have you for my divine teacher ; you open the book of my soul and help me to read about things that enrapture my powers. How good it is to go through this examination in love! ' Poor children, adds Brémond ; an examination, and, at that, an examination in love— what an attraction!—must have been the last straw.

It is not difficult to see that such ' things ' would hardly ' enrapture the powers ' of a child like Pierre Teilhard, so eager for the permanent, the solid and the durable.

In any case, he must have set a good example to his companions, for we find him prefect (that is president) of the sodality, and deservedly looked up to in the school. His devotion to Our Lady was tender and glowing, but it was now to gain in virility, and he was to assign to the Virgin Mary a dominant role in his concept of generative evolution.

At eighteen, after he had passed his baccalaureat, he said good-bye to his family and entered the Jesuit novitiate at Aix-en-

Provence. Two years later he went to Laval to continue with his fellow-scholastics his studies in French, Latin and Greek. This was in 1902, when the religious orders were expelled from France ; and he had to go abroad with the Community to seek refuge in Jersey.

He would often recall the comic epic of the move. In the hope of travelling unrecognised, the fathers wore civilian clothes. To give everyone a suit that fitted him would have been quite impossible, and so they had to make do with anything that came to hand. An appeal made to families brought the most varied collection of garments. Grave fathers and young scholastics found themselves donning a funereal top-hat with a light grey jacket, or a greenish old bowler with a long frock-coat, or a motoring-cap with a black morning coat ; fifty years later Père Teilhard would still laugh at the memory of that masquerade.

The Jersey period was an important one. He studied scholastic philosophy, becoming familiar with its methods and terminology, without, however, adopting its spirit. He had an opportunity, at any rate, of turning over new problems in his mind, and was able to give some time to his favourite subject of geology. His contemporaries recall that ' Brother ' Teilhard never went for a walk without his geologist's hammer and naturalist's magnifying glass.

In September 1905, after three years as a scholastic, he was sent to teach physics and chemistry at the Holy Family College in Cairo.

He was there for three years, during which he found time, in addition to his teaching, to deepen and extend his still imperfect knowledge of geology and palæontology. He was even able to publish in the scientific bulletin of Cairo a note on the Eocene in Upper Egypt, based on a collection he had made of its fossil fauna.

Egypt delighted his taste for the romantic. As he travelled along the Nile he must have dreamt, with the intense imagination revealed in his letters, of the exuberance of nature in unknown lands. 'The East flowed over me in a first wave of exoticism : I gazed at it and drank it in eagerly—the country itself, not its peoples or its history (which as yet held no interest for me), but its light, its vegetation, its fauna and its deserts.' Little did he anticipate that twenty-three years of his life were to be devoted to the Far East, to his 'brooding old China'.

At this point in his interior development, as we have seen, it was not man that attracted him. He had little interest in the peoples of the earth and their history. What drew him was nature in all its richness and diversity. The universe had taken bodily shape for him, but he had not yet become aware of its soul. Without realising it, Pierre Teilhard had reached a critical point in his life. He was more conscious than ever of the importance of the world, but it was a purely material world. He was in danger, if he was not careful, of succumbing to the lure of pantheism and losing himself in immensity : 'to be all, one must be absorbed in all.' 'For only three years in Jersey,' he writes, 'and then for another three years in Cairo I studied (to the best of my ability) and taught (so far as my competence allowed me) fairly elementary physics, the pre-Quanta and pre-relativity physics of atomic structure : which means that in this subject I am an amateur, a mere layman. At the same time I find it difficult to express what a sense of fulfilment, ease, and of being at home I find in this world of electrons, nuclei and waves. If we wish to escape the inexorable fragility of the manifold, why not take refuge deeper, why not get beneath it ? [. . .] Thus we may gain the world by renouncing it, by passively losing self in the heart of what has neither form nor dimension.'

If we did not know that there may be contradictions in every person's make-up, we would fail to understand how Père Teilhard could have been tempted by the eastern 'line', its self-centred passivity so foreign to his tastes. It is difficult to see how such an ardent and generous nature could have withdrawn from the contest. To let oneself be carried along passively in the cosmic eddy, to be lost in the intangible, seems completely inconsistent with a life already dedicated to action. It is important, therefore, to note that it was only at the speculative level that Père Teilhard contemplated the 'eastern' solution : it had no influence on his faith as a Christian.

From Egypt he was sent to England for the last stages of his training as a priest and religious ; and there a fuller and more satisfying view of the world forcibly impressed itself on him. It was then, one might say, that he began to direct his thought towards a philosophy of the person. The world now became for him a vast whole making its way towards a supreme personality ; he had a vision of a universe in process of self-creation in which no breach could develop. He saw the image of the absolute reflected in the filigree of nature. 'There were times when it really seemed to me that my eyes were about to see a universal being take shape in nature. Already, however, it was not by looking, as I used to look, for what is beyond matter that I sought to grasp and pin down the inexpressible ambiance, but by looking for what is beyond the living.'

The world, the whole universe, is an evolution—a genesis, to use Père Teilhard's own expression. Now every genesis presupposes inter-connections, mutual or reciprocal dependence, with no breach. It implies in the being that is forming itself a kinship between the composing elements ; thus a static cosmos, fragmented in make-up, is unthinkable. If everything forms itself, everything must hold together. Matter and spirit, then, as we know them in our universe, are not two separate substances, set side by side and differing in nature. They are two distinct aspects of one single cosmic stuff and there is between them no conflict to baffle our intelligence. Physical energy contains in itself something of the spiritual, and since the upward trend of energy is a fact we can observe and verify with the increasing complexity of organisms, the law of the universe must surely be a continually progressing, irreversible, spiritualisation. Matter has now lost its former attraction for Père Teilhard : 'the felicity that I had sought in iron, I can find now only in Spirit.'

It was during these decisive years that he was ordained priest. Marked now with the priestly character, freed from the commitments involved in theological studies, and intellectually awake to the consequences of a generalised theory of evolution, he set about building up the structure of his own interior universe. This was now the pivot on which turned all his activities, his mental attitudes and his thought. He resolved in future to collaborate with all his energies in the cosmogenesis whose reality became for him daily more resplendent. Salvation was no longer to be sought in ' abandoning the world ' but in active ' participation ' in building it up. He would approach his scientific work no longer as an amateur but as a qualified specialist ; and it would be undertaken not for its own sake (as he often insisted in conversation) but in order to release the Spirit from the crude ore in which it lay hidden or inactive.

The 1914 war did no more than delay his setting out on the great adventure of scientific research, which in his eyes was also the grand act of adoration. Obedient to the voice that called him, he was ready to plunge into another distressful adventure—an experience so monstrous and ghastly and yet, as we shall see, so exhilarating. He joined as a stretcher-bearer the 8th regiment of Moroccan Tirailleurs, later to become the 4th combined Tirailleurs and Zouaves. With the humble rank of corporal he was twice decorated, receiving the Médaille Militaire and the Légion d'Honneur.

He lived through the nightmare of war with all the generosity of his soul, with no thought for himself. Even amid scenes of death and devastation he was carried away by a sense of fulfilment. In war he breathed a new invigorating atmosphere. ' The man at the front is no longer the same man.' The shell of common assumptions and conventions was broken, and a fresh light shed on the hidden mechanism by which man's will has power to shape his development. Life takes on a new savour in the heroic devotion to a grand ideal. Père Teilhard felt that the reality he had found at the front would be with him for ever ' in the great work of creation and of sanctifying humanity.'

In 1919 he returned, this time for good, to his scientific career. He studied under Marcellin Boule at the Natural History Museum in Paris, and in 1922 his doctoral thesis was accepted. At the same time, somewhat against his own inclinations, he agreed to succeed Boussac, a son-in-law of P. Termier, who had been killed in the war, as professor of geology in the Institut Catholique in Paris. ' Rather than this academic post,' he wrote, ' I should of course have preferred research work in Beyrouth or Shanghai or Trichinopoly, where men are needed.' That those places should have come to his mind indicates the attraction to the tropics he had already begun to experience in Cairo. They were, in any case, familiar to him, for the French Jesuits had universities at both Beyrouth and Shanghai ; and Trichinopoly was one of their important missions. It was natural, accordingly, that he should have thought of them as possible fields for a career in geology.

The brilliance of Père Teilhard's scientific and apostolic work was soon manifest. His influence was becoming increasingly felt in Paris both through his geological teaching and in his addresses to gatherings of Catholics at the Ecole Normale, the Polytechnique, and the School of Mineralogy. The novelty and daring of his thought made a great appeal to the enthusiasm of young people eager to learn. It was at this moment, however, that an unexpected decision sent him to the Far East.

In 1914 one of his fellow-Jesuits, Père Émile Licent, had sailed for China with the intention of founding and building up a centre of scientific research into the natural resources of the Yellow River basin. For nine years he had been travelling over the great plain of Tchely, the Mongolian steppe which forms the Chinese border of the Tibetan plateau. He had been responsible for valuable collections bearing on its geology, botany, mineralogy and palæontology, and had built at Tientsin a museum and laboratory which he directed and inspired. In 1920 Père Licent had had one of those strokes of good fortune that sometimes attend workers in the field ; he had found a number of important fossiliferous deposits, and long camel trains had been carrying back through the provinces of Kansi and Shensi a precious store of mammiferous fossils collected in the Tertiary layers of the West.

In October 1921 Père Licent had sent the most significant of his acquisitions to the Paris Museum for expert appraisal. M. Boule entrusted the work to Père Teilhard, and a correspondence followed between the two Jesuits. In the end Père Teilhard agreed to join Père Licent in China and study the deposits on the spot. This was the origin of the ' French Palæontological Mission ', of which Père Licent was appointed director.

On 10 April, 1923, Père Teilhard embarked at Marseilles for Tientsin, where he arrived on the 23rd of the next month. He was now forty-two years old. He had volunteered for this distant assignment ; his application had been favourably received, and everything seemed to augur a successful future. He was, in fact, soon to make one of the most important discoveries in his whole career. His personal impressions, however, on arriving, betray a surprising weariness. ' I feel,' he wrote on 27 May, ' very much as though I had reached the limit of my powers ; I seem somehow unable to keep things in my mind. I have a continual feeling that as far as my own life goes, the day is drawing to a close. The only way out, I think, is to cling to a blind and absolute faith in the meaning that all things—even the diminishments—must hold for a man who believes that God is the animating force behind every single event. The further I go, the more I am convinced that the only true science—the only one we can acquire in this ocean of weakness and ignorance—is the vision that begins to take shape under and through the multiplicity of things.'

His weariness had something in common with that felt by missionaries when they first come into contact with Northern China. Everything in the North is quite different from what they expected—flat, grey, dusty and nauseating. But Père Teilhard's confidence reveals another aspect of his nature : more than once the fineness of his feelings, his reserve towards others and even towards himself, checked the violence of his deeper emotions. Later he admitted the agonising distress that attacked and came close to overwhelming him ; he lost confidence in himself ; he was tortured by scruples ; in spite of every effort of will he could not always disguise his suffering. Not unnaturally, therefore, there were times in his life when his friends noticed that he seemed to be abstracted and withdrawn.

Père Teilhard stayed for some weeks in Tientsin before setting out with Père Licent on an expedition to inner Mongolia and the Ordos desert. It was in this forgotten corner of the Chinese continent that they had the good fortune to find incontrovertible evidence for the existence of palæolithic man, hitherto unknown in these parts. Until that time nothing was known of prehistoric man south of the Yenisei. The discovery accordingly marked an essential step in the story of man.

Later in this volume the reader will find Père Teilhard's account of their adventures ; but it may be interesting to note now his reaction to the East with which twenty years earlier he had wished to become acquainted. ' I'm absorbed by the work, and very interested by the extreme novelty of what I'm seeing ; interested, but not thrilled, as I would have been ten or twenty years ago. Today what counts for me (as for you) is the future of things [he is writing to Abbé Breuil] whereas here I am plunged into the past. Mongolia strikes me as a "museum" of antique specimens (zoological and ethnographical), a slice of the past. Try as I will, I see no promise of progress, no ferment, no "burgeoning" for mankind of tomorrow. This corner of Asia (and even China outside the Great Wall) gives the impression of an empty reservoir.'

We may set side by side this a somewhat disillusioned passage from *Choses mongoles* which is conveniently included in this edition of the *Letters* : 'It is a long time, however, since I lost the illusion that travel brings us closer to the truth. . . . The more remote in time and space is the world we confront, the less it exists, and hence the poorer and more barren it is for our thought. So I have felt no disappointment this year at remaining quite untouched as I looked over the steppes where gazelles still run about as they did in the Tertiary period, or visited the yourts where the Mongols still live as they lived a thousand years ago. In what is, as in what was, there is nothing really new to be found.'

It is easy to see how deeply Père Teilhard was imbued with his vision of working to build the future. Nothing else had the power to impress itself on him. And by the future he meant more than the building up of the material world ; he envisaged the irreversible ascent, through men's efforts, to what he called the Omega Point.

It was during this expedition, in the stillness of the vast solitude of the Ordos desert, that one Easter Sunday he finished the mystical and philosophical poem, *Mass upon the altar of the World*. Alone before God, he prays with lyrical fervour : ' Christ of glory, hidden power stirring in the heart of matter,

29

glowing centre in which the unnumbered strands of the manifold are knit together ; strength inexorable as the world and warm as life ; you whose brow is of snow, whose eyes are of fire, whose feet are more dazzling than gold poured from the furnace ; you whose hands hold captive the stars ; you, the first and the last, the living, the dead, the re-born ; you, who gather up in your superabundant oneness every delight, every taste, every energy, every phase of existence, to you my being cries out with a longing as vast as the universe : for you indeed are my Lord and my God.'

When he got back to France in the autumn of 1924, an ordeal awaited him. Errors of theological interpretation had found their way into a note in which he expounded his new vision of the universe. His religious superiors had already taken alarm at the boldness of some of his philosophical views, which appealed particularly to the young, and thought it wise to bar him from teaching. Deeply wounded but submissive, he returned to China, where he became increasingly at home when he left the commercial and banking centre of Tientsin for the intellectual centre of Pekin.

It was a period of intense enthusiasm, and a succession of Chinese scientific institutions was coming into being, backed by eminent American and European scholars. Père Teilhard was completely at home in these exceptionally cosmopolitan circles. In particular he made friends with two outstanding characters : V. K. Ting, who had studied in Switzerland, and Wong Wen Hao, also with a European background (Belgium)—both geologists and both active in the new Chinese Geological Society. Ting was later mayor of Shanghai in Marshal Chiang Kai-Shek's administration ; Wong also gave up science for politics and became Minister for Communications in Nationalist China.

On Sundays, there would be a gathering at the house of Dr. Grabau, the American palæontologist. Grabau was crippled with rheumatism, and loved to see his friends around him. His lively intelligence, his kindness and the authority of his learning, carried his influence far and wide among the young intellectuals of Pekin. It was at his house that they discussed possible fields of study or publications that might be issued. I was greatly struck myself at these meetings by Père Teilhard's winning manner. Buoyant and vivacious, with sufficient command of English to make jokes in it, he was, with our host, the life and soul of our gatherings. In addition to the originality of his thought and his personal charm, he had a quality rare in men of his stamp : he could listen to others and seem really interested in their suggestions. If they were too extravagant, he simply smiled.

The circle of friends whose common interests brought them to Pekin included men of international reputation in the world of science—Black, the Canadian, who was to be the first to publish an account of the Fossil-Man of Chou-Kou-Tien ; Andersson, the prehistorian ; Sven Hedin, the explorer ; Granger and Barbour, the palæontologists ; Chapman-Andrews, Höppeli and many others. First the war with Japan and then the civil war and setting-up of the Communist regime were to destroy the organisation they had so patiently and skilfully built up.

Meanwhile Père Teilhard had been renewing his contacts in France. It was in 1928, in his laboratory at the Paris Museum, that I met him for the first time. I had been chosen by my Jesuit superiors to work with Père Licent at the Tientsin Museum, and I was at the time reading for my degree at Nancy. When Père Teilhard came back to France in that year I met him at the Museum in the Place Valhubert. His simple and natural greeting immediately put me at my ease. He offered me a chair, while he sat casually on the edge of the table. His eyes, filled with intelligence and kindly understanding, his features, finely drawn and weathered by the winds of sea and desert, the glamour that surrounded his name, all made a deep impression on me. I can still hear the friendliness of his voice as he talked to me about China and the promising future, as it then appeared, that awaited it. For over an hour I listened to a flow of stimulating new ideas. From that moment we were friends ; and so we were to remain until the end.

His stay in France was brief. He went back that same year (1928) to Pekin, including on his way a visit to Ethiopia under the guidance of Henry de Monfreid. Later followed two important expeditions into Mongolia and Western China, and a return to Paris to help in organising the ' Yellow Expedition '.

It was in China that I met him again, in the spring of 1931. I had been working in the Gulf of Liao-Tong and on the Shantung peninsula. I had hopes of being back in Tientsin for Holy Week but shipping was constantly being delayed by the necessity to guard against the sudden attacks of the pirates who infested the area. My own journey, as it happened, was uneventful but it was late on Easter Sunday morning when I arrived at our house in Tientsin.

To my great joy, as I came in I met Père Teilhard in the corridor. He had been in Tientsin for some days and was on the point of leaving for Pekin, where he was to join the Citroën Central Asia Expedition (then held up at Kalgan by a serious breakdown). Teilhard, from his long experience of China, realised that my journey, made alone except for two Chinese servants, must have been one of great hardship ; and my readjustment to normal life was made easier and quicker by his kind and tactful solicitude, exquisite tact and kindness. The next day we left together for Pekin. There I looked on while he identified the worked stones found in the jumble of fossils, and the deposits collected at Chou-Kou-Tien and placed in the Pekin Cenozoic Museum. These acquisitions held evidence that Sinanthropus might well have been responsible for their deliberate manufacture. The Abbé Breuil's more stringent examination was later to confirm the authenticity of the worked stones. Père Teilhard's keen powers of observation had not been mistaken. The rest of the story and the establishment of the near-certainty of Sinanthropus ' Faber ' is well known.

The Yellow Expedition was something of a disappointment. Père Teilhard's letters reveal the impatience of a geologist condemned to fill in time in order to forget the semi-captivity in which the whole party was kept by the hostility of the Chinese authorities.

Père Teilhard travelled later in India and several times visited America. During his brief returns to China between 1934 and 1938, he witnessed the disbanding of the Chinese national institutes he had seen come into being ten years earlier. His last work in the field was when he agreed to accompany some American friends in an investigation into the geology and prehistory of Burma. At the end of September 1938 he was back in Pekin ; thence to Japan in the hope of salvaging a future that was daily more menaced. From Japan he sailed for Paris ; and in August 1939, a few weeks before the declaration of war on Germany, he returned to Pekin.

War fastened its grip on Europe, but in China it stagnated for two years. The Japanese had occupied the North with brutal cynicism. Things were even more difficult in Tientsin, which suffered all the misery of arbitrary provocations. The territorial concessions (the districts reserved for Europeans and Americans) were isolated from the rest of the town by barbed-wire barricades guarded by arrogant sentries. The situation of the Tientsin Museum became precarious and it was decided to move it to Pekin. Père Teilhard agreed to spend some weeks in Tientsin helping to organise the moving of the collections built up during the last twenty-five years by Père Licent, whose health had obliged him to return to France for good. All we could do was to contrive to hang on in spite of everything and find some way to meet the difficulties that were aggravated for us as Frenchmen by the political and military situation.

The new house at Pekin, an annexe to the French barracks, was admirably organised. This became the Institute of Geobiology ; and although it had not been designed for the purpose, it was pleasant, and life went on smoothly and comfortably.

Père Teilhard was in his office every morning at about eight o'clock, and we used to chat together for half an hour or so, seldom longer. After I had left him he used to jot down in an exercise book (over twenty of these survive) any comment of a philosophical, scientific or religious nature he thought worth preserving. These notes, written in diary form and with no apparent connecting thread, will enable students of Père Teilhard's thought to follow day by day, for over twenty years, the workings of a ceaselessly active mind. The time from nine o'clock to half-past twelve was devoted to writing his scientific papers and memoranda, occasionally to laboratory work ; he preferred to spend his morning in writing and thinking. As far as possible we used to leave together in the early afternoon for the School of Medicine (the Pekin Union Medical College) to study its palæontological collection. Later, the whole of our time was spent at home, for all foreign institutions had been closed by the Japanese authorities. About five o'clock came visits to our friends. It was in these gatherings that you saw the real Père Teilhard ; his mere presence brought an assurance of optimism and confidence. He had, too, the sort of mind that needs to retain and even multiply its contacts with the world outside ; if he was to give substance to his thought or precision to his own personal ideas, he had to discuss his /way of seeing things with other people.

Not that his conversation was always serious or pitched on a high level. He was often, on the contrary, lively and gay ; he appreciated good cooking and a good story ; and sometimes his simplicity, or rather his unaffected frankness, could be embarrassing. Once, forgetting no doubt whom he was talking to, he embarked on an explanation that might have placed him in an awkward position. I was sitting beside him, and to attract his attention I nudged him gently with the tip of my toe. You can imagine my embarrassment when I heard him exclaim with a laugh : ' Whose was that tactful kick ? '

He had a fine sense of humour : his face would light up like a child's at a good joke ; and if sometimes he could not resist an inviting target for his sly wit—after all, on his mother's side the blood of Voltaire flowed in his veins—it was done with such unaffected good humour that no-one could take it in bad part. It was one of his outstanding characteristics that he never gave way to bitterness, not even when decisions were taken that prevented the dissemination of his ideas. No wonder that he was universally loved and admired.

Père Teilhard was not, of course, without his opponents. It was not everyone that shared his optimism and broad-mindedness. There were some even who were irritated by it ; for example, there was quite a little scene once when some remarks of Père Teilhard's caused an Ambassador to leave the table in the middle of a meal. As it happened, no harm was done, for Père Teilhard's simplicity and modesty made it easy to patch up the difference.

Living with Père Teilhard softened the harshness of our isolation, but one was sometimes conscious of how burdensome he found it to be confined within the walls of Pekin. It did violence to his nature to be thus sealed in, and his seeming gaiety was the fruit more of a victory of will and moral strength than of an inherent disposition.

Many have rightly been struck by Père Teilhard's great optimism. He was indeed an optimist, in his attribution to the universe of a sense of direction in spite of the existence of evil and in spite of appearances ; but in the daily life that concerned him personally, he was far from being an optimist. He bore with patience, it is true, trials that might well have proved too much for the strongest of us, but how often in intimate conversation have I found him depressed and with almost no heart to carry on. The agonising distress he already had to face in 1939 was intensified in the following years, and he sometimes felt that he could venture no further. During that period he was at times prostrated by fits of weeping, and he appeared to be on the verge of despair. But, calling on all the resources of his will, he abandoned himself to the supremely Great, to his Christ, as the only purpose of his being ; and so hid his suffering and took up his work again, if not with joy, at least in the hope that his own personal vocation might be fulfilled.

Six years thus went by in the dispiriting atmosphere of China occupied by the Japanese and cut off from the rest of the world. In March 1946 Père Teilhard flew from Shanghai and there embarked in a ship that brought him back to France at the beginning of May. There he returned to his old room at *Études*, 15 rue Monsieur. His friends were quick to gather round him. Then, however, came a severe heart attack which struck him down just as he was on the point of leaving for a tour of South Africa : the similarity of the terrain in which the Australopithecidae and the Sinanthropus had been found had prompted the investigators in South Africa to ask for the assistance of an expert. It was two years, however, before Père Teilhard was able to make the journey. In 1951, after his election to the Académie des Sciences, he went to live in New York as a member of the Wenner Gren Foundation. There he devoted himself to anthropological studies, and became one of their most eminent associates.

Only once did he return to Paris, and then for a short visit. Although he always gave more than he received, he derived a new spiritual enrichment from this contact. It was during this last visit, in June 1954, that he expressed a desire to see the

Lascaux caves. I had the pleasure of escorting him, and, as he had also to go to Lyons, our journey took us through Auvergne and we passed by his home at Sarcenat. Père Teilhard made no comment, but his silent absorption was sufficient indication of the memories evoked by these childhood scenes.

This was to be his last pilgrimage to France.

New restrictions had been imposed on him by his religious superiors, and it was broken by emotion he could hardly contain, and torn by unendurable anguish, that he cut short his stay and returned to New York six weeks earlier than he had intended.

In spite of the burden of spiritual distress, he took heart again and went back to work in his little New York office. I saw him for the last time a few days before Christmas. He was somewhat more tranquil, and was busy organising a scientific conference on anthropogenesis.

On 10 April, 1955, Easter Sunday, Père Teilhard collapsed to a sudden stroke just as he was about to have tea. He was walking over to the table when he fell like a stricken tree. For some moments there was an agonising silence and then he opened his eyes and said ' What's happened—where am I ? ' When he was reassured he quietly uttered his last words, ' This time, I feel it's terrible.' He did not speak again. His doctor and his friend, Père de Breuvery, were sent for, but both were out. It was Fr. Martin Geraghty of St. Ignatius's, New York, who came immediately and administered Extreme Unction. The time was six o'clock in the evening. The sky was dazzling and spring was in its full splendour.

I was in Chicago at the time. I heard the news by telephone and hurried to New York, staying in the same hotel room he had slept in the night before. The whole staff was grief-stricken, from the humblest servant to the manager.

Père Teilhard's body lay in the chapel of the Jesuit house on Park Avenue, robed in his priest's vestments as he now lies for ever. He was hardly recognisable, the features drawn, the nose in sharp relief, the forehead smooth and unwrinkled. He reminded me of his compatriot from Clermont, Pascal.

The funeral was on Easter Tuesday, a grey, rainy day. Ten of his friends were present, but I was the only one to accompany him on the ninety-mile journey from New York to Saint Andrew on the Hudson. There he was buried, with a ceremony whose only distinction was its poverty, in the cemetery of the Jesuit novitiate for the New York Province.

It remains to consider a little more deeply the spiritual powers that provided the framework of Père Teilhard's complex existence and gave it cohesion; for what is important in a man is not so much what he achieves but the basic reason that inspires his activities. Since 1912, when he had completed his theological studies, Père Teilhard's aspirations were quite definitely formulated. He was a priest and a religious, and his first duty was therefore to Christ. At the same time he was resolved, as we have seen, to ' participate ' in the world, not to live in isolation from it. It was these seemingly contradictory principles, the service of Christ and participation in the world, that had to be reconciled. The evangelical doctrine of the Redemption through the Cross had to be reconciled with the salvation of the world through active co-operation in the building up of the universe.

This is not a problem of the speculative order, but one that calls for an immediate practical solution; and at its centre lies the question of the interior unity of life.

In examining Père Teilhard's answer, one point must be borne constantly in mind: he both accepts and practises the Christian doctrine of detachment. He realises that the consummation of the world can be achieved only through a mystical death, a dark night, a renunciation of the whole being. So much we can take as established. But when he begins to look further into what constitutes renunciation, and to determine its mechanism, it may be held that he dissociates himself from ascetical practices hitherto accepted. His aim is to try out a new formula which, if it should prove effective, will enable men (already increasingly conscious of the tremendous impetus of technology) to look on Christianity not as a doctrine of impoverishment and diminution, but of expansion, and so to live as real Christians without ceasing to be artificers of the creative force. It matters little to him that God's omnipresent activity may appear as a differentiation or as a transformation, so long as Christ is attained and glorified : the problem is whether renunciation, conceived as a cutting-off of oneself from the world, is a practical proposition for the whole body of mankind.

In the life of each one of us, a vast area is occupied by the exertion of natural or social energies and it would be unfair to allow the value represented by these positive expressions of our activities to run to waste. It is not that Père Teilhard seeks to attach a permanent, absolute, value to these various human achievements : he sees them as necessary stages through which the human group must pass in the course of its transformation. What interests him is not the particular form they take but the function they serve, and what matters is that not only the self-denial of the ascetic and the renunciation of the sufferer, but also our positive efforts to achieve natural perfection and to meet human obligations, should lead us to a consciousness of our spiritual growth.

Without, accordingly, sacrificing the mystical value of renunciation, it is seen to be essential to urge on the material development of the world with passionate conviction. Looked at from this angle, detachment and attachment can be harmonised and so complement one another. As he wrote to a friend who had the good fortune to see his business affairs prosper : ' You are still having some difficulty in justifying to yourself the euphoria of a soul immersed in " business ". I must point out to you that the really important thing is that you are actually experiencing that feeling of well-being. Bread was good for our bodies before we knew about the chemical laws of assimilation. . . . How, you ask, can the success of a commercial enterprise bring with it moral progress ? And I answer, in this way, that since everything in the world follows the road to unification, the spiritual success of the universe is bound up with the correct functioning of every zone of that universe and particularly with the release of every possible energy in it. Because your enterprise (which I take to be legitimate) is going well, a little more health is being spread in the human mass, and in consequence a little more liberty to act, to think, and to love. . . . Because you are doing the best you can (though you may sometimes fail) you are forming your own self within the world, and you are helping the world to form itself around you.'

Père Teilhard was fully alive to the danger that might lie in such statements. Wrongly interpreted or understood they might engulf the Christian in a type of pantheism that denied to the supernatural its pre-eminent position. He himself, firm in his faith in the universal value of creation, was in no danger of falling into this error. 'I am not speaking metaphorically,' he wrote, 'when I say that it is throughout the length and breadth and depth of the world in movement that man can attain the experience and vision of his God.' A critic by no means over-sympathetic to this line of thought, comments, 'The driving force that runs through his thought and carries him along is that of a vigorous naturalism—impassioned and, without going so far as to say reckless, a little frightening.'

It would indeed be frightening if one left out of account the underlying structure on which he built his search for God in and through his creatures : frightening, too, for a man ignorant of the laws of organic evolution and satisfied with the out-of-date concept of a static world. There can be no doubt about the

40

ambiguity of some of Père Teilhard's statements, for the very richness and originality of his thought made it difficult to express. He himself was always alive to this difficulty of expressing in adequate and unambiguous terms the vision of 'a positive confluence of Christian life with the natural sap of the universe'. In his own self the integration of life had been achieved ; if he loved God, it was through the world, and if he loved the world it was as a function of God, the animator of all things. ' The joy and strength of my life,' he wrote a month before his death, ' will have lain in the realisation that when the two ingredients—God and the world—were brought together they set up an endless mutual reaction, producing a sudden blaze of such intense brilliance that all the depths of the world were lit up for me.'

There was no contradiction in his soul, no ambiguity between his humble loyalty as a son of the Church and the boldness of his philosophical views. But in the depths of his being there raged the excruciating torment of reconciling his complete submission to the Church with the integrity of his thought.

In the following letter, written from Cape Town on 12 October, 1951, at the conclusion of his first visit to South Africa, Père Teilhard gives an excellent picture of his state of mind at that time and of the unreserved submission of his will to the decisions of the ecclesiastical authorities. It is addressed to his General, the Very Reverend Father Janssens, in Rome.

Cape Town, 12 October, 1951

Very Reverend Father,

P.C.

I feel that my departure from Africa (i.e. after two months' work and peace in the field) is a good moment to let you know briefly what I am thinking and where I stand. I do this without forgetting that you are the ' General ', but at the same time (as during our too short interview three years ago) with the frankness that is one of the Society's most precious assets.

1. Above all I feel that you must resign yourself to taking me as I am, that is, with the congenital quality (or weakness) which ever since my childhood has caused my spiritual life to be completely dominated by a sort of profound ' feeling ' for the organic realness of the World. At first it was an ill-defined feeling in my mind and heart, but as the years have gone by it has gradually become a precise, compelling sense of the Universe's general convergence upon itself; a convergence which coincides with, and culminates at its zenith in, Him *in quo omnia constant*, and whom the Society has taught me to love.

In the consciousness of this progression and synthesis of all things in *Xristo Jesu*, I have found an extraordinarily rich and inexhaustible source of clarity and interior strength, and an atmosphere outside which it is now physically impossible for me to breathe, to worship, to *believe*. What might have been taken in my attitude during the last thirty years for obstinacy or disrespect, is simply the result of my absolute inability to contain my own feeling of wonderment.

Everything stems from that basic psychological condition, and I can no more change it than I can change my age or the colour of my eyes.

2. Having made that clear, I can reassure you about my interior state of mind by emphasising that, whether or no this is generally true of others besides myself, the immediate effect of the interior attitude I have just described is to rivet me ever more firmly to three convictions which are the very marrow of Christianity.

The unique significance of Man as the spear-head of Life ; the position of Catholicism as the central axis in the convergent bundle [*faisceau*] of human activities ; and finally the essential function as consummator assumed by the risen Christ at the centre and peak of Creation : these three elements have driven (and continue to drive) roots so deep and so entangled in the whole fabric of my intellectual and religious perception that I could now tear them out only at the cost of destroying everything.

I can truly say—and this in virtue of the whole structure of my thought—that I now feel more indissolubly bound to the hierarchical Church and to the Christ of the Gospel than ever before in my life. Never has Christ seemed to me more real, more personal or more immense.

How, then, can I believe that there is any evil in the road I am following ?

3. I fully recognise, of course, that Rome may have its own reasons for judging that, in its present form, my concept of Christianity may be premature or incomplete and that at the present moment its wider diffusion may therefore be inopportune.

It is on this important point of formal loyalty and obedience that I am particularly anxious—it is in fact my real reason for writing this letter—to assure you that, in spite of any apparent evidence to the contrary, I am resolved to remain a ' child of obedience '.

Obviously I cannot abandon my own personal search—that would involve me in an interior catastrophe and in disloyalty to my most cherished vocation ; but (and this has been true for some months) I have ceased to propagate my ideas and am confining myself to achieving a deeper personal insight into them. This attitude has been made easier for me by my now being once more in a position to do first-hand scientific work.

In fact I have every hope that my absence from Europe will allow the commotion about me that may have disturbed you recently, simply to die down. Providence seems to be lending me a helping hand towards this : what I mean is that the Wenner

Gren (formerly the Viking) Foundation in New York which sent me here (it is the same Foundation, incidentally, that re-floated Père Schmidt's *Anthropos* after the war) is already asking me to prolong my stay in America as long as I can : they want me to classify and develop the data obtained from my work in Africa.—All this allows me a breathing space and gives a purely scientific orientation to the end of my career . . . and of my life.

Let me repeat that, as I see it, this letter is simply an exposition of conscience and calls for no answer from you. Look on it simply as a proof that you can count on me unreservedly to work for the Kingdom of God, which is the one thing I keep before my eyes and the one goal to which science leads me.

Your most respectful *in Xto filius*

P. Teilhard de Chardin

Père Teilhard knew well that it was his duty to speak out and allow others to share the fruits of his own experience. ' If I didn't write,' he told me, ' I would be a traitor.' It was no doubt because he expressed himself with such frankness and unaffected simplicity that he met with so much opposition both from theologians and from scientists. Of the latter he wrote, ' I have often felt myself impelled to question the value of my own interior testimony. Friends have assured me that they have never experienced this themselves. " It's just a matter of temperament," they've said. " You feel the need to philosophise, while with us research is simply something we enjoy doing, like having a drink." ' Not a very convincing answer, it is true, and one that would by no means satisfy the scrupulous mind or soul of Père Teilhard, who felt it essential even in the conceptual order to justify his activity. ' You fail,' he replied, ' to get to the bottom of what goes on in your heart and your mind, and that is why the "cosmic sense" and faith in the world are still dormant in you. You may multiply the extent and duration of progress as much as you please, and you may promise the world another hundred million years of growth ; but if at the end of that time it appears that the whole of consciousness must revert to zero without its hidden essence being anywhere preserved, then we shall lay down our arms and there will be a complete cessation of effort. The day is not far distant when humanity will realise that biologically it is faced with a choice between suicide and adoration.'

Père Teilhard's life, his interior life, is thus seen as a witness. ' My skill as a philosopher may be greater or less,' he writes in his notes, ' but one fact will always remain, that an average man of the twentieth century, just because he shared normally in the ideas and interests of his time, was able to attain a balanced interior life only in a scientifically integrated concept of the world and of Christ ; and that therein he found peace and limitless scope for his being to expand. Today, my faith in God is sounder, and my faith in the world stronger, than ever.' Could there be a more up to date or more faithful version of St. Paul's doctrine of the ' cosmic ' Christ ? ' In him all created things took their being, heavenly and earthly, visible and invisible. . . . They were all created through him and in him ; he takes precedence of all, and in him all subsist. . . . It was God's good pleasure to let all completeness dwell in him, and through him to win back all things, whether on earth or in heaven, unto union with himself, making peace with them through his blood, shed on the cross ' (Coloss. I, 16-19, 20).

In the strength derived from the nobility of his task, he could follow a road that might have led more ill-equipped souls into dangerous misconceptions ; and this in all sincerity of conscience. It was no doubt because of this serenity that he was so tolerant, with a tolerance that bordered on weakness and often caused him to be misunderstood ; for people are more ready to give others credit for justice than for love.

Even those who were most hostile to his philosophical and religious views recognised the exquisite gift for sympathy which made him a ' catcher of souls '. Countless intellectuals, executives, workmen and humble folk caught from him the vital spark of illumination and found peace. There was one limit to his tolerance : the one fault he detested, the one he would have nothing to do with, was the deliberate acceptance and delight in disgust with life, contempt for the works of man, fear of the human effort. For Père Teilhard this lack of confidence in the efficacy of man's vocation was the real sin. Our natural weaknesses could be looked on with indulgence, so long as the desire to ' rise ', to progress forward and upward, was sincere. ' Anything that makes me sink lower—that,' he used to say, ' is the real evil.'

It was this reasoned optimism, the fruit of his interior life, that gave him strength both when he had to fight and when he obediently gave way. It confirmed him, too, in his hope that one day the whole world would enrol in the service of Christ. From a continually reinvigorated search for God he drew fresh stores of tenacity. There was nothing petty nor rigid in this tension of the will towards union, but an effort renewed from day to day—God knows in the midst of what struggles—to steep himself in the divine Presence, without which he counted everything as vanity ; and at the same time he saw that, in pushing human aspirations to the most daring extremes, man may ascend to the heights. It was this he had in mind when he used to say ' We must dare all things.'

He died suddenly, as he had prayed that he might, in the full vigour of life ; friend of all men, of all countries, he died in the most cosmopolitan city in the world. It was on Easter Sunday, in the full bloom of spring, with the city bathed in a flood of sunshine. So it was that in the joy of the Resurrection Père Teilhard was reunited with the Christ whom all his life he had longed to possess in the blaze of victory.

' Lord, since with every instinct of my being and through all the changing fortunes of my life, it is You whom I have ever sought, You whom I have set at the heart of universal matter, it will be in a resplendence which shines through all things and in which all things are ablaze, that I shall have the felicity of closing my eyes.'

THE TRAVELLER *by* CLAUDE ARAGONNÈS

(Mlle Teillard-Chambon), cousin of Père Teilhard

Pierre Teilhard de Chardin was a great traveller, as the following letters show. Now that his books are being made available to the public, and he is beginning to be well known, it is interesting to fill in the background, to see him as an explorer, a seeker, pursuing his investigations over the vast areas of the world.

In his early years as a Jesuit he had taught physics in a college of his Order in Egypt from 1906 to 1908 and had already felt the pull of the East : ' I have glimpsed and greedily " drunk in " the East—not its people and its history (which don't interest me as yet), but its light, its vegetation, its fauna, and its deserts.'

Fifteen years later he again passed it in a liner bound for the Far East. By then, after long periods in England and Paris, he had become a professional scientist and was about to take his place among the most important specialists in the geology and palæontology of China. In fact Asia, at that time still mysterious and unknown, was to account for almost a third of his life.

There seems to be a strange premonition of his journeys to the East in some notes he made during the 1914–18 war, when he was a stretcher-bearer in one of the Zouave regiments. One day in 1917, between two battles on the Champagne front, he was looking out over a vast landscape that war had transformed into a 'wilderness', and he wrote :

'If, by half-closing my eyes and letting go the reins of my consciousness, I leave my imagination to follow its old grooves and habits, there arise within me vague memories of long journeys I took as a child. I see large main-line stations and coloured lights that speed trains out into the enchanted morning. Little by little the trenches lit up with signals become confused in my mind with a vast trans-continental line leading very very far away, leading somewhere beyond everything.

'Then my dream becomes clearer.

'The devastated ridges whose purpling outline is lost in the fading yellow of the sky have suddenly become the deserted upland in which I used to nurse my mirage-like plans for discoveries and science in the East. The pale river in the valley is no longer the Aisne but the Nile—the distant, mirror-like Nile that used to obsess me like a call from the tropics. I feel that I am sitting in the twilight over towards El Guiouchi, on the Mokattam, and looking towards the south.

'I've done it . . . I've given myself away.

'The enigmatic and obtrusive "me" who persists in liking the front can now be recognised. It is the adventurous me, the seeking me, the one who always wants to go to the furthest limits of the world so as to have new and rare visions and to say that he is "in the van".' (*La Nostalgie du front*, September, 1917.)

The East, the tropics . . . From 1923 onwards, with his long sea-voyages from one continent to another—wherever his insatiable curiosity called him—he encircled the globe several times. In the intervals between his exploration campaigns into the interior of China, he carried out excavations in Ethiopia, in

Northern India, and in Burma ; he inspected collections in Java, and went twice to South Africa ; North America, after several long visits, became very familiar to him, and it was there that he ended his career. He lived there from 1951 until he died in New York on 10 April, 1955.

Pierre Teilhard was heart and soul a citizen of the universe. As Victor Hugo said of the poet : he felt at home everywhere because everywhere he was with God. In Teilhard's case it could be added : because everywhere he was with man—man, the masterpiece of creation, and the object of his patient and passionate research. Field-work always had an enormous attraction for him. Although he had to spend so much time in the laboratory, he was essentially a scientist of the open air, and to touch Mother Earth—as in the Greek myth—made him feel younger. Towards the end of his life he regretted that his indifferent health made work in the field impossible. He was always ready to go anywhere. The slightest hint of a new line of research, and off he went, however inconvenient or inopportune the move might be. His constant readiness to set out meant that he frequently found himself at just that point where his foresight, advice, and organisation of the work could result in important finds. The most memorable of these occasions was the discovery of the famous *Sinanthropus*—the Fossil-man of China—near Pekin in 1929 : one of the most important palæontological events of the twentieth century.

As an explorer, Pierre Teilhard possessed not only the flair and the initiative to put him in the way of great and significant finds, but also the physical endurance, intrepidity and burning persistence of the seeker into the earth's secrets. His correspondence bears continual witness to difficulties overcome and fatigue surmounted—victories which enabled his practised eye to make itself master of vast regions which had been jealously guarded for centuries and hardly allowed access to the foreign traveller. Often he was the first to penetrate such regions—with just one companion, and a few ‘ boys ’, and under the conditions of insecurity and discomfort that he describes with such colour and humour in his letters.

He was often a pioneer in uncharted regions. Teilhard the naturalist, geologist and palæontologist had to become an expert in topography, geography, zoology, botany and ethnography. As he journeyed he studied the different races he encountered, their mentality, habits and culture. And this over vast territories. The China which he traversed in every direction from 1923 to 1940 was still the old immemorial China in which long caravans made their way along mere tracks, the China in which road and rail were still almost unknown—the Mongolian and Gobi deserts, the banks of the Hwang-Ho and the Yangtse, the lost corners of Honan and Shansi; little towns with crenellated ramparts, pagodas with roofs like circumflex accents, sampans and pointed hats; the China that we know from screens and tea-sets. Mud villages from which resigned peasants watched their fields being carried away by storms and their livestock by brigands; lama-series with monks in their gaudy evil-smelling clothes; the classical China of plague, famine and banditry, but where the people welcomed you to their black-pig farm and the women, tripping about on their misshapen feet, their heads surmounted by a diadem of beads, served you with tea.

It is a whole aspect of China that will soon be forgotten. The advance guard of China will forget that other one, the one which very few Europeans, and still fewer Frenchmen, were able to become so deeply acquainted with as Pierre Teilhard.

For it was no small thing to lead expeditions into those lost regions. First, a caravan had to be formed, mules to carry the finds, drivers, sometimes a military escort as a security measure. For transport—sometimes a two-wheeled cart, ‘ a hellish conveyance ’; more often a horse or a mule. For shelter—the filthy inn or the Mongol yourt, or else a tent at the mercy of the desert winds. Extremes of climate had to be reckoned with—extreme cold, extreme heat, snow-storms or sand-storms, or sudden floods threatening both travellers and their baggage. There was the danger of ambushes, attacks by bandits, pockets of soldiers engaged in civil war who ruined plans and forced one to turn back in one's tracks just when reaching the enchanted borders of some unknown land. For months on end there was the complete solitude of slow monotonous days travelling across grey immensities, in which only the play of light on the bare horizon could engage the eye. No encounter with civilised people ; no post, of course.

When he emerged from the interior and arrived at Pekin, Pierre Teilhard found a totally different China, a China brimming with intellectual and political ferment and an intelligentsia avid for knowledge and emancipation. This China welcomed scientific research and hence foreign scientists—Americans, Swedes, Danes, Germans. The value of Pierre Teilhard's specialist collaboration was immediately recognised. Attached to the Geological Service of the Chinese University, at that time under the direction of Dr. D. Black, he contributed in great measure to the training of the students, and especially of those engaged in research, with whom he was to associate his work both in the laboratory and in the field. It was a period of intense activity for the Survey, the results of which were to lead to the discovery of the first Sinanthropus and to the series of important finds which were to make Pekin one of the most famous centres of palæontological and prehistoric work. Scientist friends of Père Teilhard who were to visit Pekin at his request included M. Lacroix, of the Académie des Sciences, and the eminent prehistorian and professor at the Collège de France, M. l'Abbé Breuil.

Pierre Teilhard dedicated himself to this great task with total

disinterestedness, expecting neither title nor reward.[1] Convinced
that the internationalism of science was to be one of the mind's
greatest achievements, he served as a link between the cosmopolitan elements which made up Pekin society between the two
wars. He had many friends in the Legations and Embassies.
Those among them who read these letters will surely recapture
the Pekin atmosphere of those days.

As for the political atmosphere, Pierre Teilhard was well
placed to observe the instability of a China pulled in all directions,
soon to undergo the Japanese invasion on the one hand and the
insidious penetration of the Soviets on the other. It was a time
of tragedy and suspense, the eve of catastrophe, all of which can
be sensed in letters that Père Teilhard had to make more and more
discreet and allusive owing to the censorship.

Having become a scientist with a world-wide reputation,
Pierre Teilhard was often asked to take part in congresses or
scientific missions in various countries. These journeys became
more frequent and more important as time went on. He was
familiar with all the sea-routes, with luxury steamers (in which he
never travelled first-class) or small cargo-boats. If we go back
over his itineraries before the age of the aeroplane[2] we feel quite
dizzy. He was here, there and everywhere, like a tongue of fire.
One day in Pekin, the next in Hongkong, the next in Singapore,
then Malaya, Paris, New York, San Francisco, Honolulu, Kobé,
Rangoon. . . . And the following year it would be other variations on the same theme.

He undoubtedly found travel agreeable in itself—the physical

---

[1] He was twice awarded the Légion d'Honneur. In 1921, *Chevalier* for
military services ; and on his return to France, *Officier* for services rendered
to scientific institutes in China.

[2] The aeroplane would in fact have served him less well. The leisure of
sea-voyages afforded him lon production periods, not to mention the interest of the ports of call. But he did in fact make use of aeroplanes in his last
years.

and mental relaxation were necessary to him. Now and again, however, he admitted to being a little weary of the 'endless pilgrimage'. It sometimes 'got him down a little'. But whenever, wherever, there were people to be seen, then he had to be off. It was his job. God was commanding him by means of events—'those masters given us by His hand' as Pascal said. No aspect of the earth nor of man could be neglected, in the interests of the huge, never-ending inquiry on which his work was built.

Ceaseless travel meant continual meetings. One day Pierre Teilhard came across a friend in some remote corner of the globe. He greeted him so warmly that the other expressed mild surprise. 'Why am I so happy?' said the traveller, 'why, because the earth is round!'

His capacity for making people welcome was outstanding, and it was one of his charms. He was extremely accessible; his natural and frank manner, the personal interest he took in people, the humour with which he discouraged the triteness of small talk but encouraged sincerity, won him an incredible number of friends all over the world. When referring to people, no single word came so often from his pen as 'friend'. Indeed he sometimes used this word of men well known to be his intellectual opponents—to their surprise : but he was a man who didn't know how to hate. He was intolerant only of the intolerant. He was very perceptive about people, though he was instinctively more ready to see the good than the bad. Once, when he was praising a new friend, someone exclaimed enviously : 'I see, so he's discovered yet another fine character', to which he replied, 'Come now, what are you complaining of? We are all the gainers.' And yet this man who moved in so many different circles was also dominated by a single idea, and like someone ardently following a line of research, *he was always thinking about it.*

It was by contact with new continents that his mind was

illuminated and his vision enlarged. 'It was Asia,' he said, ' that revealed to me the grandeur and beauty of the earth and its phenomena.' The earth—explored, excavated, studied with passion and religious respect—was in fact the spring-board of his thought. The earth brought him to grips with man, the living being among all living beings, that being that a unique fortune had carried to the top of the tree of life.

An interesting photograph in an American paper of 1937 shows Pierre Teilhard at a Congress in Philadelphia surrounded by foreign scientists and holding in his hands the famous Chou-Kou-Tien skull. He is telling his colleagues, who are following closely, about this ancestor of man whose age, the palæontologists tell us, is measured by hundreds of thousands of years. He was strongly of the opinion that a separate science ought to be established—anthropogenesis—the science of human origins and of the development of mankind which, in his opinion, was still in process. One step further—one of those great strides of science which sign-post the road of progress and of knowledge.

Thenceforth Pierre Teilhard was to concentrate the whole effort of his research on what he called the *phenomenon of man*, so as to pinpoint what is at the same time ordinary and extraordinary in our species as it makes its arrow-like ascent towards the summit of the evolution of species. What new thing does the presence of man bring to the scientist's view of the world? *Man's greatness lies in thought*, Pascal had already said. Does the scientist corroborate this? Science has no measure for that greatness. This strange creature is distinguished from the rest of the primates by thought *alone*. Therefore the scientists have classified him, as best they could, in a separate compartment : the Hominiens alongside the Anthropoids.

To seek the measure of man and to find his real place in nature—that was the problem which occupied Pierre Teilhard's mind all his life. He considers that on the solution adopted depends whether or not the universe has any meaning. In order to give man his true place, he must be considered in his total breadth, as alone constituting the noosphere, the sphere of the *mind*, the thinking layer of the earth (just as the biosphere is the living layer).

At the heart of universal becoming (evolution), man, the latest arrival and heir to the riches of an unfathomable past, man who has been raised to the unique dignity of *knowing* and *knowing that he knows* (reflection), has a future peculiar to himself, a future with infinite prolongations. It was on human nature and the human condition that Pierre Teilhard centred his thought, in the midst of his scientific career ; it was to those problems that he was henceforth to apply the total effort of a mind capable of the vastest syntheses. Without ever abandoning his work as a palæontologist concentrated on the past of the species, he could be seen at grips with the problem of human evolution, of socialisation (of prime importance) and of its future development. 'The study of the past,' he wrote, 'has revealed to me the structure of the future.' And he discerned, in this future, the outlines of the *ultra-human*. These were dizzy perspectives in which his creative spirit delighted, extrapolating—as he was well aware—the positive data of science, but according to the curve he thought he could draw of human evolution up to its present state.[1] Only the bold thinker, meditating on the ultra-human as he travelled far and wide, could write in his note-book : 'Are there not journeys which permit us, not merely a change of place, but a change of sphere, in the universe ?' And he added : 'The veneer of colour and place bores me to tears. What I love cannot be seen.'

This is the comment of a metaphysician, and above all of a mystic.

[1] Cf. *The Phenomenon of Man* (Collins, 1959) and *Le Groupe zoologique humain*, 'Structure et directions évolutives' (Albin Michel, 1956).

So we have the three component parts that went to make up this pioneering genius : disciplined scientific thought, a deeply original philosophic mind and a mystical temperament in which the quest for God through His handiwork was a burning passion.

At first it was my plan to publish only Pierre Teilhard's external impressions and reflections, but it soon became plain that I could not draw a line in his correspondence between the outward itinerary and the inward progress of ideas. Many of the themes of the books that were to come—and these, after all, are the most valuable outcome of the journeys—had their origin in the meditations of a mystic who, in his solitude, centred himself on God. Teilhard the explorer brought back cases of fossils and notes for scientific memoranda, but he brought back an invisible harvest too. From the long hours of recollected withdrawal, from the endless mule-rides in the desert, from the slow sea-voyages, there emerged those wonderful mystical poems : *La Messe sur le monde*, 1923, and *Le Milieu divin*, 1926–27, as well as the series of important essays of which each one marks an advance in thought on the one before.[1] These letters show us their conception and enable us to date them. From them his correspondents first learn the ideas of the essays, then hear of their completion and dispatch.

Will he succeed in ' getting his ideas across ' ? It is a question that often comes up, with alternating hope and disappointment. A few articles came out,[2] but the writings that he regarded as the essential elements of the synthesis on which he was at work were not published during his lifetime. It is a remarkable thing that

[1] *L'Esprit de la terre* (1931) ; *La Route de l'ouest* and *Vers une mystique nouvelle* (1932) ; *Comment je crois* (1934) ; *La Découverte du passé* (1935) ; *Esquisse d'un univers personnel* (1936) ; *Le Phénomène spirituel* (1937) ; *L'Énergie humaine* (1937) ; *Le Phénomène humain* (*The Phenomenon of Man*) (1938–40).

[2] In the review *Études* (Paris) and the *Revue des questions scientifiques* (Louvain).

though he was constantly trying to obtain from his superiors permission to print there is no sign of annoyance in his letters. One might have expected bitterness, *there was no trace of it.* Faced with persistent lack of understanding, the most he ever said was, ' I've worked more for the Kingdom of God than anyone seems to think ' (letter to his brother, 1933). This serenity was acquired by means of unshakable faith—faith in the world, faith in God whom he sought to reveal to his contemporaries through His handiwork once its true meaning was rediscovered. ' I have no other ambition,' he said, ' but to leave a logical life behind me, a life totally dedicated to the great hopes of the world. There lies the future of religion for humanity ; I am as sure of it as I am of my own existence.' (Tientsin, 27 August, 1927.) Or again, ' my sole ambition is to be laid among the foundations of what is going to grow '. For he saw in this future, when the deep strivings of our age have died down, a time when the world would have re-found its soul, having been reconciled with the Christian vision by ' a conquering and fully human Church '.

He was convinced that he had something to say and that one day the world would listen to him ; but like all great people who feel a call, he was divided between mission and submission. His own solution to the problem lay in personal sacrifice. He firmly believed that his message lay within ' the axis of truth ' necessary to the men of his time. The moving lines that he was to write on the eve of his death put the seal on his message : ' Once the truth has made its presence felt in a single soul, nothing can ever stop it from invading everything and setting fire to everything.' (New York, March, 1955.)

The extraordinary tension of a man consumed by such a fire can be read on almost every page of the letters. And therein lies the essence of this very rich personality made up of complexities and contrasts, one that a strong moral and religious discipline always brought back, with no loss in flexibility, to its deep interior unity.

Teilhard's letters show us the whole man as he was. We can imagine this 'fine gentleman'—as his American friends called him—with his tall stature, his vigorous and refined face, his frank and penetrating (but not embarrassingly insistent) eye, his reserved yet 'infinitely accessible' manner. Though he was called 'Father', according to custom, he was much more like an elder brother—for he never 'put off' or intimidated anyone, and one could say anything to him. Perhaps he was taciturn at times, when the company bored him, but he woke up as soon as the conversation was interesting and became the thrilling talker who dazzled a Paris reporter passing through China. It is just the same when he is writing informally.

He had the gift in his letters of talking about things and about himself with a moving simplicity which came from 'sincerity and an unshakable decision '—especially when touching on subjects close to his heart. It is an accent that can be heard everywhere —in a short, vivid, incisive phrase, though coloured by the imagination of the artist and poet. How sharp his vision was! He felt contempt only for the shoddy, and for facile exoticism ; but although landscapes, like men, bored him when they had nothing more to say to him, he was always ready with his curiosity and his wonder. He always remained the naturalist, delighted by a new flower, or, in the steppes, by the flight of a gazelle, and by the contemplation of great sweeps of land. He always passionately loved the face of the earth.

In his great philosophical and religious essays the style is quite different. Here the sentences are sometimes stretched to their utmost limits, in order to express difficult things with strength and clarity. These masterly works by ' one of the greatest minds the world has known,'[1] ' written with fearlessness, and put

[1] Jean Piveteau, in his preface to Le Groupe zoologique humain, Paris, 1956.

forward with humility ' [1] will be of inestimable value to the men of today, and still more to those of tomorrow.

The message of these letters, already received by a few but now offered to all—those who knew him and those who would like to have known him—help to restore in some shadowy way what death has taken from us : his presence.

ACKNOWLEDGMENTS

My links with Père Teilhard as cousin and close friend put me in the privileged position of receiving many notes and letters from him on his travels, over a particularly important and productive period of his life. As these seemed to me to form a document of exceptional value, I felt they should be published for the benefit of everyone wishing for a deeper acquaintance with one of the noblest and most attractive figures of our time.

It seemed suitable, too, to show the public a more intimate and personal side of Pierre Teilhard at the time when some of his important works were beginning to be known.

When I told him of my plan to publish his letters some day, I was encouraged by his answer (4 September, 1948) : ' Of course you must do what you think best in this matter. Our Lord can make use of us by means of things that seem to us unimportant—such as the spontaneous and unelaborated expressions of our thought.'

I then got into touch with other of Père Teilhard's correspondents, so as to be able to produce a more comprehensive volume. I would like to thank my cousin, Joseph Teilhard de Chardin, Père Teilhard's brother, for letting me have his letters, and also Max-Henri Bégouën, one of his closest friends. I am respectfully

[1] Ed. Boné, ' Pierre Teilhard de Chardin ', *Revue des questions scientifiques*, Louvain, 20 January, 1956.

grateful, too, to M. l'Abbé Breuil for the letters he has given me permission to publish. They are of especial interest as throwing light on their work in two neighbouring fields, and on the similarity of their outlook which over a long period made the two great scientists also great friends.

The name of the recipient appears at the head of each letter. Where no name is mentioned, the recipient was myself.

Claude Aragonnès
(*Mlle Teillard-Chambon*)

10 *April*, 1956

The Letters

The name of the recipient appears at the head of each letter.
Where no name is mentioned, the recipient was
Mlle Teillard-Chambon

At Peking, 1935

1923

On 6 April, 1923, Père Teilhard sailed from Marseilles for China. From Port Said onwards new horizons opened up before him and, like every traveller who approaches the East for the first time, he fell under its spell and recorded his impressions stage by stage.

15 April, 1913

All day long we have been gliding through the Gulf of Suez between two fantastically picturesque and desolate lands : Sinai, a great massif of granite and slashed red sandstone, and the Egyptian coast, at first regular and tabular and then bristling with all sorts of extraordinary peaks, all equally sharp and bare. Above them, dreamlike colours, strangely soft for a climate of such extremes. To the east, the sea seemed dark blue. Its line on the horizon was as sharp as a knife blade. And then, above this dark band, without a break, the pale pink of the mountains rose up into a misty green sky. At sunset, it was the western coast which drew to itself all the beauty of the evening. As the sun disappeared in a little flutter of burning clouds, so the mountains of Egypt, until then covered in mist, began to pass through every possible shade of violet, from the very deepest to the most transparent mauve. Last to be seen was a whole line of sharp points, like the teeth of a saw, silhouetted in the golden sky. But all this magic was nothing compared with what the mind was uncovering in these almost unknown lands, which hardly anyone visits and to which, perhaps for that very reason, the most mysterious phases of our religious history are linked. I would have liked to land on those rocky slopes, not only to test them with my hammer, but also to learn whether I too could hear the voice of the Burning Bush. But has not the moment passed when God speaks in the desert, and must we not now understand that ' He who is ' is not to be heard in this place or that, for the heights where He dwells are not inaccessible mountains but a more profound sphere of things ? The secret of the world lies wherever we can discern the transparency of the universe.

More landscapes, more people passed before him. The variety of passengers on board—the Chinese waiter, the negro stoker, the colonial administrator, the soldier, the merchant, the missionary, the ship's doctor (' a curious and enigmatic person who seems to have brushed up against every science and every experience ')— gave the measure of ' the heights and depths of the human layer' within this small floating universe.

' Professors of Theology would do well to have a spell of what I am doing now. I am beginning to think that there is a certain aspect of the real world as closed to some believers as the world of faith is to unbelievers. . . .'

The latter—positivists and sceptics—surprised him by their incapacity to grasp anything beyond the empirical, while his mystical attitude was equally new to them.

The interesting thing nevertheless was that he was able to discuss fundamentals with these men who had no beliefs, and to tackle with them all the major issues ; they laid bare their innermost thoughts while his only tactics were ' to be as true to himself as possible '.

In these talks Père Teilhard said that he found that ' his own reactions could be salutary for his spirit '.

' I find that the single great problem of the One and the Mani-

*fold is rapidly beginning to emerge from the over-metaphysical
context in which I used to state it and look for its solution. I can
now see more clearly that its urgency and its difficulties must be in
terms of real men and women.'*

21 April

Having passed Cape Guadarfui, we have entered a zone of absolute
calm. For the last 48 hours the sea has been smooth and oily,
except where a slight breeze ruffles its surface or covers it with a
network of minute wrinkles as regular as the weave of a tapestry.
Upon this mirror flying-fish rise up, glide, and take off again,
like swallows skimming the water. In the middle of this great
shoreless lake the evenings take on an exquisite beauty. Yesterday
I could never tire of looking to the east where the sea was uniformly milky and green, with an opalescence that was still not
transparent, lighter than the background of the sky. Suddenly
on the horizon a thin diffuse cloud became tinged with pink ;
and then with the little oily ripples of the ocean still opal on one
side and turning to lilac on the other, the whole sea looked for a
few seconds like watered silk. Then the light was gone and the
stars began to be reflected around us as peacefully as in the water
of a quiet pool.

*From Colombo, the island of Ceylon appeared under a dark haze,
but the stop was too short for the travellers to visit the wild and
mountainous part of the island. Nevertheless the naturalist in
Père Teilhard was delighted by what he saw of botanical and
zoological novelty in the gardens and streets of Colombo itself.*

27 April

The real charm of Ceylon lies in its vegetation : the heavy opu-
lence of the foliage, the luxuriance of the flowers. On landing,

you first notice the acacias, lebeks, with their large mimosa-like blooms, the ' flamboyants ' smothered in scarlet blossoms as big as nasturtiums, and other trees with clusters of golden yellow splashed with purple which, with the coconut palms, provide most of the shade. I went to admire this splendid flora in Victoria Park—the public gardens. Gorgeous butterflies hovered over the blooms, and small grey striped squirrels ran about in the branches; and instead of gardeners, it was a surprise to see little copper-skinned Hindu girls, draped in pink, walking between the clumps of flowers, or little ragamuffins begging for a few pennies in exchange for fallen blossoms, their gestures astonishingly graceful, and so quaint with their velvet eyes.

I had a glimpse of the country of *Kim*. In Ceylon there must be less variety of race than in northern India, but there is just the same swarming population. Among the proudest natives are the Cingalese, distinguishable by the comb they wear (even the men) like a half-coronet on the back of their heads. But there are other types and other castes, some with shaved heads, some with buns, and some with long hair. They are all marked by the same nobility of bearing.

In the business districts of Colombo there is constant chatter and you come across singers and musicians, sacred or secular, perhaps under a large banyan tree in front of a little Buddhist temple. In the gardens and residential quarters, on the other hand, an almost complete silence reigns ; and in the long avenues of red earth, under the leafy trees, there is no traffic except little ox-carts or rickshaws drawn by bare-foot coolies. Nothing but muffled sounds in an atmosphere laden with heavy nameless scents. No horses to speak of. The little humped oxen (often as small as calves) are the main draught animals. I have seen some of them trotting at an astonishing speed.

Penang, 2 May

I thought, when I was admiring Colombo, that I was seeing the most beautiful thing in my journey. But now I put Malaya above Ceylon, and I don't think that anywhere in the tropics you could find a more splendid spectacle than Penang between five and six in the morning. To the east, layer behind layer of conical mountains, deep blue, crowned here and there with great clouds rising up from low-lying plains where heavy vapours drift over a boundless forest. The last of these mountains, densely covered with great trees, plunge straight down to the sea, forming little islets whose woods literally dive into the water. The low-lands finish in creeks and sandy beaches lined with coco-palms ; sometimes they are enlivened with a Malayan village, the grey huts carried on tall piles, like neolithic lake-dwellings. On the sea heavy, gaily-painted junks manœuvre patiently, their copper-coloured sails roughly sewn from horizontal strips, their prows decorated with two big eyes (' to frighten off the sea devils ').

Malacca

In the strait the waters are shallow, full of currents and laden with debris torn from the coast. Instead of making our way over a heavy black sea, as in the Indian Ocean, for a whole day we have been gliding over waters of jade green, a little turbid, almost motionless. The peninsula of Malacca with its conical mountains, its islets covered with a thick fleece of big trees, and its low-lying plains lined with coco-palms, have never been out of sight. On the other hand Sumatra has always remained below the horizon, betrayed only by a pile of huge clouds, exhalations, no doubt, from the tropical forests.

In these regions the sky has none of the Mediterranean purity which we imagine belongs to all hot countries. The blue, here and there, is magnificent, but often it is just patches between huge fleecy masses or long wisps of cloud. The evening before our arrival at Singapore we had a particularly lavish sunset in an encumbered sky of this kind. Above us there was a curtain of finely-gathered draperies which turned from silvery-white to gold and then to deep red ; further off were strips of washed sky, green and blue ; and finally along the whole length of the horizon rose a mass of cumulus, dense as a mountain range, flushing with pink from north to south, like a series of Alpine peaks.

11 May

As the Lama in *Kim* said, and as I feel more and more, the world is ' a great and terrible thing '. It was civilisation that overawed the Lama. In my case, on the contrary, it is the immense mass of undisciplined human powers that overwhelms me. I feel, too, how much the exploration of the earth *in itself* fails to bring any light or point out any solution to the most fundamental questions of life. I feel as though I am going round and round an immense problem without getting to the heart of it. And I know, too, that the wider the problem seems to grow before my eyes the more clearly I see that its solution can only be sought in a ' faith ' beyond all experience. We must break through and go beyond appearances ; never perhaps more than now has their veil seemed to me so ' without seam '. . . .

Last night, a long talk with the Doctor and another passenger on questions of moral philosophy. We finally had to admit that we differed on such fundamentals as : ' Is it better to be or not to be ? '

I believe, in fact, that this is a fundamental option of all thought, a postulate which cannot be proved but from which everything is deduced. Once it is admitted that being is better than its opposite, it is difficult to stop short of God ; if it is not admitted, discussion ceases to be possible.

Père Teilhard arrived at Saigon on 13 May and continued his journey by sea from Hongkong to Shanghai, and by rail from Shanghai to Tientsin. At last he was able to send his news, from China.

Tientsin, 23 May

The last lap of my journey passed off very well. It was made in two stages : Shanghai-Nanking-Tientsin. Nanking struck me as a town of modest size looking lost within the ancient Chinese walls that surrounded it at the time of its greatness. The very green country all around has not the unbearable monotony of Shanghai, for the Yangtze Kiang, still wide enough to take large warships, is already bordered by low mountains covered with azaleas. You cross the river in a steamship to reach the terminus of the Tientsin line. There, at Pukow, I took the famous ' blue train ' which was attacked by bandits three weeks ago—a comfortable train with couchettes, dining-car and saloon coach. The timetable has been altered so that the train can pass through the danger zone in daylight, and in each coach two armed soldiers are on guard to protect the passengers : an inadequate precaution should the bandits want to repeat their attack, but it doesn't look as if they intend to re-enact their little drama ; it doesn't seem to have brought them the rewards they expected. For 24 hours I bowled peacefully along, first between splendid almost-ripe crops, then in a wild rocky region, then—on reaching the basin of the Yellow River—over vast stretches of cultivated land, still very dry, waiting to be flooded. A ' yellow wind ' brought very fine dust from Mongolia, in an atmosphere so dry that the covers of books curled up.

(To the Abbé Breuil)   *Hautes Études, Race Course Road, Tientsin*
25 May, 1923

My dear and very good friend,

As you see, I'm writing to you from my operational base where I arrived only three days ago after a good journey. I hope you received my card from Colombo. [. . .]

As regards myself, my material situation is as follows : I have landed in a China more restless than ever and almost everywhere at the mercy of gangs of insurgent troops. The train in which I travelled from Nanking had been attacked and looted a fortnight before (and it's the biggest train of the biggest line in China!) In spite of these difficulties I have every hope of leaving within a fortnight for somewhere in Mongolia, when all the preparations for the expedition—which are more complicated than I thought —have been completed. Père Licent[1] is really an amazing traveller ; there's nothing he doesn't know about what to do or what may happen when you're travelling on the road in China. While awaiting our departure, and in the time left for shopping and visiting, I'm going to study Chinese geology a little, and inspect, as a first step, the finds assembled over the past nine years in the ' Museum ' (a large three-storeyed building) built by Père Licent. I've already discovered that almost all the fossils found last year in the Ordos (in the walls of a canyon 250 feet deep) are of the Quaternary, possibly rather late : *Rhinoceros tichorhinus* (entire skulls), *Bos* (enormous), *Equus* (very small). [. . .] At the base there is perhaps some Pliocene. What I find disconcerting in China is the formidable extent of the erosion and embanking : you get the impression that, in the course of a few centuries,

[1] Père Licent, a naturalist, had already made several expeditions into Central Asia and was to accompany Père Teilhard on the latter's first.

whole countries can be born or be completely scoured away. These conditions aren't exactly favourable to ancient archaeological deposits. I'm going to watch out for quartzites or cut rocks in particular. Père Licent had no idea that it was necessary to look for anything but flints.

I would be hard put to it to give you an exact idea of my state of mind at the moment. The multitude of new things and new people that I've seen the last two months, added to the uprooting from my own world, has left me rather dazed. I haven't yet managed to master or digest the mass of strange impressions and outlooks that I have briefly and superficially come up against—at an age, too, when my mind is already losing its elasticity. My strongest impression at the moment is a confused one that the human world (to look no further than that) is a huge and disparate thing, just about as coherent, at the moment, as the surface of a rough sea. I still believe, for reasons imbued with mysticism and metaphysics, that this incoherence is the prelude to a unification. I have also noted, I think (in visiting some of the large Catholic centres of social work in Hongkong and Shanghai) that Catholicism has an extraordinary power of penetrating and re-shaping souls (I have met children, old people and nuns, Chinese men and women, who really seemed to look at me with that man-to-man communication which I might have expected to find from Europeans). The fact remains, however, that the multiplicity of human elements and human points of view revealed by a journey in the Far East is so ' *overwhelming* ' [1] that one cannot conceive of a religious life, a religious organism, assimilating such a mass without being profoundly modified and enriched by it—unless a preliminary effort to introduce intellectual and social uniformity should succeed in levelling-out the

[1] The author's use of an English expression is indicated throughout this edition by italic type in quotation marks [Tr.].

deep diversity which still separates oriental peoples from our Mediterranean civilisation.

[. . .] My impressions of this country [Northern China] are still almost non-existent. They come down to this : China, to the north of the Yangtze Kiang, is a region where there are fertile sources of interest for anyone who wants to work and search. But it is the last country in the world in which to find rest and comfort. Just as Malaya enchanted me with its flamboyant flowers and dense forests, so the valleys of the Blue River and the Yellow River strike me as austere and desolate regions in which the mind, as well as the body, is exposed defenceless to all the great winds of the earth. These immense expanses, grey and flat, out of all proportion to our plains of western Europe, and these completely bare and rocky mountains, provide no moral hand-hold. One feels lost in such undemarcated country. Perhaps I shall think differently when I get back from Mongolia.

I came to China to follow my star, and to steep myself in the raw regions of the universe. Intellectual fire is the last thing you will find in the people of these parts. The European in the Far East is normally engrossed in the ' business ' of commerce or religion. This pursuit distracts him, or arrests him at the lowest intellectual level. The deep spiritual movements that make up the life of Paris have no place here ; they would even be a little shocking. The people who come here, even the best, soon arrive at a dead end ; and I should imagine that after a few years of missionary work they are quite incapable of following the progress of our western thought : and so it will remain for as long as the Far East lacks its own religious life. In isolation a man stops either thinking or advancing.

Tientsin, 8 June, 1923

I have just returned from Pekin (three hours away by express). I spent 48 hours there getting ready for my departure on our expedition, which I hope will take place next Monday or Tuesday (the 11th or 12th of June). My brief trip to Pekin was very interesting because I was able to see one of the most characteristic places of the Far East, the intellectual centre of China. In Pekin there are no ' *buildings* ', no factories. The legations are crowded together behind fortified walls. All the rest is absolutely Manchu and Chinese. Enclosed within a huge ring of crenellated walls, the little bungalows line the roads set out geometrically north–south and east–west, so shaded by willows, thujas and acacias (often centuries old) that, seen from a certain height, the city looks almost like a wood. About an eighth of Pekin is occupied by the immense Imperial Palace whose monumental gates and successive pavilions form a huge cross (also oriented on the cardinal points of the compass) surrounded for half of its length by a wide moat full of water-lilies. In Pekin's bright sunshine, the gates and pavilions produce an extraordinary effect, with their pointed gables and varnished tiles (the decoration increasing in flamboyance with the lateness of the period), and their red and yellow colouring ; it is particularly effective when seen as a whole, from the top of a small artificial hill in the middle of the old imperial park, with ancient trees and a large lake of still water in the foreground.

I went to Pekin to get in touch with the Geological Survey of China, and there I came across young Wong [1] arrayed in a blue gown (I had last seen him in Brussels this summer in a suit). Several of the geologists of the Survey were ' *on the field* '. I shall meet them later. However, I coincided with a meeting of

---

[1] A Chinese student.

the Geological Society at which I read a paper (in English) about
Père Licent's finds. At the moment the people who matter in
these circles are the Americans and the Swedes. Outwardly, at
least, everyone was very cordial. I was staying at the large
residence of the Lazarists—the Petang—famous since it was
besieged by the Boxers in 1900.

*Finally, after countless visits to the authorities—both Chinese
and consular—and buying suitable clothes, the caravan set off.
The objective was the Ordos plateau in Western Mongolia,
situated in the great loop of the Hwang-Ho.*

18 June, 1923

I'm writing to you from a large Christian centre in Mongolia,
situated north of the loop in the Yellow River, in the plain (a
plateau about 2700 feet high) where the river flows lazily to
the south of a fine rocky barrier formed by the southern edge
of the high Mongolian plateau (the Gobi). I am in the heart of
Asia.

Eull-Cheu-Seu-Tsingti : a large mud village surrounded by
a high mud wall built by missionaries to ward off the attacks of
brigands. All around there stretches a grey plain, dotted with
mud villages inhabited by primitive Chinese, pig-tailed and
scantily clad.

We arrived at this place last night after a journey which, ten
years ago, would have taken at least a fortnight, but which a new
railway line has now made easy. We left Tientsin in the morning, and by the evening we were at Kalgan (beside the outer
Great Wall) to the north-west of Pekin. Kalgan is an important
geographical point, the centre for traffic with the Urga region,
and the starting-point for the routes going to the Gobi. We
spent the night in a Chinese inn (with our twelve packing-cases,
our two hampers, our camp-beds, our saddles and our two

servants). The next day a primitive little train with five coaches jogged us along between five in the morning and seven at night from Kalgan to Kwei-Ha-Cheng (the Blue City) across a mountainous landscape of which the central part, covered with basaltic plateaux and dotted with great lakes, was very like Auvergne, except that the pastureland, instead of being full of gentians, is covered with a very pretty little iris ; here and there it formed a positive carpet of purple.

The 'Blue City' has nothing to justify its romantic name except, perhaps, the light haze which bathes the rocky crests grouped like an amphitheatre round the horizon. It consists of a Mongol city enclosed in crenellated ramparts, and a Chinese city also built of mud and shaded by willows. Here we spent two days and were made wonderfully welcome by the Belgian missionaries who are evangelising the whole of Mongolia. Thanks to a letter from the Geological Survey of Pekin, and to Père Licent's personal connections, we had no difficulty in obtaining an audience with General Ma-Fou-Sian who commands the whole district.

The two men, dressed in khaki, were received by the powerful mandarin ; there was a ritual tea, and permission was granted to cross the Yellow River and enter the Ordos. But a complete caravan had to be organised, guides found, and further transit permits obtained from the military. 'Geology in China isn't what it is in the Alps or Spain. . . .' Moreover they were in the country of famine, brigands and plague. In playing hide-and-seek with these almost legendary scourges, the travellers both practised patience and discovered new areas of humanity.

Sant-Tao-Ho, 13 and 14 July, 1923

I really am beginning to find myself in ' *out-of-the-way*' places.

We've been travelling for long monotonous hours by mule across the steppes. We got away in the end, but by an unforeseen route : we had intended reaching Ning-Sia-Fu by cutting across the Ordos, but dangerous conditions on the right bank of the river, and the absence of grass in the desert (due to lack of rain) made us change our route ; and that is why for the last ten days our caravan has been slowly following the course of the loop in the Yellow River, to the north. The railway (and what a railway!) ends at Pao-Teo, a curious dusty city in a ring of crenellated ramparts. Beyond lie the virgin expanses of Mongolia. So the diversion would not lack charm but for the disadvantage of making us circle endlessly round and round the Promised Land and delay still more our arrival at the fossil-bearing deposits. Our caravan comprises ten mules, three donkeys, five donkey-boys, as well as Licent and myself and two servants, not counting two soldiers to act as escort. All told, ten guns which have done good service against the game in which this country abounds (pheasants, hares, gazelles) ; a highly impressive display of strength.

On the third day we arrived at an immense steppe over which we travelled for more than six days without seeing much else but endless expanses of tall grasses, tamarisk, and, at long intervals, a few mud houses belonging to Chinese settlers, or lamaseries of yellow- and red-robed monks. I no longer even notice the utter exoticism of my surroundings, and it now seems to me quite natural to drink my tea at night in the one room of a Chinese house in front of the square enclosed courtyard where black pigs roll about under the astonished gaze of great long-haired youths or women with little misshapen feet. Yet I never fail to be deeply conscious of my delight at finding myself in the middle of Mongolia's vast spaces, and in the evening I gaze at the mountain ranges with outlandish names—and which I had hardly even noticed in the atlas—as they silhouette themselves, in pearl-blue to the west and in violet to the east, above an ocean of yellow grasses. [. . .]

San-Tao-Ho is an episcopal residence surrounded by a Christian village and sheltered, with its fine large trees, by a great mud wall. In these parts the missionaries are large-scale landowners, and the Christians are, in fact, the Church's tenants. It's all a very intelligently-run organisation ; a curious legal system governs the ownership of land as between the Mongols, the only land-owners of the steppes, and the Chinese who settle there. From the top of the walls of San-Tao-Ho, where I have just climbed with my field-glasses, the view is really remarkable : directly to the south a vast area of white dunes curling away as far as the eye can see across the steppes, farther off the outline of the Ala-Shan ; and mainly to the east (only 3 or 4 miles away) the desert plateau of the Ordos, grey and red, like the mountains of Cairo, waiting for the evening to envelop it in a uniform cloak of violet. We are at last approaching the land of fossils—they are already being pointed out to us. We shall probably reach Ning-Sia-Fu by following the right bank of the river in such a way as to keep an eye on the rock outcrops. If we find deposits we shall stop to work them. And meanwhile our mail is piling up at Ning-Sia-Fu I have had no news from anyone since June 12.

Tang-Kou

I'm writing to you under canvas beside the Yellow River, with a strange half-fortified little city opposite, buried among the dunes, in the middle of the desert. We arrived here this morning after a week spent in the ' bad lands ' of the Ordos digging up fossils. For, after many difficulties, we finally found an unexplored bed— only fair as regards the quality of its specimens, but perhaps of first-class significance as regards the geology of China. We spent five days digging, and now we hope to reach the Chara-Ousso-

79

Gol, which isn't easy owing to the terrible drought in the desert. Perhaps we shall have to go right down to Ning-Sia-Fu, that is to say make a complete circle round the desert massif. The week spent under canvas in the desert wasn't without its picturesque side. We were beside a spring (a little brackish) among camels, gazelles and magnificent wild sheep (argalis) of which our Chinese servant managed to kill a fine specimen. Imagine a great amphitheatre of rocks and dark red earth, with clumps of shrubs every six or nine feet—and at the bottom two white tents and ten mules : that is the setting in which we spent some excellent days.

(To the Abbé Breuil) *Ordos (West), 16 July, 1923*

My very dear friend,

I have given you no sign of life, in spite of my promise, since my card from Tientsin on June 12. The fact is that my travels leave me much less leisure than I had anticipated. Today rain keeps us to our tent, and I am taking the opportunity of writing to you as much for my own sake as to give you pleasure. In my present isolation I feel more keenly than ever before what a deep and essential part of my life you have become.

I'm writing to you from the point marked A on the rough map enclosed. All sorts of setbacks, both climatic (the drought which has stopped the grass growing in the desert) and political (the presence of bandits to the north of the loop in the river) have repeatedly made us change the route we planned. Instead of going straight to the Chara-Ousso-Gol (whose deposits of Quaternary fossils are our main objective) we have had to make a big detour to the north, and this detour (by no means unproductive, as you will see) has not yet come to an end, though it's more than a month since we left Tientsin. There is a railway as far as Pao-Teo (extremely primitive after Kalgan, but at least it functions). At

Pao-Teo we formed our caravan (ten mules) and, since June 21, we have been jogging along with our cases through arid passes and over immense steppes inhabited by gazelles. We are in Mongolia, a country whose true landowners—shepherds living in their yourts—are gradually being ousted (all along the river) by Chinese settlers who scratch the ground and spoil the country far more than they enhance its value (because by fecklessly destroying the age-old soil of the steppes and by cutting down the few trees that still remain, they loosen the sand, cause the formation of dunes and generally accelerate the terrifying erosion of these parts). Burning days, but cool nights. Physically, I am fine. Morally, I am absorbed by the work and very much interested by the extreme novelty of what I'm seeing ; interested, but not thrilled, as I would have been ten or twenty years ago. Today what counts for me (as for you) is the future of things ; whereas here I am plunged into the past. Mongolia strikes me as a ' museum ' of antique specimens (zoological and ethnological), a slice of the past. Try as I will, I see no promise of progress, no ferment, no ' burgeoning ' for mankind of tomorrow. This corner of Asia (and even China outside the Great Wall ?) gives the impression of an empty reservoir.[1]

[. . .] And that is the key thing as regards my outward existence. Inwardly, I miss you very much, and many aspects of Paris too. But it was essential for me to come here if I was to be ' stronger ' on my return. I rather hope to find a letter from you when I get my mail at Ning-Sia-Fu in a few days.

---

[1] It must be remembered that this was written in 1923.

(To the Abbé Breuil)   *Between Ning-Sia-Fu and Yu-Lin-Fu,*
beside the Great Wall
25 July, 1923

My dear good friend,

If I write to you again so soon it is to tell you that, three days ago, about 40 miles east of Ning-Sia-Fu, in the ' wall ' of a stream, Licent and I found a typical palæolithic hearth in some perfectly stratified deposits. As the enclosed plan will show you, the hearth lies at the bottom of an old cliff of loess, beside an ancient watercourse (lake-deposit No. 1), and is covered over by an important lake or river deposit which cuts the canyon of the existing stream in several places. Man must have lived by the water at No. 1, perhaps in a dwelling hollowed out from the loess (which is still inhabited today) and his habitat has been submerged.

[. . .] We are continuing on our way towards the Chara-Ousso-Gol where last year Licent found his magnificent Quaternary fauna and a human femur. Now I hope to get a clear view of some deposits which almost certainly link up with those of the hearth we have just found. After exploring the Chara-Ousso-Gol we shall come back to the hearth if nothing takes us elsewhere. For two months now we have never gone where we meant to and yet we have always found something. I think Our Lord must be guiding us. In the end perhaps I shan't leave the Ordos and shall never get to the red Miocene lands of Kansu.

I am writing to you from a marvellous place—an inn, at a col, beside the Great Wall. In the distance there are vast sweeps of steppe. To the west the outline of the Ala-Shan. To the east a large salt lake.

This letter will go in three days, from the banks of the Chara-Ousso-Gol. It will bring you once again my deep affection *in Christo.*

Hoa-Ma-Tcheu, 26 July, 1923

There have been some wonderfully picturesque stretches since Tang-Kou, notably the crossing of the Arbous-Ula massif, a continuation of the great Gobi ranges, like a spur in the desert plateau of the Ordos. We stopped at a lamasery hidden at the base of a rocky amphitheatre, in colour and situation a marvel of art. The lamas, like monks in every country, excel in the art of finding beautiful places to live in. Seen close to, their buildings, like their purple and violet garments, are ragged and shoddy ; but seen from a distance both they and their monasteries are real masterpieces of line and colour. On our way I did quite a bit of geological work. What's more, 40 miles from Ning-Sia-Fu, we had the unheard-of luck of coming upon a very fine palæolothic hearth in a stratified bed. I think it is the first discovery of this kind to be made in China, or in the Far East for that matter. So it is, perhaps, a real find, and I have lost no time in letting Breuil and Boule [1] know about it. [. . .] All goes well with me both physically and morally. This period in Mongolia, like the war, is rather like a ' retreat ' for me, in that it leads me to the heart of the unique greatness of God.

Beside the Chara-Ousso-Gol, 14 August, 1923

The Chara-Ousso-Gol is a strange little river running 250 feet down in a canyon it has gouged out for itself in the middle of a plain of steppes and dunes.

We are camped at the bottom of the canyon in a dried-up river-bed near a Mongol ' house ' scooped out of a little promontory cut off from the cliffs (a real fortress). The Mongol is our friend, and his large family help with the digging while his goats provide us with milk. We're surrounded by horses, kites

[1] Marcellin Boule, Director of the Natural History Museum in Paris.

and cranes, as tame, almost, as garden pets. It's altogether bucolic. The Mongols wear long hair, never take off their boots, are never out of the saddle, and dislike cultivating the soil. The Mongol women look you straight in the eyes with a slightly scornful air, and ride like the men. In the south of the Ordos, where I am, even when dressed in their dirtiest clothes, they always wear in their hair a diadem of medals and coral beads hanging very prettily over the forehead, but forming a sort of helmet on the nape of the neck which is too severe to be becoming. The hair is divided into two plaits falling in front of the shoulders and enclosed in horns with quite elaborate silver decoration. This hair style makes them hold their heads very straight and very still, which is majestic though hardly comfortable, I can't help feeling.

The digging goes on. I have formed an exact idea of the geological formation in which we are (it is fairly recent for China) and I attach a great deal of importance to my conclusions. We live under canvas, dressed only in shirt, trousers and Chinese jacket. It's the real free life.

(To the Abbé Breuil)   *On the banks of the Chara-Ousso-Gol,*
19 August, 1923

My dear friend,

We have been camping since August 12 on the banks of the famous Chara-Ousso-Gol, which Licent telegraphed me in March that we would never be able to reach. The Chara-Ousso-Gol is a curious little river that winds with incredible twists and turns at the bottom of a sheer canyon 250 feet deep which it has gouged out for itself in the middle of an absolutely flat region of steppes and dunes. The cliffs of this canyon are formed entirely of Quaternary deposits. [. . .]

84

[. . .] 15 cases already (skeletons, or parts of them), a huge number of rhinoceros and gazelle, a fair amount of bison (with enormous horns), deer with curious antlers, horse, wild ass, a lamella of elephant's tooth (mammoth ?), hyena and wolf. It's curious to find these associated. And man ? Well, man was certainly there, but here I must proceed with the utmost care. . . . What is certain is that we now have two palæolithic localities *in situ* whereas three months ago not one was known in China.

But I am not saying much about the picturesque side of our time here, which is considerable. We're camping at the bottom of the canyon in the midst of a curious flora and a familiar fauna of pheasants, cranes and kites, which I'll tell you about in detail when I get back. We're keeping two teams at work : one of 13 Chinese (not very interesting), and one of 10 Mongols (the family of the owner of the land) who really know how to excavate. It would amuse you to see them working stripped to the waist and with long pigtails : a very fine type of Red Indian you'd say.

Sao-Kiao-Pan (South-east Ordos), 26 August, 1923

Yesterday we left our camp on the Chara-Ousso-Gol for good, and the day after tomorrow we're going to resume our life of caravan travel. I felt a pang of regret at leaving those wild river-banks where, after twenty-four days, we had adopted our own free and easy ways in the wide open spaces. . . . We are off with 26 large cases of fossils. Qualitatively, the results of our time there are excellent. Most important, I have found a level of human industry, admirably precise, about 60 centimetres in depth, which will surely always be one of the most valuable landmarks in Chinese prehistory.

. . . I am a little too absorbed by science to be able to philoso-phise much ; but the more I look into myself the more I find

85

myself possessed by the conviction that it is only the science of Christ running through all things, that is to say true mystical science, that really matters. I let myself get caught up in the game when I geologise. But the moment I stop to reflect I am vividly aware that this occupation (though vital for me insofar as it is a part of the 'total gesture' of my life) is by itself of no ultimate interest. I keep developing, and slightly improving, with the help of prayer, my 'Mass upon things'.[1] It seems to me that in a sense the true substance to be consecrated each day is the world's development during that day—the bread symbolising appropriately what creation succeeds in producing, the wine (blood) what creation causes to be lost in exhaustion and suffering in the course of its effort.

(To the Abbé Breuil)   *Sao-Kiao-Pan (South-east Ordos)*,
                                          9 September, 1923

My dear friend,

I received today your long and welcome letter of July 18, and it has been a tonic for me (though I must confess it gave me a pang of home-sickness by reminding me too forcibly of our thinking-den [2] in the rue Demours). I shall ponder on all you say about Père Schmidt, and primitive peoples, and Europe, as I jog along on my mule on our tedious road back to Tientsin. Obviously, many primitive intuitions have been corrupted and blunted by civilisation and speculation ; but I still believe that both these have collected, and continue to collect the elements of an intuition far superior to that of primitive men (or, if you prefer, I believe that they are collecting the elements of a much better practical application of primitive intuitions). However,

[1] Later he gave this book the title of *La Messe sur le monde*.
[2] Fr. '*pensoir*' [Tr.].

mysticism remains the great science and the great art, the only power capable of synthesising the riches accumulated by other forms of human activity.

Sao-Kiao-Pan (South-east Ordos), 12 September, 1923

Tomorrow we're at last taking the road for Tientsin, followed by twenty-three donkey- or mule-loads of finds. There is a planned halt of ten days (for digging) at a day-and-a-half's distance from Ning-Sia-Fu. There we embark on the Hwang-Ho, for Pao-Teo and the railway.

The travellers made an expedition to the interior of China and reached the region of the great loess.

After crossing the Great Wall (reduced at that point to a series of towers spaced at intervals of 500 yards) you leave the region of the Mongolian steppes and dunes and enter the astounding zone of the great loess or ' yellow earth ' (though ' grey ' would be better) of China. In the past (some thousand years ago) this area must have formed a wide undulating plateau. And then, suddenly, the base-level of the water-courses must have fallen ; from the small rivers down to the merest streams, everything that flows started to dig deeply into the soil. And since the soil in this region is formed of compact earth (loess) the gullying has taken on formidable proportions. Today the ancient plateau is cut across by an astonishing network of crevasses of which the largest are 600 feet deep, while even the smallest, owing to their sheer walls, are impassable obstacles. The few inhabitants live in caves scooped out of the walls of the crevasses and cultivate millet, sorghum, buckwheat and hemp—everything that erosion has spared. No paths except along the river-beds, or else tracks, just about wide enough for a mule that wind, corniche-wise, over the crevasses, snake their way up the slopes, or zigzag along the crests between the mouths of the crevasses. The tracks often cave in and the river-beds are danger-ous in the stormy season. I have seen with my own eyes a stream one could jump over, suddenly turn into a raging torrent 10 or 12 feet deep—and this in dry weather ; there had simply been a bad storm upstream. What an odd country! At this moment it is charming, with the black hanging ears of the millet, and the sorghum from 6 to 9 feet high. But with its great folds of impassable land, that block the view and prevent you from going where you want to, you have the stifled feeling of being in a forest. We've had an excellent haul in this northern part of the Shensi : Jurassic plants, Miocene rhinoceros, and—best of all—palæolithic implements at the very bottom of the loess. This last find, which completes and corroborates the two previous ones (at Ning-Sia-Fu and the Chara-Ousso-Gol) is important and will cause quite a stir in the world of prehistory. I've told Breuil and Boule about it, not forgetting Pekin. Taken all in all, it seems to me that Our Lord really has led me by the hand these last three months. And I can see in this Providence a sign that He really did want me to come here, and a proof that He expects a renewed activity in my special apostolate in Europe ; for, as you know, I only came to China in the hope of being better able to speak about the ' great Christ ' in Paris. I feel more and more intensely that this ' great Christ ' alone can animate my life. But what a strange and sad thing life is, isn't it ? We have to face the fact that nothing we are able to touch is the real *consistency* we are searching for, while what does seem to us to be the real consistency of the world we are unable to touch. *Beati qui non viderunt et crediderunt.* . . .

Ning-Sia-Fu, 30 September, 1923

We've been living for ten days in a small inn in the steppes, 30 miles east of Ning-Sia-Fu, continuing our exploration of the human palæolithic hearth that we found on July 23. The result : over 600 lb. of palæoliths, some of which are really very fine of their kind. It's a real triumph, the more so that the fossils enable us to fix not only the stratigraphy but also the age of the level. So, whereas three months ago nothing was known about palæolithic man north of the Himalayas, we have now found him in three places over a strip of 220 miles : a really important advance. And now we find ourselves the masters of sixty cases of spoils—over 54 cwt. of specimens—a fine caravan of 30 donkeys and mules. At the moment our cargo is in store beside the Yellow River while we are here at Ning-Sia-Fu making arrangements with the Governor about requisitioning a boat. We'd like to leave on the 3rd or 4th of October, which would land us at Pao-Teo (railway) by October 16. In preparation for the river-trip, Licent and I have each provided ourselves with a magnificent lambskin pelisse, light, soft, and as white as can be—one of Ning-Sia-Fu's specialities.

Ning-Sia-Fu is an essentially Chinese city (there are only seven or eight Europeans counting the Catholic and Protestant missionaries) and it is lost, like all Chinese cities, within great crenellated walls too vast for the houses they shelter. The position is very pretty, if not healthy : right in the middle of an oasis of rice-fields and orchards (magnificent grapes!) at the foot of the majestic barrier of the great Ala-Shan, beyond which stretches the vastness of Outer Mongolia, that is to say absolute wilderness. You feel that Turkestan is not far away, with its mixture of every sort of race come down from the west. It is the road to Tibet.

The season is remarkably mild this year, and autumn is at

its most alluring. This past fortnight the steppe has been piercingly beautiful. The sun—golden, and not so fierce—has cast a gentle glow over the great grey undulations dotted with clumps of still-green artemesia and clusters of yellowing asclipia. Here and there in the salt hollows the fat-leaved salsola formed its crimson carpet on the snow-white salt, while against the horizon stood out the jagged blue outline of the Ala-Shan, already capped with white. No sound but the calls of little red-beaked crows, or the strange cry of camels at pasture, or the tinkle of some caravan. All my memories of autumn (my favourite season) came crowding in on me : autumns on the high plateaux of Auvergne, with the Forez or the Mont-Doré in the distance ; autumns in Egypt when evening is almost cool as it falls over the violet desert ; autumns at Hastings with the golden beeches and the sea wind over the rounded ' *downs* ' or the wide saltings. I feel it all as I never have before ; but also in a rather different way : with a certain melancholy, for autumn is upon my own life, too, and yet with much greater clarity and peace, for now I am better able to discern what it was that vaguely called to me across the deep and enigmatic charm of those hours in which one feels nearer to, more enveloped in, the world.

During the long leisure of the river-trip I mean to start putting my geological travel-notes in order. If I have time (and if it ' comes ') I would like to get on paper a literary fantasy of my impressions of Mongolia, but with philosophical undertones. I'd like, within a descriptive framework, to get across the idea that historical and geographical research is, in itself, empty and deceptive, the true science being that of the future as gradually disclosed by life itself ;[1] and I should end by saying that, in order to see Central Asia with an assured and confident eye, you

[1] See pp. 92-103. Later on Père Teilhard developed this into a comparison between oriental mysticism (Hindu) and western mysticism (Christian): *La Route de l'Ouest* (1932) and *L'Apport spirituel de l'Extrême-Orient* (1947).

must see it at dusk when the sun, taking with it all the glory of the Far East, sinks behind the mountains to the west, to rise on our western civilisation.

Tientsin, 15 October, 1923

The last days of my journey were picturesque enough but very monotonous. We settled down in a sort of large barge, deep and rectangular, in which Licent very ingeniously arranged our beds and camp-chairs. Our 72 cases and mess-chests formed the cargo. In this primitive vessel we gave ourselves to the current and, thanks to a good pilot and fine weather, we were at Pao-Teo in seven days. And I watched the stages of the outward journey as they passed swiftly before my eyes. [. . .]

On the river hundreds of ducks and geese were chattering and flying, with here and there a few swans and pelicans. It was cold, but fine, and the sun cast golden tints over a landscape which was uniformly grey, yellow and russet. The evenings were magnificent. I remember in particular a gorgeous sunset over the Ala-Shan. Behind the purple range of mountains the sky was blue-green to the north, crossed on the south by fiery clouds, and, every now and then, against the ever-reddening background of the sky, a skein of wild geese was silhouetted in black—just as they are painted on screens.

[. . .] The journey was over, and I felt keenly how little, of itself, mere displacement in space adds to a man. On returning to his point of departure, unless he has developed his inner life—a thing which doesn't show outwardly—he is still exactly like everyone else.

During the leisurely river trip Père Teilhard had written, as he had said he hoped to do, the pages [1] *that follow :*

[1] Later published in *Choses mongoles*, 1923.

On the Surface, June, 1923

A few days ago we left Pao-Teo, the terminus of the railway by which, from Pekin through Kalgan and the Blue City, the traveller proceeds more and more uncertainly from Europeanised and maritime China right to the Mongolian marches. One evening we passed through the crenellated walls by the Western Gate (the one used by caravans bound for the Ala-Shan and Tibet)—the walls within which huddle the grey flat-roofed houses of the little city—and thence made our way, at the pace of the ten mules that carried our equipment, along tracks which, by a long detour, lead to Ning-Sia-Fu.

Almost at once we left behind the first of the rocky barriers separating the valley of the Yellow River from the really high Asiatic plateau. Our second stage brought us to the gorges of the Ula-Shan—garnet and white marble gneiss. Just the day before we had still been at the foot of the Lang Shan where layers of folded rock rise to storm the old crystalline shelf of China. I must confess that at that moment the north drew me like a magnet. Just a few more stages, I thought, across these grey expanses stretching in front of us, a few more steps up this stairway of mountains, of which we have already climbed two, and the door will open on the solitudes of the Gobi ; we shall enter a wholly mysterious land.

Our caravan's course should have lain southwards. The goal of our journey was not in fact the great Mongolian desert ; we were trying to reach the land of the Ordos, the little-known plateau north of Kansu and Shensi which forms a sort of square massif, doubly enclosed on three of its sides by the waters of the Yellow River and a long mountain range. We were travelling so far to the north only because the drought and the activities of bandit gangs had made the direct route across the sands impracticable.

Then we turned our backs on the Gobi and my eyes had soon forgotten the wide torrential valleys where herds of gazelles could be seen, nose to wind, among the pebbles and the meagre grass. We were making our way over the low-lying steppes of San-Tao-Ho.

All around as far as the eye could see, over a vast plain levelled in the past by the Yellow River, waved the grass of the steppes, the sighis, with its hard swelling stalks sometimes as high as a man on horseback, while here and there were clumps of a small white-blossomed shrub whose fruits like pomegranate seeds we were to taste later. Now and again some tamarisks marked a mud hut inhabited by bronzed half-naked Chinese. There are no Mongols left now—herdsmen with the simplicity of children, they are gradually surrendering their ancient domain to the shrewd tenacious farmers from the east. We could hardly expect to see a single one of their yourts in the whole of San-Tao-Ho.

The season of the yellow winds was over. The sand blown from the west no longer darkened the sky, but seemed content to whirl around in little dust-devils. We sometimes saw ten or twenty of these miniature tornadoes, 150 to 300 feet high, drifting over the steppe, and I was instinctively reminded of the columns of smoke which used to mark the fall of a heavy shell on the plains of Flanders.

One evening, from the back of my mule, I was looking over the straw-yellow sea of sighis to the pearly-blue jagged crest of the Khara-Narin-Ula, the eastern confine of the high Mongolian plateau. And when I turned my head to the left, there, above the yellow expanses, I saw another land—russet and purple under the rays of the sinking sun. At once I recognised the colour—I had seen it so often from the banks of the Nile when looking eastwards towards the Red Sea. It was the colour the burnt stones of the desert and the sand of the dunes take on at dusk. It was the Ordos at last—the Promised Land.

July

Our tent was pitched in the middle of the desert, in the north-west corner of the Ordos. Around us curved a large ring of red earth cliffs, some 300 feet high. It was very hot and we had nothing to drink but water drawn from a spring whose banks were crusted with salt. There was no greenery but isolated tufts of strange desert plants with woody stems and fat or prickly leaves, and we were astonished to recognise here and there, bindweed, buckwheat, or some common labiate—familiar plants in a strange guise. No neighbours but a Mongol hidden in his yourt a mile away behind a ridge. We were camping in the Bad Lands.

There is no shade and no cool in the Bad Lands. On the other hand the torn naked earth provides here, as in America, an incomparable field for palæontology. In the paler layers running in stripes through the red cliff near our camp, the remains of mighty pachyderms lay side by side with those of small rodents. All day we were bent double over the white sand, while the treasures piled up in the tent. Fauna was abundant in the Ordos in the Pliocene age, and still is, in its own way, to judge by the fine female argali, as big as a young ass and with a shiny grey coat, which was brought with some difficulty to our camp one evening. The lusty fawn was still at large, bellowing from the top of the amphitheatre.

We hadn't expected to start the fossil hunt so soon. But Mongolia is full of surprises for the student. It still had more than one in reserve for us that month as, by short stages, we went down towards the south across the Arbous-Ula and to the fertile plain rich in magnificent fruits. Here Moslem Ning-Sia-Fu, too small for its encircling wall, sleeps among rice-fields at the foot of the blue range of the great Ala-Shan.

Of this part of the journey, the crossing of the Arbous-Ula

will stay in my memory as being the best stage. The countless strata of this wild mountain, a bastion of the Ala-Shan on the right bank of the Yellow River, bend softly into two long concentric folds which seem to unfurl over the solitudes of the east. At the broken crest of the most eastern of these waves, erosion has isolated a vast platform several miles in length and breadth—Genghis Khan's Anvil, as the Mongols call it. Not far from the Anvil, a lamasery nestles at the base of a sandstone amphitheatre, near a stream. We sought a day's hospitality there. Like all monks everywhere and always, lamas have an infallible instinct in choosing the setting for their dwelling-places, so that it is always a delight for the eye to come upon one of their monasteries suddenly, deep in a most unexpected recess. Gilded flagstaffs glistened in the sun over the geometrical group of red and white rectangular buildings. Now and again a monk went past, in a purple or yellow robe—a sight which delighted the eye and filled the heart with peace. But to admire the lamas and their lamaseries one has, unfortunately, to see them from a distance. As soon as one draws near, the gleaming façade is seen to be tarnished and the vivid garments dirty and torn. The people who first created these desert retreats were doubtless really great men, prophets who discovered something of great beauty in the world, and beyond the world. Today one scrutinises the dull faces of their successors in vain to find the most fleeting trace of that long-faded vision.

August

After crossing interminable hills covered with fragrant artemisia, liquorice trees with acacia-like leaves, and sea-grass with its horsetail stems and raspberry-like fruit, we finally reached the south-east corner of the Ordos, the goal of our journey. Once again we pitched our tent in the middle of the desert, within a circle of earth cliffs. But here the desert was smiling and the cliffs were grey, yellow and green instead of white and red. We camped at the bottom of a winding canyon carved out in the steppes to a depth of 250 feet by the Chara-Ousso-Gol, whose waters—liquid mud—gurgled beside us over a stony bed. Close by was the unusual dwelling that the Mongol Wanschok had scooped out for himself in an island of earth separated from the cliff. Access to the inside of this little fortress was by an underground tunnel, and from the top of its ramparts could be seen the whole of the little alluvial plain formed at the bottom of the canyon by the river in the days when its bed was shallower. What could bandits hope to do against such a citadel ?

We owed a great deal to our friend Wanschok, for he welcomed us to his estate and allowed us to excavate some deposits belonging to him. Better still, he became our prize digger. We had to open a separate site for him and his five sons. It was a curious spectacle to watch the old Mongol sitting by the mound, gravely inspecting the extracted fossils, carefully putting on one side the flakes of palæolith, and paternally directing the industry of the young workers with their long hair and bronzed bodies.

Meanwhile the mistress of the Mongolian castle had come out of the keep, shepherding her flock of frisky black goats and stolid white sheep. Like all the women in these parts she wore the helmet of coral beads with silver medals falling over the forehead; and beneath this heavy headdress, which forced her to hold her head still, she walked stiff and straight, with perfect balance, like an amphora-bearer. She climbed the highest of the dunes which encircled the ravine like a golden crown, and then, unfastening her scarf, she waved it as she sang to herself.

We spent a whole month on the banks of the Chara-Ousso-Gol where a lilac-coloured broom was in flower and a sort of lavender with deep blue flowers which the Mongols call incorrectly, but so prettily, argalis' artemisia. Between the dunes a dense growth of a small garlic with pink flowers spread a carpet of watered silk, like that which, I am told, cheers the melancholy of the Gobi at this season.

All those things smelt good and sparkled gaily in the hot light. The steppes are really very lovely in the short-lived beauty of the last days of summer.

September

We left Mongolia for a week and made an exploratory incursion eastwards into China proper. For us, to enter China was to cross the Great Wall. At the point where we crossed it, the ancient rampart was almost entirely destroyed and submerged in the sand. And yet from *li* to *li* [1] the towers indicating its line were still proudly standing, and from right to left as far as the horizon we could see their diminishing outlines spaced along the mountains bordering the Mongolian steppes to the east and south.

These mountains, among which we travelled for ten days, are of loess, the famous Yellow Earth (though it is actually grey). Not so very long ago this yellow earth, accumulated by the action of wind and water, must have formed a barely undulating sheet over the Shensi and the Kansu, to a depth in places of 300 feet or more. And then, as a result of the sudden and violent scouring action of all the rivers and streams, this sheet was split, as it continues to be, to a great depth. The country today is nothing but an unbelievable network of fissures with vertical walls in the midst of which one feels as lost and paralysed as in the middle of the trees of a forest or the waves of the sea. It is impossible to proceed in a straight line. The only paths are the river-beds or the narrow tracks which sometimes snake up the earthen walls of the fissures and sometimes zigzag along between their mouths. These tracks are naturally hazardous, and as for the river-beds, you have to be

[1] A Chinese measure of distance (one-third of a mile).

very careful indeed. After a storm has broken upstream, sometimes a long way up, a harmless stream can suddenly be transformed (we saw it happening) into a raging torrent many feet deep, the first waves arriving with the speed of a galloping horse.

Since it is difficult to move about, the inhabitants live in caves scooped out of the hillside. The land still unaffected by erosion is assiduously cultivated. Millet, sorghum, buckwheat and hemp ripen in the strips of field between the clefts in the soil. Nothing is more poignant than this agony of a splendid land struggling against a destruction that nothing can arrest. In some favoured corners the waters have not yet accomplished their cruel work. Then the hills swell with pride, adorned here and there with clusters of jujube trees, or oddly crowned by a solitary ailanthus. And when the traveller finds himself in one of these clearings that chance has spared in the heart of this tortured country, then he recognises with delight the smiling China of the picture books.

We two geologists, however, coming here—as to the Ordos— in search of the Bad Lands, were not to be side-tracked by the comfortable peace of the gently undulating fields. We plunged down into the deep crevasses of the mountains where the red earth looks like wounded flesh beneath the thick grey layers. There lie the bleaching bones of the rhinoceroses and giraffes and antelopes that used to roam here in the Miocene age as they roam today in the tropical prairies of Africa. There too, beneath the high walls of loess, are scattered the remains of a Man whose eyes had looked on China before she had put on her mantle of Yellow Earth.

But already in the fields the gently folded ears of the millet, and the heavy stiff heads of the sorghum were turning black. Autumn and the cold were soon to come down over the plateaux of Asia. The time had come for travellers to make for the more temperate plains of Eastern China.

At a deeper level, October

In a heavy rectangular barge which is following the current of the
eddying waters, we are going down the Hwang-Ho from Ning-
Sia-Fu to Pao-Teo. Rapidly, by water, we are going over the
ground we covered with such difficulty by mule four months ago.
And beyond the banks thronged with swans, pelicans, ducks and
hundreds of wild geese, I am trying to identify the various stages
of our outward journey.

Here are the piled-up folds of the Arbous-Ula, and then the
red desert cliffs where we killed the argali ; next the yellow sea
of sighis of the San-Tao-Ho. Here, following the Ala-Shan,
the desolate ranges encircling the Ordos : first the Khara-Narin-
Ula running from south to north, then the Lang-Shan, followed
soon by the Ula-Shan from west to east.

And as I watch these austere shapes passing before me under
the clear light of a cold sun, the inevitable question presents itself
to my mind : What am I bringing back from my four months'
travels in Mongolia ? Here, all around me, in the bottom of the
barge, there are sixty cases piled up, full of fossils and stones.
But all that is on the external, material side. . . . What gain has
there been to my innermost being during this long pilgrimage in
China ? Has the great continent of Asia any profound message
for me ?

Had I undertaken such a journey twenty years ago I would
have set out, I think, with the ill-defined hope that, as I made my
way over an unknown land in an effort to read its history, I
might slightly raise the curtain which hides the great secret from
men. I was rather like those simple people of the past who
thought that the gods inhabit the hidden places of the world and
that long ago they used to reveal themselves to men.

It is a long time, however, since I lost the illusion that travel

brings us closer to the truth. I knew it when I left Europe—that
space is a veil without seam which we can go over indefinitely
without ever finding the least aperture through which to glimpse
the higher spheres of existence ; and that the light we think we
see shining in the depths of the past is no more than a mirage or a
reflection from above. The more remote in time and space is
the world we confront, the less it exists, and hence the poorer
and more barren it is for our thought. Indeed I have felt no
disappointment this year at remaining quite untouched as I
looked over the steppes where gazelles still run about as they did
in the Tertiary period, or visited the yourts where the Mongols
still live as they lived a thousand years ago. In what is, as in what
was, there is nothing really new to be found.

And yet, when I landed in China, there was one hope I still
retained. If, I said to myself, to explore history and geography
is to labour in a vacuum, and if the only true knowledge of things
lies in foreseeing and building up the future as life gradually
brings it into being, then what better opportunity to initiate
myself and associate myself with the building-up of the future
could I hope for than to go and lose myself for weeks on end in
the fermenting mass of the peoples of Asia ? There I could count
on meeting the new currents of thought and mysticism in process
of formation, which were preparing to rejuvenate and fertilise
our European world. To reach full maturity the earth needs
every drop of its blood. What kind of sap is it that still runs in
the age-old human branches of the Far East ?

For long weeks I have been submerged in the deep flood of
the people of Asia. And now, as I come to the surface and collect
my memories and impressions, I am forced to admit that in that
direction too my quest has been vain. Nowhere, among the
men I met or heard about, have I discerned the smallest seed
whose growth will benefit the future of mankind. Throughout
my whole journey I have found nothing but absence of thought,

senile thought, or infantile thought. A missionary from Tibet, returning from Koko-Nor on the Himalayan border, assured me that out there there still survived, to his knowledge, two or three solitaries who nourish their interior life by contemplating the cosmic cycles and the eternal re-birth of Buddha. But a chance passer-by like myself is not in a position to recognise these infrequent heirs of a venerable tradition of thought whose fruit is reserved for some new season.

For myself, I have seen nothing in Mongolia to awaken the ' other life ' within me.

I am a pilgrim of the future on my way back from a journey made entirely in the past.

But isn't the past, viewed from a certain angle, transformable into future ? Isn't a wider awareness of what is and what has been the essential basis of all spiritual progress ? Isn't my whole life as a palæontologist sustained by the single hope of co-operating in a forward march ? Mongolia seemed to me asleep—perhaps dead. But can't even the dead be made to speak ?

Perhaps it was on the eve of my departure that I heard the hidden message I was waiting for China to utter, as I leant over the battlements of the small fortified Christian community of Belgaçoum and watched the sun set in the fiery sky of the steppe.

To my left the smooth and fissured mountains of loess were picked out by the sun's slanting rays ; to my right, where the fields of buckwheat were still pink, I could just make out the ruins of the ancient city of Si-Hia, razed to the ground long ago by the Mongol hordes.

And I thought about the desperate struggle to live that had been made in these parts. In a setting hardly different from the one in front of me, splendid herds of animals had searched avidly for grass and light. Then man—a man whose remains lie buried 180 feet under the sand near the Chara-Ousso-Gol—had grappled with elements that still remain baffling and ruthless. Much later Genghis Khan crossed this plain, in all the pride of his victories.

And what is left today of this tremendous thrust towards a little more life? Nothing—nothing but a few poor fields struggling to keep the invading sands at bay.

Nothing?

I stood and watched our golden star as it sank behind the dunes taking with it the whole wide range of colour. And it seemed to me that it was no longer the fiery sun I saw, but the very focus of terrestrial life setting over the Mongolian desert —to rise again *on us*. And, from the whole of sleeping Asia I thought there rose a voice which whispered, ' Now, my brothers of the West, it is your turn.'

Our turn. Yes, sleep on, ancient Asia ; your people are as weary as your soil is ravaged. By now your night has fallen and the light has passed into other hands. But it was you who kindled this light, you who gave it to us. Have no fear : we shall not allow it to die. Your labour will not have been in vain. So long, too, as a few wise men still have your life (your own life—not a life we would seek to impose on you) in safe-keeping, it is not extinguished. Tomorrow perhaps it will shine once more over your ravaged plateaux.

It is our turn. Yes, I believe this more than ever.

The sceptics, agnostics and false positivists are wrong. Within all this shift of civilisations, the world is neither moving at random nor marking time ; beneath the universal turmoil of living beings, something is being made, something heavenly, no doubt, but first something temporal. Nothing here below is lost to man, nothing of his toil. As I am convinced that the only real science is that which discloses the growth of the universe, I have been distressed to find nothing in my travels but the traces of a vanished world. But why this distress? Surely the wake left behind by mankind's forward march reveals its movement just as clearly as the spray thrown up elsewhere by the prow. . . .

This evening, as I watch the flight of wild geese showing black against the play of gold and red clouds above the river, I repeat to myself again and again : if we want to understand the Far East, we must not look at it at dawn, nor at high noon ; we must look at it at dusk when the sun, bearing the spoils of Asia with it in its glory, rises in triumph over the skies of Europe.

It must be borne in mind that these pages were written on Père Teilhard's first contact with China, the China of steppe and desert. His outlook was to undergo a profound change in the years to follow. In close touch with intellectual movements in Pekin, he frequently expressed his certainty that a real awakening of Chinese national consciousness was taking place behind the confused political crises that shook the whole Far East. The evolution seemed to him inevitable though what form it would take might still be uncertain. Of one thing he was sure : 'Sooner or later, the unification of the human race is bound to come, and if the world wishes to survive there must be an end to racial conflict. For its maturity the earth needs every drop of its blood.'

(To the Abbé Breuil) *Hautes-Études, Race Course Road, Tientsin,*
23 October, 1923

My very dear friend,

I received the announcement of your mother's death yesterday, and I have just said Mass for her and for those she has left behind. Coming after your July letter, the news of this fresh bereavement was not unexpected. You were expecting it, too, but even so such a break with all the past must be a blow to you. I pray that Our Lord may help you to find strength in your isolation : was it not He who said that once you have set your hand to the plough you must never look back ? The longer I live the more certain I am that individual events count for nothing ; all that really matters is devotion to something bigger than ourselves. I feel sure that this trial will have thrown you back with added determination on the great tasks that have grown to be your real interest in life.[1]

[. . .] Tientsin is pleasant enough just now. But the cold we left behind us in Mongolia will soon be with us here. I hardly leave the Licent Museum, where I shall have enough to keep me busy for several weeks. At the moment I'm writing a geological note on the journey, and then I shall get on with the stratigraphical part of a note on the anthropological aspects. From the palæontological point of view, I haven't with me here the necessary books and specimens for comparison fully to develop our findings. The rodents in particular I am anxious to sort out.

Apart from that, I'm trying not to drop ' the interior life '. In that, I rather miss the atmosphere of Paris. I can't help feeling that my Mongolian journey has not been any direct ' crack of the whip ' ; indirectly, however, it has confirmed me in my faith in the future. The world holds no interest for me unless I look forward, but when my eyes are on the future it is full of excitement. I miss your conversation—write to me.

Goodbye, my very dear friend. I pray for you daily when I ask God's protection for those who are nearest to me ' in heart, in thought, and in science '—and you are included in all three categories.

---

[1] Elsewhere he writes : ' There's great strength, I believe, in having emerged from the cloud-zone in which most men live—but only so long as the sun continues to shine in a clear sky. To hold fast to only one thing—but a really precise, concrete thing, so exalted and so great that it sheds its light over all the rest—therein, I am sure, lies the summit of happiness.'

1924

Père Teilhard had been thinking of returning to Europe in the autumn, but on 13 October, 1923, he was back in Tientsin, where the results of his first expedition were such as to commit him to extending his researches during a second expedition in the spring. An immense and almost entirely new field was open to him, whose wealth he was beginning to suspect. How could he abandon the enterprise when it was barely started? He accordingly applied to Marcellin Boule and the Rector of the Institut Catholique in Paris for an extension of leave, and prepared to divide the winter between Pekin and Tientsin.

The only cloud on the horizon was the possibility of conflict between Mukden and Pekin. If, as was feared, the new President should go to war with Manchuria travel in the interior of China would become difficult. Meanwhile his days were filled with examining the finds, writing geological notes, and preparing for a Congress of Russian and Chinese geologists to be held in Pekin. With the re-opening of the Trans-Siberian railway, letters to France were now taking only thirteen days. ' How limited and narrow the material world seems to be becoming. The only thing that really interests me now is the universe of the future—the world of living ideas and the mystical life. And so I often yearn to find more people with whom and to whom I can talk about such things. . . .' (24 October, 1923)

20–21 November, 1923

I have now been three days in Pekin. At this time of year the city is much less beautiful than in June. The trees, of which there are so many that the thousands of low gabled houses look like rows of tents pitched in a forest, have shed their leaves. You no longer see the red and gold of the Imperial city reflected in the moats full of water-lilies ; the Chinese have left off their blue robes and are muffled up in thick black tunics. However, the old capital is still very picturesque in the cold autumn light, and, what is more important, it is still, summer and winter alike, the one city in China where you find most intelligence and intellectual life : and that is more than enough to make up for the inclement weather. I have been immersing myself in this spiritual warmth and it has been like a breath of fresh air to come back to the conversation of men who think and work as I do. Yesterday, for example, I spent the day with the American and Chinese anthropologists, palæontologists and geologists. I saw practically every single scientist of this sort in China. It's a great deal in itself, don't you think, to have had the opportunity of finding them all collected at the same place and time. The man who interested me most was Dr. Granger, the palæontologist of the big American expedition to the Gobi. People here are inclined to treat the Americans as a joke, but the more I see of them the more I admire their ability to work and get things done, and the kinder and more approachable I find them. This is one of many discoveries that make me bitterly hostile to ' accepted ' judgments. No-one, at any rate, can deny that the Americans did a wonderful job in the Gobi. My own finds, in another field, were just as valuable as theirs, but compared with them I had only the most puerile means at my disposal. In my own branch of science it's the Americans who are showing us how we must set to work on the earth if we are to read its secret and make ourselves its masters.

I am going to lunch at the Legation, where I expect to meet Mr. Deniker again, my colleague from the Institut français d'Anthropologie who drove me about in his car in June. If he offers to take me out tomorrow I shall stay another day in Pekin. [. . .] I find it a real restorative to see something of the outside world and not just the world of Paris. [. . .] The reception at the Minister's (M. de Fleuriau) was most hospitable. He had even invited the Nuncio, so that dinner was a very diplomatic affair.

4 December, 1923

[. . .] The end of my stay in Pekin was as pleasant and fruitful as the beginning. To wind up, there was a most friendly (and by no means prohibitionist) dinner given by an American attached to the Geological Survey of China, which brought together three Chinese, two Americans and one Frenchman (myself) in the most warmly cordial atmosphere. I greatly enjoyed the contact that was established between such diverse elements ; it was really natural and deep-rooted, and its sole basis was our common, dedicated, search for some small measure of truth. There's no doubt that the mind has a far greater power of bringing people together than we can ever imagine. But if that power is to operate it must be under perfectly simple and natural conditions, and not under a cloak of formality and convention.

Pekin, 8 January, 1924

The end of my stay in Pekin, like the beginning, was most interesting. The Geological Conference was very lively ; I made a number of new contacts, learnt a great deal, and greatly enjoyed the frank intimacy that was born between Chinese, Americans, Swiss and French. A continual succession of dinner-parties consolidated these new friendships. If you'd been here yesterday you'd have laughed to see ten rickshaws, each carrying a gentleman in a fur cap, plunging into the narrow lanes under the eyes of the dumbfounded Chinese, and all looking for the scene of the banquet. These little lanes are perhaps the most picturesque of the memories I'll retain of my time in Pekin. About eleven o'clock in the evening the day before yesterday, my rickshaw man couldn't find the Petang (the Lazarists' house) and I spent a good half-hour being taken round narrow alleys, absolutely silent, almost pitch-black, under a magnificent starry sky against which rose the silhouettes of the little gabled roofs and the great twisted trees where the crows were roosting.

27 January, 1924

Dinner at Dr. Ting's : a most interesting dinner, and very picturesque.

There were three of us : Dr. Ting, director of the Geological Service, Dr. Lee, an anthropologist, and I. The meal was served in the proper Chinese style, except that I had been given a spoon and fork instead of the chopsticks my friends used. Then came the series of little dishes containing all sorts of different things to eat cut up into little cubes and all with the same rather insipid dressing. I finished with trepang soup and the customary bowl of rice.

Ting is a very intelligent man, in constant touch with all the ' *leaders* ' of young China, and I had a really interesting conversation with him about the intellectual state of modern China. We came to the following conclusions : at present there is nothing that can properly be called Chinese thought. Their philosophical traditions have been broken, and they are still too much under the influence of western teachers. In the end, however, they will ' find their own feet ' again. From the religious angle they need, as every man needs, something to ' justify ' (*sic*) life, but at the

present moment they are going through a ' reaction ' against a
religion that has been found wanting—rather like France in the
eighteenth century. The present phase is anti-religious ; that will
sort itself out, but it's still a fact that the Chinaman is by nature
pragmatic and agnostic. These conclusions agree pretty well with
what missionaries have told me, but they, unfortunately, seldom
have a chance of coming into contact with people like T. With
him, I have never felt that there was in his soul any really religious
domain, only an intense and noble curiosity to learn. I have
always had the impression that to discover a religion would for
him be too much like a great, long-term, scientific enterprise.
[. . .] At any rate, he has a lofty conception of the greatness of
the problem by which man is faced.

*A visit to the mission at Tcheli, south of Tientsin, gave Père
Teilhard an opportunity of seeing at close quarters the life of the
Chinese and their missionaries.*

Tientsin, 10 February, 1924

I am just back from Sien-Hsien, from the depths, that is, of the
Tcheli mission. I am not sorry to have made the journey, for it
has added considerably to my knowledge of the Chinese and their
missionaries. Physically, it's a long and monotonous journey.
After four hours by train in a bleak grey plain dotted with mud
villages and tombs, we got out and spent the night in a town
where the mission has a rest-house. At five the next morning we
were each climbing into a Chinese cart : a square box with a
curved roof, resting on two wheels without any springs ; and it
was only at half past eleven, after jolting as you can well imagine
over roads worse kept than a French cart-track, that we finally
reached our destination. Sien-Hsien is a large fortified dwelling
similar to the one I saw in Mongolia, but older and therefore
bigger. It is quite a shock when you're inside its walls or stone

ramparts to find, in the middle of a sea of cultivated fields, a little Christian city with a huge printing works, a college, a brewery, a mill, and nuns. From the outside you'd imagine you were coming to a Trappist monastery. The house was rather cold and I immediately adopted the dress they all wear, a quilted tunic and fur coat.

[. . .] During the few days I spent there I appreciated more vividly than during my time in Mongolia (which is too sparsely populated) what it means to a missionary to be plunged into the Chinese mass—a vast, inert, stolid mass, instinctively hostile to foreigners arriving with new ideas for changes it doesn't want. Everybody I spoke to seemed to have the same underlying impression of being up against a humanly speaking thankless and unending task.

In February 1924 Père Teilhard, accompanied only by a young missionary, made a second journey, on foot and by mule, to the further limits of Tcheli and Honan, during which he became more intimately acquainted with the native population.

I have been moving from one Christian settlement to another, and I have seen at close quarters just what a missionary's life is like, not in the big settlements but in the remote country parts. I have thus been able to verify what I had already been told, that the greatest trial for a missionary in China is to find that he is lost in a sea of primitive beings, kind and affectionate, no doubt, but as inquisitive, persistent and tactless as savages. Unless he takes steps to defend himself, the missionary can't call his life his own. Moreover the people who invade his life are not human beings with sharp edges that you can appreciate distinctly and love or reject. Relations between Chinese, and still more between Chinese and Europeans, are predominantly a matter of convention or approximation, and this makes you feel that the whole atmosphere is woolly—you can't get hold of anything. Even so, I can understand how men dedicated to this work can love their life and their wretched converts in spite of their flagrant defects : they are poor creatures, with no evil in them, quite defenceless, and their life is hard. They live in what are no better than dens, have nothing to eat but cereal pastes and millet—boiled—with a very occasional dish of rice or corn, and hardly ever any meat. It is a movingly picturesque sight to see them travelling dozens of miles behind their little donkeys, to the coal mines where they hope to pick up a hundredweight or so of fuel. When you see such things you understand the strength there can be in a really deeply experienced feeling of pity. If only men loved one another—in the context of something greater than themselves— how changed the world would be, how invincible and armed for every conquest.

There were difficulties in the way of the projected spring expedition, for which Père Teilhard had postponed his return to Europe : the danger of war between Pekin and Mukden, the problem of obtaining the necessary funds, the inaccessibility of the objective (the southern edge of the Gobi in eastern Mongolia), exaggerated by a month's drought and the presence of bandits. However, Père Teilhard and his companion made up their minds to go through with the plan.

Sung-shu-tsui-tzu (Notre-Dame-des-Pins), 12 April, 1924

I am writing to you from the real starting point of my expedition which is where we are assembling our mule caravan. Notre-Dame-des-Pins is the central (episcopal) residence of the vicariate of eastern Mongolia, 40 miles west of the Tientsin-Mukden line. [. . .] The country I am in now is quite different from that in which I was travelling last year. Imagine a chaos of lava mountains, fairly high but bare and rocky, separated from one another by wide valleys with the river-beds three-quarters dry but liable to devastating floods. Here, more than anywhere else in China, deforestation has brought swift ruin to the country, and it is not difficult to foresee the time when the people will have to abandon it as uninhabitable. The exodus to Manchuria has already begun.

In ascending stages they reached the Mongolian plateau, one of the marches of the Gobi : vast grey expanses over which, for much of every week, howled an icy wind, the ' yellow wind ', which filled the air with dust. Geologically the country was practically unexplored, but on this occasion it was the palæontological interest of the Gobi farther west that they were counting on. They stopped at several Christian settlements, and visited the local mandarins, who insisted on providing an escort of ten soldiers. Père Teilhard notes, ' Some days ago we passed close to some bandits on the move, but they seemed anxious to avoid us. Apart from the more considerable operations of insurgents, the bandits are not inclined to attack armed caravans, and the missionaries have nothing to fear from them.'

(To his parents, M. and Madame Emmanuel Teilhard de Chardin)
Chifang, 26 April, 1924 (Eastern Mongolia, or, in Mongol, Hata)

Père Teilhard had already written on Palm Sunday from Notre-Dame-des-Pins. He was now 100 miles to the north-west, only some three or four days' journey from the Gobi, and it was necessary to reorganise the caravan.

Chifang is a large Chinese city, with a population of nearly 100,000, lying in the centre of a wide plain surrounded by basaltic plateaux. I did no more than pass through it : it's very spread out and is based on seven main streets crossed by smaller transverse ones. The former are as wide as avenues in European cities, but they are lined with small, low, single-storeyed houses, mostly little shops. The city is a busy centre of commerce, but all on a small scale—the small shopkeepers have boycotted any attempts to establish big stores.

[. . .] With no railway and no good roads, this is the real essence of China. Nor is there anything else to suggest that you are in Mongolia. The Mongols are now either to be found farther north or have become completely Chinese. But soon we'll be seeing the Mongols as they really are. We came in sight of this plateau one evening at dusk. As we emerged from the col which leads to it, we saw a great plain, bleak and yellow, from which blew an icy wind. The sun was setting behind the tall mountain peaks of Mongolia, and the scene was most impressive. On the whole the country, particularly at this time of the year, is rugged and grim. Since we have been here, high cold winds from the north or north-west have been getting up every second or third day, bringing clouds of dust. You'd take it for fog or an approaching rain storm, but it's simply that the air is laden with very fine sand. There are still great masses of ice in the torrents where it's beginning to thaw. [. . .] As we are crossing a country that is almost unknown geologically, I am collecting a great deal of valuable evidence. Traces of a considerable number of Quaternary animals (rhinoceros, horse, deer, musk-ox) are to be found here and there, but no important deposit. All our hopes are centred on the Gobi.

I am finishing this letter after a short walk to the 'red rock', which turned out to be scattered with neolithic remains and— more interesting—with shells of ostrich eggs—a bird that must have been living here until comparatively recently.

Lin-hsi, 26 May, 1924

I am writing from Lin-hsi, but tomorrow or the next day we are off with six Mongolian bullock carts we managed to find eventually : primitive carts with only two wheels, but they can go almost anywhere. We shall be six weeks without any communication with the civilised world, but work will prevent me from feeling isolated.

The last fortnight has been spent in exploring the neighbourhood of Lin-hsi. [. . .] It's a countryside of great grandeur. From south-west to north-east it is broken by a whole series of saw-toothed porphyritic ridges separated by wide rolling valleys in which, apart from the Chinese settlements, you can see nothing but a vast expanse of pasture and steppe with here and there a Mongol yourt (tent). One evening, just as the last rays of the sun were disappearing, I saw all these ridges lit up at the same moment like a series of screens, the intensity of their purple fading as they receded into the distance. At one glance you could see the whole geological structure, displayed with all the poetry you could conceive. The grazing grounds along the river Tchaga-mouren are particularly lovely. Hundreds of oxen and cows wander over them, and at night these great herds come in docilely, led by a Mongol on horseback, sometimes with a lasso on a long pole.

On the banks of the Shiling-Gol, 2 June, 1924

Here I am, close by my tent, in a setting at once wild and biblical, with Mongol shepherds not far away. To the west and south runs a circle of rolling hills, bare but covered with turf, which represent the remains of an ancient plateau dominating the valley of the Shiling-Gol from a height of 300 feet. To the north and east I can see nothing but a sandy plain covered with the grasses of the steppe, through which winds the bright ribbon of the Shiling-Gol, to be lost in the sand some miles to the north. Just beside us stands a group of Mongol tents (yourts), planted in the middle of the steppe like black mushrooms. The air is full of the bleating of lambs searching for their mothers, for the flock has just come down from the mountain. Long-haired, big-booted Mongols, and a couple of lamas—one red, one yellow—are walking around us with childlike curiosity. The sky is bright blue, with a few large white clouds.

We arrived last night, after a five days' journey from Lin-hsi. The road first crossed a mountain range and brought us to a wide green valley between walls of rock. Then this valley climbed again to its original height, ending in a narrow col which led to the high Mongolian plateau. And there almost at once, where the cranes were strutting peacefully, we came on the marsh-like expanses which are the sources of the Shiling-Gol we had been following all our way down to the north-west.

For the last four days we haven't seen an inch of cultivated ground : no trees, nothing but virgin pasture. In the valleys there are plenty of yourts, savagely guarded by their dogs—even the Mongols never approach them without a cudgel in their hands. Apart from the running streams it is one vast emptiness. From the peaks you can see nothing but a regular sea (a tide-rip) of green hills, fold upon fold running in every direction, the full length of the horizon.

It's most picturesque, but it's quite different from the ' ravaged ' country, the ' bad ' lands of the Ordos and the western Gobi which I was hoping to find. During the coming week we'll find out what the plain we move into tomorrow holds for us. So far I rather feel that from the point of view of palæontology I have lost the game I started this spring. Geologically, at any rate, I believe that I am doing valuable work ; but it's not exactly what Boule and I were hoping for from this expedition. However, there's no need to lose hope.

10 June, 1924

Today we found our first Gobi fossils : nothing much—a few fragments of horse, gazelle and rhinoceros, but very much fossilised and supplying a key to a new chapter in the Tertiary period in China. The mass of these sand expanses is enormous, but fossils are very infrequently found in the debris, and I am wondering if we are ever going to enrich our meagre collection of specimens. However, we have at least one significant find, which is some satisfaction.

Since the Shiling-Gol we have been travelling over a vast grazing-ground, pretty well dried-up and desolate, but still with the same top-growth.

There isn't a single cultivated field, not even the size of a pocket handkerchief ; and outside the valleys you never, or hardly ever, see a yourt. On the other hand, as you follow the track (the stages are strictly determined by the wells) once or twice a day you meet convoys of Mongol carts—anything from 100 to 200 in single file—carrying salt to China from the salt-pans (Nor) in the north-west, or making the return journey. There are very few animals apart from any amount of small hares about the size of a rat (lagonnys), and eagles—I find a nest or eyrie on practically every rock I climb. It's quite different by the waters of the Shiling-Gol. There you find a concentration of living creatures—the gazelles are the most numerous, as well as every sort of duck and wader. The Mongolia of the Gobi is every bit as wild as Central Africa, and the inhabitants are just as primitive. At long intervals you come across a lamasery, and on every prominent rocky peak you find a heap of stones called an obo—at once an altar and a landmark—to which the devout Mongol adds a stone as he passes. There's one of these obos about a mile from our camp ; it has a dozen cairns, each with a branch stuck on top which the wind from the west has blown sideways like the flame of a torch.

In these silent symbols, these ever-lonely altars, scattered over the wilderness, there is something really mysterious, really wild and impressive. The nights, when ours is the only caravan encamped by the well, take on a wonderful colour and majesty. We have been having very warm weather, but yesterday there was a little frost. It's Whitsun week, and I like to think that ' the Spirit of Christ has filled the earth ', as the Church says at this season. I include you in my prayers.

A fortnight later (25 June), in the sandhills between Kalgan and the Dalai-Nor.

A fortnight has gone by without my adding a single line to this letter. [. . .] We have made a lot of progress during the last two weeks. Two days took us from the Shiling-Gol to the Dalai-Nor (the western extremity). [. . .] From the palæontological point of view, this last period has been satisfactory. Our most westerly excursion brought us right into the fossil country : no fine museum specimens, but plenty that enable us to deduce a variegated fauna for two types of country almost unstudied, in Mongolia (Miocene and Pliocene) and much further south (around Kalgan) ; we found them over an enormous area and in great profusion. These finds will enable us to pin down an important date in the geology of the Gobi and of Asia generally. On top of that, for over 60 miles along the Dalai-Nor and further to the west, I was surprised to find a chain of Quaternary volcanoes, as perfect as our conical peaks in Auvergne. I wonder whether anyone has ever noted them—I rather think not.

I am at last becoming able to ' understand ' and love these vast expanses of sparse grassland, cut by rivers and Nors, in which I have been lost for the last month. The Dalai-Nor has real majesty. It is, in fact, a small sea—over 25 miles in length—with billowing waves and gulls crying, and it is a continual surprise to find that the water throws up no seaweed and not a single sea-shell.

In the steppe, ten days north of Kalgan, 30 June

We are camped in what used to be a river valley, now dry and covered with grass. Six miles to the south a line of hills, round, smooth and grassy, which we shall cross tomorrow, stands between us and country in which we shall find Chinese settlers and cultivated fields : various foodstuffs, too—rice, eggs—we have been without for some days since our Chinese servants failed to lay in the necessary supplies. Until the 25th of June it stayed cold ; it's now warm again, but still wild weather—storms and squalls nearly every day. Licent is always inventing a new device for securing the tent. It took us four days to cross the sandhills. Although we were sorry to leave behind us the delightful clumps of willow and the little lakes between the sandhills, it was a relief to get out of that ocean of sand. My last sight of it provided an astonishing spectacle : from the top of a hill that overlooks the neighbourhood from a height of some 500 feet, I was faced by a most unusual scene—a rolling succession of white waves, tipped with green, which filled a good semicircle of the horizon and ran away into the distance as far as the eye could reach—just like the sea. Three or four miles to my left lay a large Nor. To my right, at about the same distance, a string of five or six still larger Nors. Behind me the line of green mountains we'll be crossing tomorrow. Finally, all around me a grassy hill, with ancient twisted elms, dotted about like apple trees in an orchard over an area of four square miles or so. And with this, not a sound, not a living soul. Three tall obos, with their apparel of boughs and poles, were a silent testimony to the sacredness of the spot. Standing there, I offered up the world of Mongolia to Christ, whose name no man has ever invoked in that place so completely beyond the reach of any missionary. Less majestic but more poignantly romantic are the little lakes or Nors, sleeping in a circle of hills, where cranes, swans, geese, spoonbills and beautiful ducks with dazzling plumage nest and swim almost as fearlessly as the birds in a public garden. Only yesterday, too, our tent was pitched by one of these Nors. It was a delightful evening—an uncommon occurrence in the wild climate of this country, where hardly a couple of days can go by without squall or storm. As I watched the sun setting over the vast ridges, low and smoothly rounded, that marked the horizon, I witnessed a strange effect : a single large black cloud, alone in the golden sky, was releasing a shower of violet rain.

All that was remarkable in the rest of our journey was the magnificence of the landscape as we came down to Kalgan. For weeks we had been making our way over a country of rolling ridges, and as we emerged from a wide marshy depression, we suddenly found ourselves at the edge of a shelf overlooking a drop of some 2500 feet. Below us lay a chaos of broken rocky peaks—mountains below the plain!—and beyond them the green ribbon of wide fertile valleys. Spread out before us, in a scenic design that was completely new to our eyes, lay China—the ' great diamond' as the ancient Mongols called her, fascinated by the Promised Land from which the Great Wall shut them out.

They completed the return journey rapidly and comparatively uneventfully. Père Teilhard felt that the expedition had strengthened his conviction that 'without knowledge and research, there can today be no possibility of any human progress or real mystical life. I am deeply convinced, with a conviction based on reason, of the fundamental spiritual importance of an effort to reach consciousness ;

for consciousness is the sap of the tree of life, and of that tree our own privileged species is the topmost bough.'

On 10 September, 1924, Père Teilhard was in Shanghai where he visited the grave of his elder sister, Sister Marie-Alberic of the Sacred Heart, superior of the Little Sisters of the Poor, who had died there in 1911 of smallpox at the age of thirty-two. As he thought of his sister who, after ten years' work in the poorest quarters of Shanghai, had given her life for Asia, he felt that he, too, might well be called to the same sacrifice. Three days later he embarked for France. His next visit to the Far East, in two years' time, was to open a long career culminating in the completion of an important body of work.

1925-1927

This was a period of intense and varied activity all round. The Museum was the centre of Père Teilhard's scientific researches; it was suggested that he should join the staff, but he preferred to retain the independence of a free-lance. His teaching at the Institut Catholique brought him into contact with geological students, and other lectures extended his influence even beyond the young people attending the big colleges: the U.S.I.C. (Catholic Engineers' Society) and the Talas (the Association of Catholic Students at the École Normale Supérieure). He was widely known, too, in the intellectual and religious world of Paris.

In the latter there were at times indications of violent partisanship. He had his warm supporters, but there were others who were hesitant or even bitterly opposed to him. Père Teilhard neither invited nor refused argument. He was always ready, when asked, to explain his views on the great problems of the day. There were some with whom he could discuss these profitably, but there were others who were unfamiliar with his idiom and unable to follow him in his new avenues of thought. He was, in fact, faced by the difficulty encountered by every man whose ideas are in advance of his time.

Some of his more 'cautious' superiors were alarmed by the boldness of these new views, and their rapid spread among believers and unbelievers alike. Père Teilhard was instructed to confine himself to his scientific work, and sent to China to continue his already distinguished career.

He accepted the decision without demur, and thereby gave proof of his loyalty to his Order. He was in any case attracted to Asia and looked forward to the wide field of exploration and research it offered. China was to be the centre of his activities for many years to come, and he was later to be recognised as the leading expert in its geology and palæontology.

In the life of the Far East his mind found a new freedom. The grandeur of nature in a vast new continent, the multiplicity of human types he met on his travels and in the cosmopolitan society of Pekin, gave depth and richness to his thought, and continual reflection ripened the harvest of his vast experience.

His observation of the great ferment of societies and races, alternated with strict solitude, meditation, and concentration on God.

The trenches of the 1914 war had been for him what the cell is to the monk or what his ' stove ' was to Descartes. Père Teilhard now became the wandering hermit of the Asian deserts, a background that facilitated the ascent of his powerful spirit, and gave full scope to an outstanding personality and an outstanding destiny.

On board the ' Angkor ', 26 April, 1926

For the third time since 1906 I am passing Cape Bonifacio. Today the sea is grey and rough, instead of the deep blue lake that I crossed on the way to Egypt, where my first awakening lay in wait for me. But my ship is more powerful and has a longer passage before it than the one which was then carrying me to the same East. I have certainly grown older even in the last three years—even in the last eighteen months. Ideas no longer bubble up inside me with the same exuberance, the same perennial intoxication as before. In a man's life such exuberance, such fertility of mind, can last for only a limited period. On the other hand I don't think that I have changed fundamentally. I am still as eager to make the world my own, but there's a coolness, almost a joylessness, in my search. Twenty-five years' experience has taught me to define more exactly the nature and meaning of the charm that I used vaguely to feel woven into matter.[1] My vision is more direct, and my grip firmer, but I feel less. It's still the same charm that I seek, but it can no longer act on me as a charm.

Before, the light used to make the whole surface of things sparkle for me, and I found immediate delight in everything ; now it is as though the light were dimmed. The veneer of colour and scene bores me to tears ; what I love is hidden. In all men, no doubt, it is thus that the first steps are made towards the migration from one sphere to the other. It is a pull towards another zone that draws us towards maturity and death. Does the ageing of our bodies necessarily bring a detachment of the soul as a natural accompaniment ? Perhaps.

[. . .] Air and sea : a thick, living envelope, in which life swarms and hovers, as fluid and dense as the medium that holds it. Astonishment before the shape and the wonderful flight of the gull : how was that craft built ? The worst failing of our minds is that we fail to see the really big problems simply because the forms in which they arise are right under our eyes. How many gulls have I seen, how many other people have seen them, without giving a thought to the mystery that accompanies their flight ?

[. . .] May God grant it to me always to hear, and to make others hear, the music of all things so vividly that we are swept away in rapture.

During the voyage Père Teilhard made the acquaintance of Henry

[1] In 1919 he had written an essay on the spiritual power of matter.

*de Monfreid, who was on his way back to his estates in Abyssinia.
Although so different in many ways, the two found much in common. Monfreid has described the impression Père Teilhard made
on him. ' I observed with interest his long face, forceful and
finely drawn ; the features, emphasised by premature lines, looked
as though carved out of some tough wood. There was a lively
twinkle in his eye ; humour, too, but no hint of irony. On subjects that moved him he spoke with vivacity and animation. He
was a fascinating talker ; his words went straight to your soul,
with the persuasive force of an apostle. . . .' [1]*

*When Monfreid left the ship, he bade Père Teilhard a cordial
good-bye, and invited him, as soon as he had the chance, to include
Abyssinia in his researches, where he could be of great assistance
to him. Speaking of such meetings, and of how they disclose such
diversity of human natures in all parts of the world, Père Teilhard
notes : ' The more I knock about, the more aware I become of
the richness and variety of the lives and temperaments that we try
to force into the same mould.'*

[. . .] What a colossal thing the world is for a religion to assimilate. Travelling through these exotic peoples, this strikes me
even more than last time : you feel that you come up everywhere
against water-tight bulkheads between minds, and you have to
dive down to the absolute depths if you want really to make
contact with souls and to ' convert '. ' Conversion ' always
seems to me a very difficult problem to understand.

*Sailing along the coast of Egypt and remembering his days at
Ismailiah, when he was twenty-five, he notes sadly, ' Had I been
able to look into the future then, how surprised and excited I
should have been. Now I think that I might get something really
worth while done if only I were ten years younger.' He landed at*

[1] Henry de Monfreid, *Charas.*

124

*Saigon and took the little railway that runs through Annam to
Hanoi : he saw some forests being burnt.*

[. . .] Invasion and destruction, the subjection of all life to
human life and its ally—fire, the symbol of all the other forces.
Some years ago I would have been broken-hearted to see the
jungle swept away and a magnificent fauna (buffalo, elephant,
tiger) disappear. But now I realise that another era of the world
is beginning and I believe that the new forms of life are more
interesting than the old. So you see where palæontology can
lead you!

*After spending his first days at Tientsin in cataloguing the fossils
collected during his absence by Père Licent, Père Teilhard went
back to Pekin, which was to be increasingly his centre of operation.*

19 June, 1926

I have dropped straight back into a circle of very warm friends,
Chinese and American, the latter practically at full strength since
Mongolia unfortunately is closed to them. The photographer
of the Third American Expedition [1] took me with Andrews,
Mathieu, Granger and Nelson. The last three came from Pekin
yesterday evening in the same train as I did, and I spent an
interesting morning showing and discussing with them the
collections which I had spent the preceding days in arranging.

I saw quite a few people in Pekin : M. de Martel (the French
Minister), the Lazarists, the American Benedictines and their
embryo university—a fine princely mansion, strictly in the Chinese
style, which means a series of doll's houses, but very prettily
decorated and painted. I came back more puzzled than ever
about China, where the situation is really quite impossible to
define. There is in fact no central government any longer, and

[1] Organised by the New York Museum of Natural History.

things, including trains, muddle along as best they can. The Chinese-Bolshevik troops are a few miles from Pekin, while the nationalist troops are in quite peaceful occupation of the capital, though they make it most uncomfortably crowded.

You never saw anything so flabby-looking, or childish, or vicious as these Chinese troops. To look at them doesn't give you much confidence in the country. At the same time there's a Russian armoured train actually in the station at Pekin ; but the city still displays the usual scenes of animation. The world of the European concessions retains its brilliance ; only the tourists seem to have been scared off. You see none of them about and the two big hotels seem to be empty.

Old China, new China—dead religion, religion being born. If anything could give me hope, it would be letters such as that I received yesterday evening from my friend Ting the geologist, now promoted to be ' mayor of greater Shanghai '. I had left a note for him as I went through. He has just sent me a few lines in reply, and I was greatly touched and impressed by the cordiality and sincerity of his tone. No European of ancient family could have had a nicer thought or expressed it better. I wonder whether such cases are not symptomatic of a really new China, as different from that of the old scholars as it is from that of the bandit-marshals who at present control the country. It is really very difficult to form any idea of what goes on in these oriental hearts and heads. Recently I was shown two little idols given to a missionary by a young convert (from a famous family)—his own idols : two delightful little idols, the size of my hand, carved in hard wood. One represented a jolly, rather pot-bellied Buddha stepping out in a light-hearted dance. The other was a *female* Buddha, praying, a little marvel of human and heavenly beauty. In the first there was nothing spiritually inter-esting—rather the contrary—but the second held the real frag-rance of prayer. Now, when the young Chinaman was asked what sort of worship he gave these objects he could only answer that he honoured them ' to protect his body '—to avert any evil physical influence. He seemed never to have wondered how one could reconcile the veneration of two such different symbols—nor to have felt anything of the nobility of contemplation. And yet these little figures are still being made. Is it just the mechanical transmission of an ancient art ? or does some religious ideal still circulate among the masses ? I rather fear the first answer is nearer the truth.

Side by side with this dead religion, is there not a parallel development, only vaguely to be discerned, of 'a vast spiritual activity, still either formless or appearing under confused or disquieting forms' ?

There is a vast quantity of goodness and beauty outside the Church, which will come to fruition, no doubt, only in Christ ; meanwhile they are still there, and we must give them our sympathy if we are to be fully Christian ourselves, or if we are to assimilate them to God.

The day before yesterday, before a mixed audience of Chinese and Americans, a very likeable Harvard professor gave a simple and modest explanation of how he understood the dawn of thought in the animal series. I couldn't help thinking of the abyss that divides the intellectual world I was in and whose language I knew, from the theological world of Rome with whose idiom I am also familiar. At first it was something of a shock to realise that the latter could be, and indeed must be, just as real as the former ; and then I told myself that now perhaps I was capable of so using the first language as to make it fairly express what the other contains but puts into words that most people can no longer understand. However far-fetched the notion might appear at first, I realised in the end that, *hic et nunc*, Christ was not irrelevant to the problems that interest Professor

Parker ; it only needed a few intermediate steps to allow a transition from his positivist psychology to some sort of mystical outlook. This I found a heartening conclusion. There, I felt, lie the Indies that call me more strongly than St. Francis Xavier's. But what a vast problem to be solved, no longer of ritual but of ideas, before one can really convert them!

The expedition planned for the summer of 1926 was about to start. The objective was Shensi, enclosed in the loop of the Yellow River. 'A train will take us directly south of Pekin to the other side of the Yellow River (18 hours in the express). There a line still under construction (running east to west) brings us to Shensi. Then comes the tricky problem of how difficult or easy it will be to make up a caravan, and to get through. If we can, Licent anticipates that by the end of July we should be at Lanchow in Kansu, within reach of Chinese Tibet.' The purpose of the expedition was more geographical than geological, but palæontology had its place too.

Near Tungkwang, 8 July, 1926

A town situated at the bottom of the great loop of the Yellow River. We left Shanchow only yesterday by caravan. We had been hanging about for more than a week at Shanchow before finding the mules we needed. These endless confabulations are most exhausting. But now we're well set to reach Lanchow (20-25 days). We had a good journey as far as Shanchow, without too much difficulty. We were greatly delayed in Pekin, where we were on the very day of the 'historic' meeting between Chan-So-Lin and Ou-Pai-Fou—I had a most friendly luncheon that day at the legation with Madame Herriot.

In the evening I was present at the departure of Ou-Pai-Fou, who got into the train at the very station where our train should have been (but which was ten hours late). It was an odd sight such as hardly any European has ever seen : about a hundred cars dashing by at full speed, headlamps blazing, dark inside, armed soldiers on the running boards, the station taken over by armed troops and military bands in cream-coloured uniforms plastered with braid, a great turn-out of portly officers or lean, spare mandarins in long Chinese robes. The whole thing had an air of childish play-acting or conspiracy. The question between the two war-lords was to see which could bring most troops and show the least confidence in his partner. What the result of the meeting will be, I don't know. Meanwhile I am crossing a district that has been fought over all during the spring. Ou-Pai-Fou's people have driven out the bolshevising Kuominchun from the west, but they have yet to come up against peasant societies banded together to fight the scourge of militarism, and all you hear talk of is of throats cut. There is no feeling against foreigners. Honan is an impoverished countryside, overrun for centuries by bandits, and, for the past year, by soldiers, in indescribably awful conditions.

It is a bare landscape ; after the jagged mountain chains you have nothing but vast expanses of yellow earth, fantastically fissured. As far as Tungkwang we are following the line of the European engineers' staging-posts for the projected railway line, and we are admirably entertained. We expect to be at Tungkwang tomorrow and leave the next day, passing to the north of Sian-Fu, where fighting is going on at the moment. I've had time to make some interesting geological observations, but the real work won't begin—in theory, at least—until after Lanchow. We are moving through the most ancient parts of the Chinese empire. Laoyang was the first capital, and Sian-Fu the second ; so the countryside has nothing in common with wild Mongolia. Until today, the drought has been terrible. Everything is dried up and burnt. We spent all day yesterday shrouded in dust, in a burning atmosphere.

The road to the west is completely closed and it's impossible to get through. We have got as far as three miles from Sian-Fu, that is, up to the firing line—if you can call it that ; and the big military bosses have told us quite definitely that there is no road by which we can get through the front. So, to our great disappointment, we have had to go back over the devastatingly tedious 90 odd miles we had to cover from Tangyuan.

To European eyes this Chinese war may hardly have seemed a serious military operation. But it was a great set-back to Père Teilhard's palæontological work. However, the journey suggested some far-reaching problems in geology and when it was over he felt that he would be able to ' button up ' an important piece of work on the Quaternary era in China.

Ho-ching, on the Hwang-Ho, 29 July, 1926

Every inch of the valleys is cultivated (chiefly cotton), and they are very thickly populated. In places the fruit-trees, particularly the lovely dark-leaved persimmons, are so numerous as to form regular woods. More often than not the fields are quite bare and it's a very tedious business crossing them. We made a very pleasant trip into the mountains, surrounded by flowers, nearly all of which were new to me [. . .] You see pagodas everywhere, generally dilapidated, and at the entrances to the village stand miniature ones, full of ferocious-looking Buddhas. The local people appear much more devout than those of Hanon or Shensi, but I doubt whether their piety looks further than the birth of a son or the coming of rain. I have never seen so much of Chinese China as I have this last month. In these parts you really get the impression of an enormous mass of concentrated peasant ; but who can foresee the speed with which the leaven of the towns will work in the mass ? We are following a projected motor road, and are beginning to meet cyclists on the most primitive tracks.

Between Shensi and Shansi,[1] 29 July, 1926

Yesterday we made a detour to an extremely interesting place, where the Yellow River emerges from the rocky defiles that lie between Shansi and Shensi. The river bed is only 120 to 150 feet in width but it suddenly widens until it covers a mile or so. The effect is quite staggering. The place is guarded, of course, by two fine Taoist pagodas, one in Shansi and the other in Shensi. The officer commanding the little garrison regaled us with melons, sweets and various snacks.

On 26 August they were back at Tientsin : then north towards San-Ko-Ho (two days west of Pekin) to investigate some fossil-bearing deposits they had visited on an earlier expedition. Their stay was cut short by the cold weather and the unpleasant proximity of a group of bandits who held up the neighbouring villages to ransom. But they obtained a good load of interesting and probably important fossils.

The countryside is extremely rocky, the ground cracked, the houses the same colour as the earth—which gave the appearance of an absolute desert. Only a few golden poplars lent a touch of gaiety to the yellow and red of the earth and the sombre background of the mountains. But the light was of a heavenly purity, and brought out in strikingly sharp relief the serrations of naked rock and the vast ramps characteristic of Chinese mountains and valleys. One corner of the horizon was shut off for us by a chain of mountains, 9000 feet high, completely covered in snow. In another direction a lake perched up on the plateau threw back an enchanting dazzle of colours from the setting sun. Through gaps

[1] Two provinces in the loop of the Yellow River, Shensi to the west, Shansi to the east.

to the north you could catch glimpses of the platform of the Gobi which always fascinates the eye. We were comfortably lodged in a little Chinese house where they gave us three small rooms to ourselves. This was real village life, right among these simple kindly folk, still smiling and unmoved after being plundered at least twice this year and spending every night with the threat of a bandit raid hanging over them : poor things, they had lost nearly all their livestock and were living off meagre plots of ground, painfully and precariously saved from erosion. I had never appreciated until then how terribly China suffered from the scourge of militarism. Bands of soldiers disorganise and destroy every single thing, and the war-lords think of nothing but carving out loot for themselves, without any thought for improving the country.

Tientsin, 1 September, 1926

Since I got back to Tientsin I have been busy arranging and deciding how to make the best use of the hasty notes I made during our expedition. I have sent for Pekin's use a long memorandum, with numerous sections, on the Chinese Quaternary, and another on the older formations is practically ready. There are two fossil forms collected from the latter which are new for China ; one is particularly interesting, since it was found in the country's most ancient strata. One way and another I feel that I have got something done ; but these results are really material for specialists.

Now that that's done I'm more or less free. I shall take advantage of this to type out my manuscript on Evolution, written during the voyage out. I am dominated by the complex feelings that the earth is too small, and yet that this very narrowness is nevertheless the essential condition of our centration and co-penetration as men, and so perhaps of our emergence or

' exstasis '. *Nothing but the earth,* said Paul Morand : which is
true in more than one sense. It has called for nothing less than the
whole earth to produce man ; and the real man is the man who
gathers, or will gather, within himself the consciousness of the
whole human stratum. But it is precisely when that stratum is
being formed or welded into shape by the check on our continued
outward extension that we feel that our domain is absurdly con-
stricted. We feel increasingly driven to find some way out ;
' Nothing but the earth ' becomes too little. What I want to do,
in short, is to express the psychology—the mixed feelings of pride,
hope, disappointment, expectation—of the man who sees himself
no longer as a Frenchman or a Chinaman but as a *terrestrial.* The
further I go the more determined I become to live above political
and national prejudices of any sort, and to say openly what I think
without taking any notice of what others say or have said. I
believe that the time has come when, if men are ever to achieve a
common understanding, they must do so at a point which will
be reached only by breaking, reversing or re-framing a mass
of conventions and prejudices that enclose us in a dead outer
shell. We all now need something quite different. You know,
of course, that there is nothing anti-Christian—far from it—in
the direction my thoughts are taking ; I see it simply as a call for
the appearance of an even Greater Christ, and for that there can
be no substitute.

*During an unusually tranquil period at Tientsin, Père Teilhard
had completed ' an important palæontological task ' and was
planning a very different undertaking.*

7 November, 1926

I have finally decided to write my book on the spiritual life. I
mean to put down as simply as possible the sort of ascetical or
mystical teaching that I have been living and preaching so long.

I call it *Le Milieu divin*, but I am being careful to include nothing esoteric and the minimum of explicit philosophy. What I intend to do is to confine myself to the realm of a moral attitude, vigorously presented but still incontestably Christian. I really mean to try to ' get across ' and to have the book read. I think that if I could manage to get it printed, it would do good in two ways : it would spread ideas which I believe might open new frontiers for many minds, and at the same time my efforts might be rewarded by some sort of approval from the Church.

I have settled down to my little book. I want to write it slowly, quietly—living it and meditating on it like a prayer.

Père Teilhard's normal routine was now to alternate between Pekin and Tientsin, with Pekin as the real centre of his work and contacts. In December he took part in a Pan-Pacific Congress, including Australians, New Zealanders, Americans and French, at which he was particularly engaged in escorting his old friend, M. Lacroix, permanent secretary of the Académie des Sciences.

5 December, 1926

The Congress routine is the same as usual : receptions, with a big Chinese dinner, in two Universities ; a dinner (European, fortunately) given by the Minister of Education at the Winter Palace ; other private dinners for geologists in the houses of friends or at some big Pekin restaurant. That's one side of the programme. It isn't the cocktails or the rose-scented wine that have made me join in. I have seen a really imposing number of congenial or useful people about, new or old, foreign or Chinese ; I have been weaving, I hope, some strands into my fabric—the fabric of potential influences—and at the same time I have been feeling the intransigent internationalist, or rather the *terrestrial*, growing stronger in me. What I find most interesting, perhaps, in these meetings is to realise to what an extent for a great many people the step has already been taken. Everyone, no doubt, remains first and foremost a man of his own country and continues to draw from it his motive force. Yet the geographical and racial gaps are practically abolished, and it seems incredible that China, for example, can still seem to some people a wild or inaccessible country. The tendency soon asserts itself in Pekin to govern one's life by the same preoccupations as in Paris, and these various visitors whose lives have criss-crossed practically the whole earth, including the Antarctic, behaved almost as though they were at Harvard or Sydney—just as unexcited, just as wrapped up in their usual jobs.

Pekin, 17 December, 1926

For the last two weeks I have been practically all the time in the company of M. Lacroix, with whom are his wife and Madame B., sister-in-law of Sylvain Lévy, the director of the Franco-Japanese Centre at Tokyo. I was heartily delighted to meet my old friend and teacher again. He is one of the three or four finest examples of a man of science that I know. He has been greatly fêted almost everywhere here ; at first the tributes he received were perhaps rather done to order, but they soon became a spontaneous gesture of friendly respect. I went with him, last week-end, to Kalgan. It was a most interesting trip, both from the point of view of geology and for the picturesque landscape, but it was by no means a comfortable one. It was a fifteen-hour train journey each way, in very broken-down railway carriages, and in icy weather; and it was only through the personal intervention of the director of the Geological Survey, who accompanied us, that we were able to find seats. However, we took it in good part and got through with nothing worse than a few colds, which I personally escaped. I have never seen Kalgan look so intensely Asiatic and Siberian as in this wintry weather and state of siege. There were no Europeans, except for a few Russians : Mongols everywhere in great fur caps driving long lines of carts as they galloped along on wild little shaggy ponies. Thanks to our passports obtained through the American consul, we were able to drive out of the town by car and go some twenty miles down the Urga road as far as the edge of the Gobi, so that M. Lacroix was able to see its first undulations. I knew it all, but in the company of three geologist friends, among them Lacroix, it was as if I were looking at it for the first time. I was not sorry too, from a more selfish point of view, that M. Lacroix should be there to appreciate the difficulty of geological work in China and at the same time see for himself the position I have come to occupy in the Chinese geological world. He will be the more ready to realise both these points in that at Tokyo he felt that France (for lack of a representative) was on the point of being elbowed out of the field of pan-Pacific sciences. Kalgan, then, has been the important item in the Lacroix programme, almost the only geological item. Tomorrow we are going again to look at some rocks in the Summer Palace, but transport is so disorganised that we have had to give up excursions in the hills even though they're less than 25 miles from Pekin. On the other hand I have seen a great deal of *chinoiserie* but I can't muster up any interest in it. Anything large the Chinese have made (palaces, gates, walls) is built of mud, and their only work in durable materials (jade, bronze, porcelain) is no more than pretty trifles. The most massive and intricately carved statues are revolting anatomically. The awful grinning lions that stand at the entrances to palaces have a terrifying number of teeth, and they all have a little bell round their necks. I feel that wherever you go in old China you see and hear that little bell. . . .

But China is in a bad way at the moment. Chinese and Europeans alike are all pessimistic and people anticipate that six months from now it will be Cantonese influence that dominates

Pekin. What we hope is that the north's contact with the south may cool the bolshevik fervour of the latter. It is possible that the people in the west and south, once they are masters of the situation (and unless they start fighting among themselves), may say thank you to the Russians and wish them good-bye. For very much *a priori* reasons perhaps, I still think the south's victory will be the first step in the reorganisation of China. But, as a leading Chinese personality very rightly said to Mgr. Fabrègue, China has three revolutions on its hands at the same time : political, social and intellectual. It's a very grave crisis, and one year won't see the end of it.

In February 1927 Père Teilhard was invited to supervise the work on vertebrate and human fossils in China. The invitation, initiated by Chinese, Swedish and American scholars, came to him from the Carnegie Foundation. Hitherto he had been assigned to his researches by the Paris Museum, and the resources at his disposal were limited. He was still the Museum's representative, but now that his appointment gave him the direction of so wide a field of work, with the power of American money behind him, he was finding that he was able to greatly extend his activities.[1]

20 February, 1927

I now find myself (with several colleagues of course) in charge of geological work in China. In my own special field my concern is now to clear up some geological formations over an area as large as half Europe. That is work I must keep in my own

[1] The International Research Organisation at Pekin included three centres : the Geological Survey (Chinese–American–Swedish), the Rockefeller Medical Institute (American–Chinese), and the Free Chinese University (an American foundation). The staffs, who were more or less shared in common by all three institutes, were grouped again in the Geological Society and the Natural History Society, to which had just been added the Institute for Prehistoric Research (a Carnegie endowment). Besides these, there were visiting missions, such as the Andrews (American) and the Sven Hedin (Swedish).

hands. [*He is thinking of the repugnance shown by M. Boule, director of the Paris Museum, to his incorporation in a Chinese organisation instead of working primarily for Paris; this separatist attitude, the direct opposite of Père Teilhard's universalist views, seemed to him very petty.*] Without me, by which I mean without what I represent, the Museum has no existence in the Far East, whatever Boule may think ; with me, it balances Nagasaki and Uppsala. [*In fact Père Teilhard's work was to do more to convince his old friend and teacher, Marcellin Boule, than any tedious discussion could have done.*]

I have often told you of the cordiality of these gatherings in Pekin. There were ten of us, all friends, and almost all intimate friends ; four Chinese : Ting, Wong, the director of the Survey, Lee, a professor at the University, and King, an amateur of natural history ; several Americans : Dr. Grabau, my great friend the palæontologist, Dr. Black of the American University of Medicine, and Granger, the palæontologist of the American expedition ; two Swedes, Andersson and Sven Hedin ; and myself. As usual, there was a more or less conscious feeling of achievement in meeting on the level of common humanity, man to man, transcending all national, racial or even 'confessional' barriers. But on that occasion, with the meeting a prelude to many partings, and in a Far-Eastern atmosphere charged with passions and hatreds, a feeling of poignancy overlaid our talk. The table was strewn with apple-blossom, a sign both of spring and of its storms ; we each spoke in turn of friendship, of collaboration, of our hopes for small or great things. I am quite certain, for I can feel it or detect it continually in others, that though the world is full of potencies, it is floundering and suffocating ; the reason is that there is no-one at hand, not even the Christian, to set an example and show how men may learn to act and live in a way that will be human in the fullest sense, passionately and actively receptive of everything good and beautiful and true. There is only one contact charged with an irresistible centripetal and unifying force, and that is contact of the whole of man with the whole of man.

Père Teilhard was really happy working in collaboration with the Chinese University. 'What I find so attractive there is not at all the idea that I can introduce denominational or national influences in a place from which they have hitherto been excluded, but that I can surmount many wrong-headed barriers and join up with men of very different types on a footing of real humanity, sought for in our common pursuit of truth. [. . .] I should much prefer, of course, to try to let a spark fall into the Parisian bush, but one must be faithful to life, and then the one will perhaps help the other.' (12 March, 1927.)

The idea that his authority as a scientist may win him a hearing in both non-Christian and Christian circles, reappears frequently in his letters, and with it the idea that his religious constancy is the strongest evidence he can offer : ' It is my view of the world and of Christ which is put to the test in my own life.'

In the spring Père Teilhard undertook another ten weeks' expedition towards the Dalai-Nor ; this had already been explored in 1924, but the geology was still little known. There were doubts about the safety of the countryside but ' it would be silly to be actually on the spot and then give up '. The first stage was at the mission of Notre-Dame-des-Pins. Thence the column moved off with a military escort towards the mountains at the south-eastern extremity of the Gobi.

Chan-wan-tzu, 11 June, 1927

Everything is going well and the country is quite peaceful. More often than not, it's true, we have found that little groups of bandits have set up a sort of private toll-post in the cols, but these gentlemen have a wholesome respect for an armed party and have kept their distance. We have no idea, or only a vague one, of what is going on in China.

For the last three weeks I have been completely absorbed in geological work, but we have not yet emerged from a chaotic mountain mass whose structure we have to determine as we progress without losing the thread ; and although we do no more than 25 miles a day, this calls for care and attention. Fortunately I have a good little pony who consents to trot along without cavorting first to one side of the caravan and then to the other. I have already collected the material for an important piece of work. [. . .] The country is picturesque : it is simply an enormous plateau cut up by multiple valleys into a network of abrupt rocky chains. But what is really heart-breaking to see is the stupid, wicked deforestation the country has suffered at the hands of the Chinese settlers, so that what less than a century ago was heavily wooded is now completely bare. Huge cracks appear on all sides, down which the storms carry torrents of stones and earth. For the geologist, nothing could be better, for you can see the bare rock, but for society it is a crime. Licent says that botanically and zoologically it is a sacrilege. But, basically, I feel oddly indifferent to this devastation. My interest has wandered so much further afield, even when I am most absorbed in geology. It is the Other that I now seek, the Thing across the gap, the Thing on the other side. Is this no more than an effect of age ? Or have I really broken through some barrier ?

As a result of being so tied to geological work—perhaps also of a certain lassitude which arises from an element of uncertainty about what I may be doing in the future—I am ' thinking ' less perhaps this year than on my earlier expeditions. My most active moments are still when I am saying my ' Mass upon the altar of the world ', to divinise the new day.

This mystical poem is a longer version of that which Père Teilhard wrote during the war, and which he then called ' The Priest'. The essential theme is the same.

' Since once more, my Lord, not now in the forests of the Aisne but in the steppes of Asia, I have neither bread, nor wine, nor altar, I shall rise beyond symbols to the pure majesty of the real, and I shall offer you, I your priest, on the altar of the whole earth, the toil and sorrow of the world. [. . .]

' Receive, my Lord, this one whole victim which creation, drawn by your power, offers up to you in this new dawn. Bread, our toil, is in itself, I know, no more than a vast dismemberment. Wine, too, our sorrow, is alas, no more than a draught that dissolves ; but in the heart of this form-less mass you have planted an irresistible and sanctifying urge which makes each one of us, from the godless man to the man of faith, cry out " Lord, make us to be one! " ' [1]

Tong-Kia-Yingze, 4 July, 1927

The last three weeks have been spent in excursions into the sur-rounding countryside under the protection of an imposing force of mounted and armed Christian troops, bursting with pride at having to escort us, and equally pleased at having a chance to get around and hunt. First we spent some time under canvas in the woods and pastures of Weichang ; then we pushed as far as Ting-Pang, a little frontier town standing isolated on the Gobi border, only 50 miles from the Dalai-Nor, where I had been in 1924.

Weichang is extremely picturesque country, in many ways very reminiscent of the Haute-Auvergne. Imagine a vast plateau of basalt, with an average height of 5400 feet, dotted with shreds of forest (pines and bamboos) and covered elsewhere with magni-ficent pear-trees. Most of the Chinese and Mongolian settlers

[1] *La Messe sur le monde.*

141

had left the year before, after the troubles ; where we camped there wasn't a living soul in sight as far as the eye could reach. There are stags in the woods, roebuck and black-cock, and in the open country you find some gazelle. But the flora, especially, was magnificent ; with some variations it reminded me vividly of our woods and meadows in Auvergne : a carpet of red and yellow lilies, scarlet primulas, white-striped rue, wide single peonies, lady's-slipper orchids with flowers as big as walnuts, and masses of iris. In this botanical Paradise, where the thermometer twice fell to 2° [Centigrade], I was able to collect some fine rock specimens for my friend Lacroix—delightful excursions on my own in a setting of intense, even if apparently infra-human, life. But is it not the Spirit that animates everything, even the plants, even the stones ?

Tientsin, 7 August, 1927

Our journey ended happily enough, but there was some difficulty between Jehol and the Great Wall. The country was full of bandits ('big' bandits, this time) and we were only able to cross the last cols in the wake of a military convoy we providentially met. And we took care not to lag behind.

Here I found an accumulation of mail that has brought me back to the realities of my other life—not that it was forgotten, but a little pushed into the background by the daily work of the expedition.

Nothing official, but from various quarters—Lyons (theology), Paris, England—I have letters that disclose the thirst of believers and unbelievers alike for a conquering and fully human Church. Even if I have not had time these last three months for reflection, I feel on the other hand that my ideas have been consolidated and clarified, so that the important factors receive their real value. Thus I can see more distinctly how much my interior life is dominated by these twin peaks : an unbounded faith in Our Lord, as animator of the world ; and a clear-eyed faith in the world (particularly in the world of man) as animated by God. *In season and out of season*, says St. Paul, and I feel that my mind is made up to declare myself a ' believer ' in the future of the world in spite of appearances, in spite of a false orthodoxy that confuses progress and materialism, change and liberalism, the perfecting of man and naturalism.

My sole ambition now is to leave behind me the mark of a logical life, directed wholly towards the grand hopes of the world. There lies the future of man's religious life. I am as sure of it as I am of my own existence.

1928-1930

On 27 August, 1927, Père Teilhard embarked for France where he was to stay for a year. On 7 November, 1928, he left again for the Far East, but on the way he spent a couple of months in Ethiopia.

Henry de Monfreid had invited Père Teilhard, with his colleague M. Pierre Lamare, to make a detour into Ethiopia by way of the Red Sea. Monfreid was a sort of feudal chieftain in the country, a nuisance to the local authorities but friendly with the native population. He cruised about those parts in his little Arab dhow, with his own crew, and it was almost impossible to get hold of him. He seemed to be ubiquitous, for at one moment he would be at sea and a moment later on land, and vice versa. He had a house at Obock, a power-station and a mill at Diré-Daoua, and an estate in the Harrar. He had no love for the Negus and still less for the Governor of Djibouti, who returned the feeling. Monfreid, in short, was the Monfreid you meet in his own books : the liveliest and most fertile teller of real-life stories, which Père Teilhard was the first to hear and the success of which he predicted. Monfreid was proud to show the two scientists round the colony and take them to little-known parts, but he found the road barred by the Governor, C. B., who refused to allow him into the Tankali country.[1] The three men decided to dispense with his permission

[1] This short hold-up gave Père Teilhard an opportunity to collect some specimens. Life in the colony was extremely primitive, but this troubled him little.

144

and left Djibouti by boat in broad daylight and in full view of the local authorities. The next day the chief customs officer and the askaris, the native guards, were at their heels. Monfreid was suspected of gun-running, and this suspicion also fell on his guests.

Obock, 26 November, 1928

If I go further than a radius of half a mile, an askari falls into step behind me. It's quite farcical, and everyone takes it as a joke. Straightaway we found our popularity, Lamare's and mine, firmly established with the Tankali, who are ready to welcome us with open arms (we have seen several of the chiefs here) ; but unfortunately it is going to be impossible for us to take advantage of this, for even so we cannot disobey the proconsul's (C. B.'s) formal instructions. We have written to the Minister to complain, for it is really tantalising to see the Mabla Mountains rising up a few miles away—where no white man has been, and where the natives are expecting us.

Monfreid's large, airy house stands right on the edge of the sea : there's a small anchorage separated from the open sea by a coral reef, with a few dhows at anchor. Apart from a small French post, where an administrator lives, there is nothing else at Obock except a Tankali village. Their picturesque huts are grouped around us. Monfreid is quite at home there, and his two little blonde children, Amélie and Daniel, toddle around all day chattering with the little negro boys and girls.

However, Père Teilhard persisted, and succeeded in getting as far as the Mabla foothills accompanied by a Tankali who had taken a liking to him ; and so was able to have a look at the country-side.

(To the Abbé Breuil)   *Obock, 4 December, 1928*

My dear friend,

I am writing to you from Obock, where I have been more or less immobilised for the last fortnight owing to the ill-will of the Governor, who—out of jealousy, spite and so on—did not want us to go through the Tankali country with Monfreid, the only man who can go about there in safety. It would take too long to tell you all about the marvellous battle we have been having with the authorities. But briefly, instead of exploring the Mount Mabla massif, I have had to be satisfied with having a look at the foothills—and even that surreptitiously : I went about alone, hands in pockets, with two Tankali, which proves the absolute security that Monfreid's protection confers—the Tankali take me for his brother-in-law. Even so I was able to do some useful work. In two days' time I am going up to the Harrar, where I'll be at liberty to go where I please.

Obock is no more than a village of negro straw huts on the edge of a vast coralline plateau (average height 90–120 feet), itself dominated to the west by the eruptive massif of the Mabla : an absolute desert, dotted with small umbrella-like mimosas.

Generally speaking the ' savages ' of these parts, from every sort of different tribe, are of a very fine type, but apart from the Tankali they are said to be rather a cowardly lot given to treacherous murder and ambush.[1]

According to people here, the government of the Negus is paralysed by the clergy (heretical, and violently reactionary) and the old chiefs, who still persist in refusing to travel by train—a whole world of extreme primitiveness. One amusing touch :

[1] He adds immediately : ' My experience in China has taught me not to take literally the accusations Europeans make about the Ethiopians.'

the bishop ordains priests (a pack of good-for-nothing parasites), by blowing on them. Recently the bishop of Diré-Daoua, who is asthmatic, has been having trouble in performing this ceremony: so the opportunity was taken when his breathing struck a good patch to have him breathe into a leather flask, and when the candidates for ordination presented themselves, the flask was squeezed over them to deputise for the episcopal lungs.

The Harrar, Diré-Daoua, 28 December, 1928

Diré-Daoua is a third of the way between Djibouti and Addis Ababa—a two days' journey by train (which pulls up for the night). Later they went up with Monfreid to his estate of Araoui on the Harrar plateau, some 6000 feet high, an interesting spot for geologists.

Long low ridges, yellow in the winter drought ; the winter here is the dry season. An implacable blue sky, and a north wind that can bring the night temperature down to 5° [Centigrade]. In front of me, a pretty lake covered with water-fowl, and surrounded by cattle. On the horizon a vast purple tabular chain, that must be at least 9000 feet high. If you disregard the fact that the houses are completely circular huts with thatched roofs pointed like corn-stacks, and that the background vegetation consists of large cactiform euphorbias, and finally that the commonest birds are thrushes with metallic blue plumage and little scarlet sparrows, then you might imagine that Balla was next door to La Godivelle.[1] But Balla is not the whole of Abyssinia. If you go south, the country begins to drop gently in height and grow hot. At Harrar (an extraordinary, ancient little Arab town, with narrow winding streets, enclosed in walls and with gates that are shut at nightfall) begins a strip of cultivated land, planted

[1] A village in Auvergne.

with bananas, coffee and khat—a shrub whose leaves the natives chew all day long as a stimulant.

If from Balla you go towards Diré-Daoua—north, that is— you drop abruptly several hundred metres to the Afar country, which lies across the line from Djibouti to Addis. Between those two are stretches of appallingly burnt-up desert, in which herds of gazelle somehow manage to survive. Leaving Diré-Daoua you come to fine bush country, a vast expanse covered with scattered mimosas and masses of bushes, where you find antelopes and countless dazzling and fantastic birds. Through this bush the little train from Addis ambles quietly along for days on end.

Up here on the Harrar plateau the Galla peasants seem to be a very peaceful lot. In the Afar they seem more warlike and you never see them—alone or trotting along in single file—without a long spear and a broad-bladed knife. In fact all along the railway line the lands of various tribes adjoin one another—Tankalis to the north, Hissas and Gallas to the south, etc.—who spend their time squabbling with one another. All these natives are exceedingly handsome : magnificent bronzed bodies that blend with the landscape like the gazelles and the many-coloured birds. It would be fascinating to get to know their customs and cultural habits, but I greatly doubt whether they will ever be in the van of human progress.

Père Teilhard had a few days' rest in Monfreid's house at Araoui. On Christmas Day he went to say Mass at the good Capuchins' at Harrar, 'short fat men, for the most part, lost behind their beards'. A zebra-skin served as an altar-cloth. The servers ('levites') had bare feet under their cassocks. Then back to Obock to wait for a ship. Père Teilhard writes of their last days in Ethiopia, the two of them along with Monfreid, in the old house lapped by sea and desert, among the native huts.

Since I've long ceased to take any notice of Citizen C. B. (the Governor) I have been going about by myself among the Tankali, in any odd corner that took my fancy, and I have done some useful work in geology and prehistory. Last week was spent in sailing in the Gulf of Tadjoura, to try out Monfreid's boat, a very successful and picturesque trip. Monfreid and I have practically left anything European right behind us. At night we anchored under basalt cliffs on which grew incense-bearing trees. The men went out in canoes to catch outlandish fishes on the coral reefs. One day some Hissas sold us a kid and some camel's milk. The crew took the opportunity to 'christen' the boat. The dried-up old negro who has been Monfreid's servant during all his adventures smeared blood over the tiller, the bows, and the mast, and later, in the night, we heard the chant of the Koran rising up from a thick cloud of incense. . . .

(To Max and Simone Bégouën)   *Diré-Daoua, 8 January, 1929*

I am right in the middle of an exotic picturesque world—every type of country : the deserts fringing the Red Sea, the high Somaliland plateau (6000 feet above sea level), the bush of the Aouache and the Harrar. I have spent a little time in every part ; and it really is pleasant and unusual to be wearing as few clothes as possible in the middle of winter (except at nights on the high plateau), living among the birds, the different coloured monkeys, the mimosas, the coffee-bushes. I'm still thrilled by this African life, so different from the austerity of Mongolia—not that I am forgetting the latter.

The human inhabitants would make an interesting study. Moreover, unlike the Chinese, they are well worth looking at : Tankali, Hissa, Caragan, or Galla—they all have magnificent copper-coloured bodies, so that they really blend with the landscape and the fauna. They suddenly appear, springing from nowhere, armed with spear and knife ; or they pass by in little groups (even when going about the town ; in Harrar, for example) in single file, men and women, and nearly always at a trot. It's a survival of a splendid human type—but how ill-fitted, it would seem, to follow our forward march.

They will merge or disappear—like the zebras and elephants. J. will say that I'm cruel and insufficiently catholic, but the truth is that the more I look about me and the more I consider the matter, the more I realise that thought and action can lead only to faith—ill-defined, perhaps—in the progress of thought (or, if you like, of spirit) ; and that progress itself implies an unquenchable force that insists on the destruction of everything which has outlived its time. My whole outlook is governed increasingly by this physical realness of thought, which is stronger than (or rather includes in its own self) all the boundless properties that a century of research has attributed to matter.

Obock, 19 January, 1929

The end of my stay in Abyssinia was marked by two considerable triumphs. Quite apart from a fine store of rocks and observations collected for Lacroix, I found within a few days, around Diré-Daoua, (1) a cave, with an important petrified filling of fine tools, probably palæolithic, and several paintings ; (2) a stratum rich in ammonites, a thing unknown so far in this part of Abyssinia and most valuable from the geologist's point of view. In each case, then, I have something completely new. I lost no time in letting Boule know and I am hoping that a case of specimens will reach Paris safely and speedily. So altogether I am in a position to draw up at least two useful little memoranda on Ethiopia and Somaliland.

On board ship for China, Père Teilhard was reading Malraux's
' Les Conquérants '.

In it [*Les Conquérants*] the atmosphere, the noises, the feeling of
China are evoked with extreme exactness and intensity. But it
is the general key of the book that I find so enchanting : tension
and vigour in a work whose value may be debatable but which
is conceived on a grand scale—the pursuit of a grand ideal in
a supremely concrete effort. One weak point—the anarchist
individualism of Garine : it's difficult to see in what way the
Canton he dreams of would be better than the Hongkong he
destroys. The mystique of destruction is indeed an odd and
complex thing.

Physically and morally at peace, I have again reached a sort
of ease and liveliness in ' thinking '. The fact is that now only
one sort of world of the spirit exists for me—but not a meta-
physical spirit in a Hegelian sense, I think. The spirit which I
think I can discern is loaded with the spoils of matter. I now see
all the grandeur, all the physical and historical attributes with
which science has been loading matter for the last hundred and
fifty years—I see all these transferred to one characteristic stuff
which includes all things. Entropy has been replaced for me
by ' the highest consciousness ' as the essential physical function
of the universe. The world seems to me to ' tumble ', if I can
so put it, forward and upward upon the spiritual ; and this
inversion of cosmogony has the consequence of giving a cosmic
consistency to the centres of consciousness—to the monads : this
personal treasure, the centre within every soul, is imperishable,
and the supreme Centre must be both lovable and loving.

Père Teilhard's return to Pekin (or Peiping, as it was to be called in
future) was marked by closer contact with the official world. He
normally lived now with the Lazarists in Pekin, but his working

headquarters were with Dr. Grabau, ' father of all the natural history institutes in China ', or with Dr. Black, director of the Sino-American laboratory for human palæontology.

Having decided to accept ' the supervision of the Geological Service ', he realised that the Chinese attitude to foreigners had changed greatly, and that in future they would look askance at European organisations. He decided accordingly not to hold back but to collaborate openly with the Chinese National Service. As he had complete freedom in every field he felt it his duty to do so. Moreover, the Propaganda,[1] with an eye on peaceful penetration through native clergy, would be glad to see a French religious attached to a great Chinese institute.

In future he would have the control—virtually the complete direction—of the younger students and research workers, both in the laboratory and in the field.

Just at that time the Sinanthropus had been discovered in the Chou-Kou-Tien caves 30 miles from Pekin (December 1928). It was an important date for the history of human origins. For Père Teilhard it was one of his great ' strokes of luck ', and he remarked that on several occasions he had had the good fortune, unusual in a scientific career, of happening to be on the spot when one of these cardinal finds in the history of fossil man had come to light.

He set off, with camp-bed and stores, to direct the work, living entirely with the Chinese and seeing to the orderly exploitation of the site. His work in the field was interrupted from time to time to return to Tientsin, where he habitually went for important feasts and Easter, and to make his annual retreat. Although this was on the whole a period of calm and spiritual concentration, yet he sometimes suffered from a feeling of exile, from uncertainty about the future, from misunderstandings and procrastinations that delayed the diffusion of his ideas, for with Père Teilhard, ' mystical

[1] The Roman Congregation for the Propagation of the Faith.

vibration is inseparable from scientific vibration and calls as urgently for expression'.

Tientsin, 17 March, 1929

I have been here since the day before yesterday.

I am writing to you in the same room, and from the same table, as two years ago, with the same greyish marsh on the horizon and with the whistle of the same eternal wind of China in my ears. It is an odd mixture of pleasure and pain, and difficult to analyse, to find myself again in this setting : old, happy memories of this place, mingled with a certain nostalgia for Europe, and saddened a little, too, by an awareness in mind and body of departing youth. These are the ingredients that combine to make a potion that I find not enervating—not that at all— but just a little harsh. 1923, when I first arrived at Race Course Road,[1] seems to me to belong to another era. Hardly anything had been built in those days and I cannot help feeling that my own 'soul' then was practically brand new. But now I give myself the impression of a veteran fighter, not exactly sceptical, but pretty tough, a man who has no use any more for anything but the activity—and the friendship—that science brings, in so far, of course, that it allows me scope for action.

Pekin, 13 April, 1929

I am back in Pekin for ten days or so, very busy arranging a consignment of more or less fragmentary fossils collected in the last eighteen months from our celebrated Chou-Kou-Tien fissure. The Chinese Survey is in fact trying more and more to monopolise me. If my superiors at Tientsin raise no objection (and I don't think they will) I shall accept an invitation for June or July

[1] The Jesuit house at Tientsin.

to accompany a young Chinese palæontologist as an expert guide
to the deposits beside the Yellow River, between Shansi and
Shensi. I have in fact come to realise during this last stay that it
is becoming increasingly difficult for any foreigner to do geological work in this country without official liaison with the
National Service. This probably means a quite fresh orientation
to my life, but it is, I hope, what life expects from me. [. . .]
Who knows whether in a few years' time the big foreign
institutes (universities, museums) will be able to retain their
independence ?

[. . .] The end of my stay in Pekin has been interesting and
busy. I have been to see Sven Hedin. We had three hours of
friendly and even intimate conversation. Hedin is a ' *most fascinating man* ' who is obviously lavish with his charm. But I had the
impression that with me there was a more personal touch, and
that for a reason I didn't suspect. When he was getting ready
to go to Turkestan in 1926, Hedin came up against Chinese
touchiness about rights in scientific material, and he was the first
to accept the conditions they insisted on for expeditions and
researches in Chinese territory. He was criticised at the time, I
am sure, and thrown over by even his best European friends, who
accused him of going over to the Chinese. Just then I met him
and urged him to trust the Chinese and work in with them. He
is still touchingly grateful to me, as though my words had kept
him going during the long months that preceded his success,
which is now complete. He now has the full confidence of even
the most anti-foreign Chinese and every single one of those he
took with him is his devoted friend. Once again it has been a
triumph for faith in the spirit, or the good. I came away from
my talk with Hedin confirmed in the line I have decided to take ;
for I too (like the Church, for that matter) am going over to the
Chinese. My friend Wong, at present in Nankin, is looking
after the formalities of my official attachment to the National

Survey. Is this just a little unimportant side-turning I am stepping into, or is it the main road? I still have no idea, but what I can see quite clearly is that I must follow it further and find out.

Tientsin, 6 May, 1929

I got back yesterday from another trip in the Peiping area, and tomorrow I am going to join Licent in Manchuria. [. . .] Things have so turned out as to make me take a further step in the direction I was telling you about—a new co-operation with the Chinese. A letter from Ting urgently begged me to get down to Chou-Kou-Tien, 30 miles south of Pekin, to study with two Chinese the geology of the site and supervise the organisation of the year's new excavations. To take charge of Chou-Kou-Tien is too important a job for me to think of refusing. So I started back for the capital with my camp-bed and some provisions. A little Ford took me and my two companions over impossibly bad roads to a village near the dig. Well, one way and another, I'm pretty satisfied. In the first place, from the technical point of view, I think I have been able to throw a little more light on the history of what will in future be a very celebrated site. Then, too, I have been very touched by the good will and gratitude of my new pupils. The experiment gives me courage to face the Shansi expedition, which I am sure will be much more interesting for me and my companion than the rather thankless task we have just been working at.

In Manchuria

From May 1929 Père Teilhard, with Père Licent, was in charge of an expedition to Manchuria. It was his first, and rather arduous, experience of the northern country: a 36-hour train journey to Mukden and Kerin, and then two days in a cart to a

Christian medical mission, but not without being bogged down in
the swamps, with nothing in sight but squalid Chinese peasants.

From the Gulf of Petchili, and on towards Karbin, one is in Sino-
Russian territory. So far the country is simply an immense grey
or black plain, crossed at intervals by undulations between which
lie the bogs that herald the tundra. Before the Chinese came
the Mongolian steppe stretched out into a limitless expanse ;
but today it has all been reclaimed ; fields stretch to the horizon,
with isolated clumps of willow, poplar, elm, and wretched mud
villages with incredible ' roads ' along which the carts progress
with great difficulty, drawn by seven or eight oxen, all under a
sky that often pours down in a torrent of rain. Towards Kirin,
in the east, the Korean mountains begin, once magnificently
afforested but now stripped bare by the Chinese settlers. To the
west lies the great Khinghan range, the southern part of which I
know, though I haven't seen it yet this year.

Here at Karbin flows the mighty Sungari, nearly a mile in
width, whose waters roll down to meet the Amur. I am not
dissatisfied. This fearsome Manchuria forms a single massive
sedimentary unit, but no-one, so far as I know, has yet tried to
determine its stratigraphy and still less its connections with the
neighbouring Chinese formations. I am beginning to clarify
my views on it and I now have an important new contribution
to my theoretical reconstruction of Far-Eastern Quaternary geology. During my various moves I have had friendly assistance
from the Fathers of the Paris Foreign Missions.

He then left with a Russian engineer, ' an agreeable and majestic
Baltic ex-baron ', for the Chalai-Nor on the Mongolian plateau,
which meant a long journey by the Trans-Siberian railway almost
to the Siberian border.

' *A picturesque and interesting journey. The Chalai-Nor is six miles from Siberia and nine days from Paris. I saw Mongols again, and gazelles, all the background of my 1924 expedition. I believe I have done some useful geological work.'* He was able to co-ordinate his work with the Russians' and help in the interpretation of their findings. He gave a lecture, and felt that collaboration between Russians, Japanese and Chinese could be profitable.

'*I have learnt a tremendous amount about the ancient and recent geology and prehistory of this country. My whole work in China has been illuminated and my conclusions confirmed by these new observations.*'

He was back in Tientsin on 10 June and found that it was already time to organise a new expedition to Shansi, unless it should be prevented by danger of war between Chiang Kai-Shek and Fu-Yu-Shiang. . . .

'*Since November 1st* [he is writing in June] *I have never been more than a fortnight in the same place, and often much less.*' *There was a pile of letters waiting to be answered at the 'lab'.* '*I feel rather overwhelmed, but there is nothing for it but to bow one's head and press on in the Faith.*'

They left on 6 July: Père Teilhard, his young Chinese assistant, three 'boys' and six mules.

Everything is going well; even the cooking is improving. Geological work is entertaining when there are two of you and I think we are getting some really valuable results. I am writing to you from a little town, typically Chinese, surrounded with tall crenellated walls and chock-a-block with pagodas. The advantage of travelling as a Chinese official with a Chinese companion is that one is much less of an 'outsider'. Everyone is immediately co-operative.

Pao-Teo is a little fortified town perched on the banks of the Hwang-Ho, against an unreal setting of grey loess and burning sky. We had an admirable reception from the authorities : a real Chinese dinner, which puts your resistance to alcohol to a severe test ; and a lodging in a little pagoda on the bank of the Yellow River.

Between Shansi and Shensi, July 1929

The expedition ranged between Shansi in the east, and Shensi in the west, in the great loop of the Yellow River. A fortnight's excursion to the north of Pao-Teo brought ' some cardinal observations for determining the geology of the Yellow River, going back probably to the palæolithic, and extending by several hundred miles my 1923 finds.' They re-crossed the river after sending off cases of specimens, and came downstream south-west towards Shensi.

A deluge has for the time being ended the terrible drought which northern China has been suffering from for the last three years. Suddenly all the roads have opened up into cracks, sometimes several yards deep. Fields have been washed away into the bottom of the ravines, and in the valleys the maize is buried up to the ears. In spite of all this, the people are pleased, and we were able to cross the greatly swollen river. We were then in Mongol country again as far as Chungar, whose ' king ' gave us a magnificent reception in his sort of combined farm-house and castle, crowded with lamas, which stands in the middle of the sands : a fine hefty fellow, with a completely simple and open manner, but for all that very shrewd in his dealings with the Chinese. We are starting our wanderings again from one inn to the next, over the ridges and furrows of loess. Delightful welcomes in the towns—they fall over themselves to make us comfortable and offer us meal, jam and syrup. The only thing is, there are too many flies. The dinners consist always of the same ceremonial dishes—if only they weren't at such an unearthly hour, three to four in the afternoon, I'd find them quite excellent. I have got right back into my ' form ' as a traveller. Everything is going splendidly.

Taiyuan, Shansi, 16 September, 1929

In his mail Père Teilhard found letters which reminded him of Europe and his apostolic work. A young priest (and by no means the only one) was kept in the Church by him : ' I have just had the opportunity of using my own experience and my own method of apologetics to help a young colleague through a religious crisis.' There was a letter, too, from Père Charles telling him that the ' Milieu divin' was going to the printers at any moment unless some unforeseen contingency should turn up. ' I hardly dare to believe it yet. But what I do know is that all the official reports have been favourable, and that is a most valuable indication.' [1]

I am thinking of a third draft, considerably fuller, of *La Messe sur le monde*, and also of an essay on *La Physique de l'esprit*. In the latter I shall try to show (as I believe I can see myself) that in future science will be constrained—particularly since the notion of evolution and duration has invaded the physics of matter—to build its explanations of the experiential world on the spirit. This will lead me to a general presentation of a sort of spiritual cosmogony—but not a metaphysic—of *the person*. Approached from this angle, it seems to me that the immortality of the soul and of the personality (hyper-personality of God) ceases to appear as anthropomorphic or self-interested expressions of the truth ; it takes on an essential significance in the structure of the world. I am trying to pin down this idea, or at any rate to find some first approximation.[2]

[1] In fact it was not published during Père Teilhard's lifetime.
[2] In the essay entitled *Esquisse d'un univers personnel*, 1936.

159

I have been tremendously ' *excited* ' by this autumn's finds in the Chou-Kou-Tien fissures : jawbones and fragments of skull of a very strange anthropoid or hominid ; the dentition is completely human, the shape of the jawbone typically simian, and the cranial dimensions completely human(?). If that last point is confirmed —so far the fragments have been only partially sorted out—it will be the conclusive answer to the opponents of transformism as extended to man ; and so I've told Le Roy.[1]

30 October, 1929

The longer I live, the more I feel that true repose consists in ' renouncing ' one's own self, by which I mean making up one's mind to admit that there is no importance whatever in being ' happy ' or ' unhappy ' in the usual meaning of the words. Personal success or personal satisfaction are not worth another thought if one does achieve them, or worth worrying about if they evade one or are slow in coming. All that is really worth while is action—faithful action, for the world, and in God. Before one can see that and live by it, there is a sort of threshold to cross, or a reversal to be made in what appears to be men's general habit of thought ; but once that gesture has been made, what freedom is yours, freedom to work and to love! I have told you more than once that my life is now possessed by this ' disinterest ' which I feel to be growing on me, while at the same time the deep-seated appetite, that calls me to all that is real at the heart of the real, continues to grow stronger.

Physically I am very well. It was not physical fatigue that I felt at the beginning of my June expedition, but a sort of spiritual weariness, as though everything were growing old (which gave

[1] Édouard Le Roy, professor at the Collège de France, and a personal friend of Père Teilhard's, by whose views on evolution and human origins he had been profoundly influenced, as he acknowledges in *L'Exigence idéaliste et le fait de l'évolution* (1927).

me a curious surge of excitement, and yet at the same time cast a shadow over some of the world's horizons). There are times, you see, when you have to be blind and deaf to what is going on within you and will soon be lost in action, in a passionate and blind abandonment to life's currents.

(To Max Bégouën)   *Tientsin, 11 November, 1929*

My dear Max,

My diary tells me that I have not written to you since the end of April. During this six months' silence I have been almost continually on the move : from May 10 to June 10 in Manchuria, as far as the border of Transbaikalia ; from June 20 to September 20 in western Shansi and northern Shensi in the midst of the great loess country. This second journey, which I made with a Chinese companion as a member of the National Geological Service of China, gave me plenty of hard work, but with excellent results : palæolithic information (in isolated items) covering an extensive new area, and an important contribution to the Upper Tertiary stratigraphy of China. I spent the whole of October in Pekin at the Survey, where I now have my ' *office* ' (although I am not tied by any contract). There, with a Chinese colleague, I prepared the first geological and palæontological report to be made on the famous Sinanthropic site at Chou-Kou-Tien. All this is quite absorbing. At the moment I am taking a little break at Tientsin, for spiritual rest and to help Licent at his museum. But I foresee a winter at the Lab. (Tientsin and Pekin), and some journey to the West in the spring. But whether I'll see Paris in 1930—that I don't know yet. But I shall try to get back to the West, at any rate for a certain time. I still, you see, don't know where life is taking me. I'm beginning to think that I shall always be like this and that death will find me still a wanderer as I have always been. But really I believe that I'd rather have it so, than sink at my moorings. But perhaps that's just vanity.

Your long letter of September 20 (which came only a few days ago) gave me great joy, and indeed I thank you for it. One thing, of course, distresses me, to know that you still have to drag B. around behind you.[1] But what, in fact, is that encumbrance compared with the inner fulness you have attained—partly, no doubt, in return for having been so ill-used! You hold the real treasure within yourself—a soul that has grown in stature and has been renewed. Watch over this treasure, and that you may do so put all your trust in the great higher Presence who has given it to you. It is only natural, particularly in you, that you should try, probably with some anxiety, to find a way of extending and applying this force ; and I pray that life may grant you the great joy of falling ' like a spark on a bush ' (*sicut scintilla in arundineto*, the Scripture says somewhere). But if you are to preserve the fulness of your peace and your strength, remember that you would already have sufficient justification for your existence even if you never succeeded in spreading the fire within you as far as you might wish. We spend our lives, all of us, waiting for the great day, the great battle, or the deed of power. But that external consummation is not given to many : nor is it necessary. So long as our being is tensed, directed with passion, towards that which is the spirit in all things, then that spirit will emerge from our own hidden, nameless effort. There lies the unswerving trust that should dominate the forces whose influence you feel—should overlie them, I might say ; whether they be fated to remain for ever enclosed within your own self, or to be confined to a narrow circle, it is already a great deal—it is in fact the essential thing— that they should be born in you and that they bear the world's homage to God.

[1] Referring to a professional embarrassment.

At the beginning of 1930, Père Teilhard had to leave again for Shansi, to escort the American geologist Barbour. This was a little bit of a drag, at least mentally, for physically Père Teilhard had said that he was very well. ' I must get going—all my life urges me forward.' ' A comfortable journey, too, on the motor road : 48 hours for the 400 miles that before took me a week by mule. Interesting result. Barbour endorses all my views—a most valuable check.'

They pushed as far as Tong-Kuan, in the south-eastern corner of Shansi, and saw Honan in the distance, as they had in the ill-fated Tibetan venture of 1926. They were joined by a new companion, a young graduate from the École Normale, a pupil of Martonne, who had won the university ' Tour du Monde ' scholarship.

' We stayed in the quite sumptuous house of a Swedish friend. Dinner with the Governor. Nearly everywhere we were given hospitality by the Protestants : excellent people. But what can they give the Chinese of the hinterland beyond a little money, some grain, and hygiene ? '

They were back in Pekin for Washington's Birthday. Père Teilhard's friend Grabau took him to a party given by the American colony at the Grand Hotel. ' It was brilliant and not a little original. At one in the morning, under the probably rather astonished eyes of the French Minister, I was having a discussion with Sven Hedin on the meaning of life.'

(To Max Bégouën)   8 April, 1930

You are still having some difficulty in justifying to yourself the euphoria of a soul immersed in ' business '. I must point out to you that the most important thing is that you *do* have that feeling of well-being. Bread was good for our bodies before we knew about the chemical laws of assimilation. But granted what you have already understood of the world and of Christianity, you can certainly go further and give a religious and philosophical reason for what you feel. ' How ', you ask, ' can the success of a commercial enterprise bring with it moral progress ? ' ; and I answer, ' In this way, that since everything holds together in a world which is on the way to unification, the spiritual success of the universe is bound up with the correct functioning of every zone of that universe and particularly with the release of every possible energy in it. Because your undertaking—which I take to be perfectly legitimate—is going well, a little more health is being spread in the human mass, and in consequence a little more liberty to act, to think and to love. Whatever we do we can and must do it with the strengthening and broadening consciousness of working, individually, to achieve a result which (even as a tangible reality) is required, at least indirectly, by the body of Christ. As you say yourself, to the value of the work done is added the value of the actual doing, which by its fidelity creates in us the personality expected of us by Christ. Our own soul— in itself and in its being at the heart of the universe—is the first of the tasks calling for our efforts. Because you are doing the best you can (even though you may sometimes fail), you are forming your own self within the world, and you are helping the world to form itself around you. How, then, could you fail from time to time to feel overcome by the boundless joy of creation ?

Gobi expedition, May, 1930

A new expedition : this time with a group of Chinese geologists to Mongolia. ' Immense austere plains. The rash of Chinese houses and cultivation is spreading over what was yesterday a boundless steppe. There is something dramatic in it, if it is looked at as a human effort to exist and multiply in conditions of the most extreme severity. Here you see the very lowest strata of humanity.'

Père Teilhard returned to Pekin only to set out again to the eastern Gobi with American colleagues. ' We went as far as Kalgan, and then north : a vast plateau with a few yourts scattered over the endless grazing grounds. An advance party of 50 camels has been sent on a hundred miles farther north.' There he had the ' good luck ' to find a solution to one of the main problems he had gone there to study.

My companions are pleasant and charming. Andrews, the organiser, is a wonderful talker, full of real-life stories of hunting from the Yunan to Siberia, and by no means his least valuable quality is that when we are short of meat, he can take his car and his rifle and come back in an hour's time with a couple of gazelles on the running-boards.

These men have done real prodigies of exploration in the Gobi in the last six years, and they save their energy and know how to live.

This is a very different experience from last year's, when I was the master of my ten mules. I am in excellent shape physically. Rain, storms and dust and icy winds have only whipped up my blood and brought me rest. Andrews has presented me with a thick fur coat and a sheepskin sleeping bag which enable me to face the cold, until the time comes when we're roasting again.

' Wolf Camp ', Gobi, 29 June, 1930

We are now a hundred miles farther to the north-west, well into the Gobi. Our blue tents are pitched at the edge of a fossil-bearing cliff, looking out over the immense flat surfaces of Mongolia : the terraced levels, uniformly grey with a tinge of delicate green, have a look of magic when the rays of the setting sun skim over them. There is nothing in sight but a few yourts beside the streams, and we work in absolute solitude, our only companions the wolves, eagles and gazelles, which last always provide the bulk of our diet. The same gaiety and family spirit prevails in the camp. The facilities and amenities of the expedition are much as I foresaw. The weather, of course, is not always as pleasant as it might be. Except for the last three days, we have had incessantly to put up with all the gales of Mongolia. About the 23rd, after a night during which our tents had been almost uprooted in the icy rain, we were all in furs! But we always manage to see the comic side of these trials. In short, physically I am going through a really toughening course. But even so I still think, if you can believe it, that I'm putting on weight. The work goes well. We have got hold of some authentic mastodon deposits—strange mastodons with an elongated jawbone rounded into a huge spoon. Personally I am managing to link together satisfactorily the geologies of China and Mongolia (my principal objective) and I am vastly extending the horizons I include in my vision.

Cut off from any correspondence, I feel that my Paris and Louvain hopes and preoccupations, others too, are necessarily dormant.[1] Yet I feel too that all that world is living and growing unseen, in the depths of my being. When I turn my eyes in that direction it seems to me that I have never attained such simplicity, clearness of vision or controlled tension in my interior effort. I look more and more to God to find the best point at which to apply it all most fruitfully, when the time comes. And meanwhile I can see quite clearly that I am still gathering my strength for action. If the action has to be brief—well, no matter.

[1] Concerning the publication of the *Milieu divin*.

1931

Père Teilhard returned to Pekin at the beginning of August, and prepared to leave for France in early September. He spent only a short time in France and left again for America at the end of January. Business connected with the Citroën mission [1] made it necessary for him to stop in the United States, where he was pleased to meet again his friends Osborn and Andrews at the Natural History Museum. In religious circles, on the other hand, he found that there was still opposition to the scientific attitude now adopted by naturalists of every country, and that evolution was equated with materialistic monism. Père Teilhard was to devote his life to combating this misunderstanding by showing that evolution must be given a spiritual orientation. ' In Paris the attitude is less crude,' he adds without bitterness, thinking of his predecessors such as Lapparent or Termier, or friends such as Henri Breuil, who had advanced along the same road as he was himself to follow.

Passing through New York he gave two lectures in English, one to the staff at the Museum, the other at Columbia University. In New York, too, he met Paul Claudel.

' I spent an hour or more with Claudel, on the thirtieth storey of the hotel at which he is staying. My visit was in connection with Haardt and Point, but in fact we talked chiefly about religion. The great poet was most charming and friendly.' Claudel was to

[1] Père Teilhard had agreed to join the Yellow Expedition, in preparation since 1929, and had been in touch with the organisers in Pekin and Paris.

Père Teilhard ' the pure poet, for whom everything is a question of aesthetics [. . .] He sees no difficulty in the vastness of worlds —they dance for our delight ; no difficulty in the Biblical presentation of history—that it is a wonderful enrichment of our thought is enough in itself; he sees no adversary of Christianity in sight at the moment—for Christianity alone has the power to influence the minds of men of good will. The idea that at this moment there can be an intellectual crisis for a man seems to him an anachronism. Claudel often, and with great intuition, reaches new and valuable concepts : the necessity, for example, of giving primacy to the final end rather than to the effective means in the creation of the universe ; but now that he has escaped from determinist evolutionism himself, he imagines that there is nothing left of what he believes he summarily annihilated by his " conversion ".' Père Teilhard, on the other hand, believed that the Christian cannot afford to overlook or neglect the tremendous diversity of minds and the difficulties they raise, if they are to be brought to one single faith. ' The world must have a God : but our concept of God must be extended as the dimensions of our world are extended.'

(To his brother Joseph Teilhard de Chardin)

New York, 8 February, 1931

I must confess to having been quite unmoved by my contact with New York : no feeling of repulsion, of course, such as Duhamel had, but none of admiration either—just a deep appreciation of the order and majesty of the city. The skyscrapers are very beautiful, especially at night when their summits are lit up like light-houses, but you immediately get accustomed to their scale. I spend practically all my time at the American Museum of Natural History, where I had a delightful welcome from Osborn [the director], Andrews and others. At one of the two luncheons given in my honour, I was welcomed by Osborn as an ' adopted son of the house ' and I think that expresses the situation perfectly. My visit is much too short, of course. All the same I shall have done quite a number of things in these few days, and when I take the train for Chicago I shall have achieved all that was essential to my purpose in coming here.

Père Teilhard returned to China by San Francisco and the Pacific. San Francisco seemed to him a giant Riviera, with the Pacific as its Mediterranean.

(To the Abbé Breuil)
On board the ' President Garfield ', 23 February, 1931

I had the pleasure of visiting the rather new but enormous Field Museum in the company of the founder's grandson, Henry Field (with whom I had dined in Paris in November). The only corner of Chicago I saw, the Michigan Avenue district on the shore of the lake (which is a regular sea), seemed to me magnificent. In his vision of the future, *Au pays de la vie future*,[1] Duhamel really has overstepped the bounds of emotional partiality. I had chosen the southern route for San Francisco, through Santa Fe, so that I could have a look at the deserts. But through lack of time I had to pass within 60 miles of the Grand Canyon without being able to visit it. However, I did well to leave time for San Francisco. I made new friends there at the great University of California, where I had as excellent a reception as at the American Museum in New York.

One of my young colleagues (an S.J.) is finishing some palæontological studies there. We found ourselves very much in agreement on every plane. In France we can hardly imagine a University like that of San Francisco, where hundreds of students live rather in the way we associate with the Greeks, bursting with

[1] Georges Duhamel's *Scènes de la vie future*.

health in the glorious sunshine. We console ourselves with the thought that these hefty athletes don't give a damn. But this isn't completely true, for in my own sphere I found several keen young workers.

One way and another, then, I realise that I did well to return to Pekin through the United States. In the course of this short visit I have strengthened any number of half-formed contacts, and scores of possible new ones have come to light. If only I were still forty. . . . If for any reason Pekin should fall through, I could take my choice of the offers I'd certainly get from America.

[. . .] Yes, I liked America : doubtless, of course, because I was made a fuss of (excessive admiration, in fact, which displays the rather ' young ' side of the country), but still more because everyone engaged in research gave me the impression of freshness and keenness without an eye on a Chair or some other academic advantage. I should only have to turn up in New York, or Chicago, or San Francisco, this very moment, and I'd immediately find work or an appointment. However, my future seems to be tied to China.

At the end of this letter, Père Teilhard passes on to the Abbé Breuil an invitation from Dr. Black, the director of the Geological Survey, to visit Pekin. He hoped the two of them might be together there in the coming autumn. Père Teilhard was committed to accompanying the Yellow Expedition, but expected to be back in October.[1]

On board the ' President Garfield ', 24 February, 1931

[. . .] The end of my stay turned out in much the same style as the beginning. I was made a tremendous fuss of at the American Museum, where I gave two ' lectures ', one to the staff of the

[1] His return, as will be seen later, was delayed six months.

Museum, the other, at Columbia University, to the geological students ; and I had the discussion with the experts in Mongolian geology for which I had come to America. I felt very much ' at home ' at the American Museum—at least as much so as at Boule's.

Leaving then for Chicago, I had twenty-four hours' experience of travel by Pullman. Whatever Duhamel may have found to say, Chicago—or at any rate Michigan Avenue and its neighbourhood by the lake, which was practically all I saw—is a magnificent place. In fine weather, the modernity and unselfconsciousness of the skyscrapers and the great wide avenues running along the shore of a real inland sea, are quite fascinating. Young Field did the honours for me and entertained me to a delightful dinner at his home—a friend of Breuil's with whom I had dined in company with the Bégouëns in November. He is the grandson of the millionaire Field who founded the Field Museum at Chicago (the rival of New York's American Museum). He seemed delighted to do me the honours of that vast collection, where I learnt a great deal and met a great many people.

The same evening a Pullman on the California Limited was taking me through Santa Fe to San Francisco (three days and three nights). I chose that route so that I could see the Colorado desert : and—just imagine—I passed within 60 miles of the Grand Canyon and didn't have the time to see it !

16 March, 1931

I greatly enjoyed the Hawaiian Islands. They are a real little paradise in spite of the influx of Americans who have made it one of their most pleasant ' *centers of resort* ' : the soft climate and luxuriance of the tropics ; the greenness, the fragrance, the flowers—extraordinary flowers covering the tallest trees and turning them into huge bouquets.

To introduce me to all these wonders, a geologist, Dr. Gregory, director of the Pacific Services, put his car at my disposal, with himself and his wife for company, which ensured me a delightful day. Garlands of flowers as we arrived—that's the routine ceremonial. Lunch at the Honolulu Club, and an excursion into the lava mountains, clothed in forests in which you see some uncommon species. Tea—a very ' social ' affair—in one of the villas to which these fortunate islanders can retire at a distance from the town. In a few hours I was able to make real contact with both the scenes and the people of this interesting little land lost in the middle of the Pacific.

Back, then, to my journeying : twelve days at sea in the excellent *President Garfield* where I became more and more appreciative of the peaceful comfort and even of the society on board [. . .] but in spite of these contacts I still had plenty of time on my hands, and at last I succeeded (after a few days in getting started) in writing a paper—only moderately long but very compressed— on *The Spirit of the Earth*. More than anything else I could have written, I look on it as a sequel to the *Phenomenon of Man*.[1] It's an essay in the interpretation of the world—more particularly of the earth—taking as a starting point the spiritual forces manifested in man. I haven't made it my business to introduce any scientific or religious teaching, and yet I believe there is nothing in it that is not entirely Christian or capable of being Christianised. I'll send you a copy, of course, when I've typed it out. There's a great deal in it that you're already familiar with, but there's a good deal that I've never yet put precisely into words, and the general approach is from a new angle—hardly anything of the scheme I used for my lectures at the École Normale in November.

We arrived in Japan in cold but beautiful weather. Kobe is only a fairly interesting place, but while I was waiting for my

[1] The article previously written for the *Revue des questions scientifiques* (Louvain).

ship I went to spend a day at Kioto, a curious, typically old-fashioned Japanese town. I saw a whole series of classical temples, more sombre in colour than the Chinese but very clean, built of a most magnificent wood and nestling in such a wonderful green background of tall dark-foliaged trees. (Unfortunately I was not alone—a missionary was my guide—so that I couldn't linger as I should have liked to in front of the gilded altars, *without* idols.)

1931-1932

In 1929 Père Teilhard had been sounded with a view to his taking part as geologist in the Citroën Central Asian Expedition, later popularly known as the Yellow Expedition.[1] Although the original purpose had been to demonstrate the adaptability of the Citroën tracked vehicles, which had already proved their value in the Black Expedition of 1925, there was the wider objective of re-opening to economic and political exchanges the ancient silk route across the vast central Asian depression.

The enterprise received encouragement and support from Governments and from learned Societies in France and other countries. There were two parties. One, led by Georges-Marie Haardt, who had already led the Black Expedition across the Sahara to Madagascar, was to travel through the Near East, Persia and Western India to the Pamir massif, which was to be the climax of the test ; the Chinese party, led by Lieutenant Victor Point of the French Navy, was to leave Pekin, cross the Central Asian steppes and deserts, enter Sinkiang (hitherto strictly closed to all foreigners) and join up with the first party at Kashgar. Both would then return together to Pekin. The teams included engineers, scientists, two doctors, a painter, a cinema photographer, a well-known reporter, Georges Le Fèvre, and a staff of mechanics. It

---

[1] Cf. Georges Le Fèvre, *La Croisère jaune*, Expédition Citroën Centre-Asie, 1933.

*had been anticipated that the journey would take six months;
in fact it took nearly twice as long.*

*The Chinese party was to set out at the beginning of April.
Victor Point and Père Teilhard were to join it by train at Kalgan,
but there was a breakdown at the very beginning.*

(To J. T. de C.)   *Pekin, 19 April, 1931*

You may be thinking of me as on the Gobi road, but I am still in
Pekin. The *Yellow Expedition* had hardly left Pekin before there
was a serious hitch. After 90 miles the rubber of the caterpillar
tracks, burnt apparently during the crossing by the tropical sun,
began to collapse. It's a bad break-down. [. . .] But apart from
that I must say that the equipment is impressive and the morale
of the team astonishing. This set-back is a great blow to my
friends. We're waiting for spare tracks from Siberia.

Meanwhile I am writing various memoranda or notes on
subjects that range from the lower Cambrian to the Neolithic,
and I ' *enjoy* ' this familiar old Pekin which a good spell of rain
has just washed from the half-inch of loess deposited by the recent
dust-laden winds. Blue skies, yellow roofs like circumflex
accents, peach-trees and pink lilacs, the cry of pigeons on the
wing—it's still all the old China, or rather it's still just the old
setting ; for one of the first results of the comparative peace that
has prevailed between North and South for the last eight months
has been to bring out how profoundly the spirit of the country
has changed since 1925. The Chinese now definitely have the
self-awareness, if not the capabilities, of a modern nation. It
means an end to privilege and to everything which has no fundamental spiritual value. On the scientific side, too, the days of
foreign expeditions in China are numbered. Only occasional
individuals like myself are going to be admitted, and they may
even be sought after. Sometimes I would very much like to be

able to tell myself that some reason will ultimately make it necessary for me to leave China ; but in point of fact, when I think of the work to be done here, I feel just the opposite, that the country ' breathes me in ' more and more.

While waiting for the tracks to be repaired, Père Teilhard was trying to complete his ' Spirit of the Earth' to his satisfaction.

4 May, 1931

I believe I have collected a great deal of new material in these pages, and that they answer a number of questions that are often only vaguely formulated. I have been realising this recently in two contexts : one was when looking through a book by the English astronomer Jeans, *The Universe around Us*, and the other when reading an autobiography which was given to me last week by its author, Hu-Shih (almost a friend now), the young well-read philosopher who has behind him the whole Chinese undergraduate world. Jeans's book (a popular work, a sort of very superior Abbé Moreux) is being widely read just now. But it absolutely makes one despair. He believes that he is offering us hope and something to live for when he tells us that with a certain amount of luck we still have some million million years of humanity before the final and utter end (humanity petering out on a frozen earth where no problems exist any longer). It's the most explicit (and hence to me the most interesting) statement I know of the attitude diametrically opposed to my own, and in it you can see laid bare all the weaknesses (a complete misunderstanding of the phenomenon of life) that distort his thought. It is precisely the antithesis I need to use as a concrete individual illustration of my thesis. Hu-Shih, on the other hand, has arrived at a *Credo* which he is offering, and having welcomed by, his fellow-intellectuals in China : faith in the world but in a world conceived in a childishly immature and imprecise way. [. . .]

He fails to see that the 'universal energy', if it is not to be inferior to our own selves who form the advance guard of the world, must be a 'thinking energy'; in other words he doesn't see that the cosmos holds together not by matter but by spirit. I have been deeply interested to see even Chinese thought, in its own way, taking the same direction as my own and that of my friends. Moreover, it's a most encouraging confirmation of the idea—very close to my heart, as you know—that in future the faith of Christ will never hold its own or be extended except through the intermediary of faith in the world. In fact I cannot help regretting not having two months' peace to round off what I have in mind. Perhaps the fruit will be riper by the autumn.

I am going on ahead to the west with two supply trucks. The 'fleet', which now appears to be 'seaworthy' again is not to set out until the 17th. A solemn moment—but shall we ever reach Turkestan? There is every sort of political cloud on the horizon, for we are obliged to include in our convoy representatives of the Nanking government, and these are looked on as 'undesirables' in the practically independent provinces. I am in extremely interesting company, and I find that I have an important part to play while at the same time I am having to experience all sorts of salutary mental reactions. The three of us, the chief engineer, Point and I, have endless conversations on 'basic' topics.

After so many years of continual contact with every sort of temperament and mentality, Père Teilhard notes :

I have been struck by the difficulty of making certain universalist lines of thought intelligible to men who have never been Christians or who have escaped any deep-reaching Christian influence : for Christianity emerges as the only spiritual current capable of developing in souls the sense of the Absolute and the

Universal, conceived above all as personal,[1] in other words the true 'mystical sense'.

Pai-ling-miao, 22 May.   North of the Yellow River

Since the 12th of May we have already covered 500 miles of this wonderful Mongolian country : on the second day a snowstorm, on the third a sandstorm, and now beautiful weather. In these few days I have already gathered a considerable store of geological data really ' *illuminating* ' for the structure of the Gobi, which is encouraging for the future. The type of quick research that I was envisaging turns out to be both possible and rewarding ; and on top of that it has been pleasant going. This vast ocean-like expanse, furrowed by sharp ridges of rock, inhabited by gazelles, dotted with white and red lamaseries, and trodden by Mongols in clothes as filthy as they are colourful, is extremely ' taking ' ; the more so perhaps that being obliged to get to understand it, I am settling down as though I were quite at home. My companions, too, are delightful.

Pai-ling-miao is an important junction of tracks that run to all the chief centres in China—long files of camels carrying opium disguised as inoffensive loads of hides ; it's an organised trade between the Chinese Governors, the Mongol princes and the bandit-chiefs. The place itself consists of a fine lamasery, red, white and gold, and two Chinese inns, the whole set in a granite gorge on the banks of a crystal-clear stream ; a few stunted elms in the ravines and some enchanting apricot trees covered with pink blossom ; and a swarm of lamas in their long red robes.

On June 16th we were at Suchow, west of Kansu, and comparatively close to Turkestan, after covering 750 miles of the

[1] These considerations were the basis of the essay *Esquisse d'un univers personnel* (1936).

most astonishing and sombre wilderness of solitude I have ever encountered : sandstorms, gazelles, wild sheep and above all fascinating geological work. We expect to move off in two days for Hami and Turfan. The tricky part is getting into Sinkiang (Turkestan), which is a hotbed of political trouble [. . .] Meanwhile we are enjoying the lush vegetation of Suchow, whose poplars and fresh streams variegate the eternal sand at the foot of the snowy barrier of the Nan-Shan (on the northern borders of Tibet).

In an appendix to the account of the Citroën Central-Asian Expedition, Père Teilhard notes one of the illuminating geological aspects of this meeting point, where the Gobi plateau merges with the foot of the Nan-Shan Celestial Mountains.

The setting changes, just as during a film one sequence fades into another. A ridge higher than any we had yet seen marks the 12,000 feet and more of the Karlik Tagh. At its foot the country falls away to the west as far as the eye can reach. The balance is disturbed to give way to a new structure. Instead of the unending corrugations of the Gobi peneplain, two features hold the eye : the huge ridge of the Celestial Mountains, and at their foot, starting with the Turfan deep (600 feet below sea level), the vast depression in which the Tarim, rolling through a jungle of wild poplars in a torrent as mighty as the Yellow River itself, loses itself in the shifting basin of the Lop-Nor : one single chain and one single basin. By pure simplification and interlocking of the contours you find that you have passed almost without noticing it from the monotony of Mongolia to the monumental formations of Upper Asia.[1]

---

[1] *La Croisière jaune*, pp. 361-2. This contains two maps showing the route from Pekin to the meeting of the Pamir and China parties at Aksu, Turkestan.

Turfan, 7 July

I am writing in a temperature of 40° [Centigrade], stripped to the waist, facing a most impressive view :

In the foreground rows of tapering poplars ; behind them a wall of red and grey cliffs encircling a depression below sea-level which is our present position ; beyond them a long snow-capped barrier, the Bogdo-Ula, a continuation of the Tien-Shan. So here at last we are, at Turfan in the heart of Chinese Turkestan. It has been a long long road from Suchow, across deserts more deserted than any I knew. The whole countryside becomes more majestic in outline. When, at the end of the trail, you arrive at the oasis of Sinkiang it is a shock to find yourself among people who remind you more of the Near East than the Far East : a negligible minority of Chinese, and a predominance of Arab, Turkish and Persian types. They are practically all Moslems ; you see mosques and minarets and hear the muezzin. The men dignified, grave and bearded. The women wear a little round cap on their heads, their long hair falling in two plaits over long gaudy dresses—they look exactly like gypsies. I'll tell you, but it will have to be later, how it turned out that we were able to cross the jealously guarded frontier of this lovely district. Victor Point is certainly an outstanding leader ; we are now received with delightful consideration and kindness. The work is more and more absorbing. I am in the heart of one of the most mysterious and sacred of geological regions, and I think I am finding the key to it by establishing step by step its connection with eastern China.

Any moment now we start on the last long lap, the 750 miles we still have to cover to the Pamir ; we no longer feel that reaching Kashgar is only a dream.

They were doomed, however, to be disappointed. Georges Le Fèvre has described the difficulties caused by the ill-will, touchiness and suspicions of the Chinese contingent, without whom, on the other hand, the Europeans would not have been allowed to cross the Turkestan border. Père Teilhard, as the one best known to the Chinese, took part as an intermediary and peacemaker in the difficult negotiations that followed on the Nanking party's demand that the control of the expedition should be divided, and signed the agreement reached between the two groups on 20 June. There were still, however, omens of trouble to come. One day they found a flat post erected in a completely deserted spot, near a dismantled fort. On one side was written in Chinese, ' Do not advance westwards. Danger. Hide your camels in the mountains and wait.'

' It was obviously a recent message left by the leader of a caravan to warn his friends : a " desert gazette " giving the news that is mysteriously passed along through uninhabited country.

' On the 28th June, having covered 65 miles the day before and seen the snowy peaks of the Karlik Tagh, we arrived at the first village, lying on the edge of the Hami oasis. We found it abandoned and in flames. Two terrified Shantus (eastern Turks) came out to meet the vehicles. Terror made them quite unintelligible, but Petro [1] finally managed to understand their abominable Chinese, " Don't go there, don't go west, there's fighting there ", and the two Shantus fell to shadow-boxing with one another to show what they meant. " But who's fighting ? " " Everybody ", they said, " everybody's fighting."

' It was perfectly true : there was no doubt about the reality of the fighting. Even then we could hear in the far distance a staccato rattle punctuated by heavy thuds—shell-fire and machine-

---

[1] Petropavlosky, the expedition's interpreter.

guns. *Sinkiang was being left in no doubt about the advantages of modern civilisation.'* [1]

In his notes and correspondence, Père Teilhard was unable to do more than allude to the situation without comment, for the Europeans were looked on with suspicion by the Asiatics and were obliged to observe the utmost discretion.

Urumchi, Chinese Turkestan, 1 August

Having made a surprise entry into Sinkiang under cover of various political troubles, we have now been held up for a month at Urumchi, the provincial capital. We are loaded with attentions but we are prisoners, and there appears to be no more hope of advancing further towards Kashgar. At the bottom of all this lies Nanking's hostility to any foreign expedition in China. I have been expecting this all along and I didn't hope to get even so far into central Asia.

Urumchi lies at the foot of the Tien-Shan, on the northern slope, and is much cooler than Turfan. Countless details give you a foretaste of Europe—the people's faces, the types of crop, the look of the flowers and trees.

The crux of the situation was that the Chinese party had to wait for Haardt, the leader of the expedition, to give the order to turn back. He, however, would be unable to understand the position until he had seen the gates of Kashgar close against him : and they were forbidden to use wireless telegraphy. It looked as though they had stirred up a hornet's nest.

27 August, 1931

We have installed ourselves in a pagoda set in the middle of some big trees and overlookin ; Urumchi. A wonderful view—the

[1] Georges Le Fèvre, *La Croisière jaune*, pp. 113-15.

endless chain of the Tien-Shan with its 15,000 and 18,000 foot peaks glistening with snow. A few days ago I went into the pinewoods that lie in the 6 to 9 thousand foot belt. You would have thought yourself in the Alps if the Kirghiz yourts had not replaced the chalets. A carpet of geraniums, aconite and arnica.

Unfortunately such excursions are the exception, and on the whole we are having a tedious time here. I find it annoying to have to waste time when I'm fifty, with so much work waiting for me in Pekin : but wasting time is what everyone has to put up with here—part of the price you have to pay if you adventure into Sinkiang.

In the end, then, the inexorable force of circumstances has thrown me back on myself—without any tangible exterior compensation—and I find I can only immerse myself in the Unique Necessary. The least expected and the most substantial result of my journey seems to me to be this : that I have progressed further in a zest for and an appreciation of what actually happens, independently of its agreeable or disagreeable content : the event becoming ' adorable '[1] precisely and only because it is privileged to be the form taken by the nascent real. So it is that in the bustle of camp life I am beginning to collect my thoughts and write a little. I am making a first rough draft of a memorandum on the results of my researches between Kalgan and Urumchi. I think, too, I shall in the end write a series of reflections under the title *Prière dans la durée*.[2] It is to be at the same time an interpretation, a making one's own, an acceptance and a transfiguration of the world, put forward in the context of the deepest and most commonly shared of man's questionings, anxieties and emotions : those of discovering, undergoing, growing old and waiting—all of which are effects or forms of duration.

[1] Père Teilhard was fond of quoting a saying of the great geologist Pierre Termier, ' Everything that happens is adorable '.
[2] Never, so far as is known, completed.

Two other subjects also are rather tempting : ' L'Univers personnel' (for which there is a sketch in the papers I sent you in the spring), and a work on 'La Conversion du monde' (a review of the present state of the various religions). But that must wait till later.[1]

Urumchi, 27 August, 1931

Apart from being cut off from the civilised world (Sinkiang is probably the most impenetrable frontier in the world),[2] we are not too badly off here. The season is gradually developing into a magnificent autumn, with almost continual sunshine : radiant dawns, and at sunset the overlapping ridges are shrouded in astonishing purples, with the snow cap of Bogdo-Oula emerging like a flower from its calix. Moreover, thanks to the maintenance work which keeps the party of mechanics busy, the team are working together pretty well even though inactivity tends to exaggerate certain ' cleavage planes'. The arrival of the Pamir party with the big chief will improve the atmosphere again. Meanwhile Point, the doctor, the engineer Brull, the young naturalist Raymond and I, are intellectual company for one another. [. . .] In fact I have never since the war found myself so immersed in the raw complexity of human relations.

We're still in just the same position, confined to our camp by the smooth-spoken hostility of the Governor. By diplomatic pressure we have obtained permission for M. Haardt to join us here, but the bulk of our caravan will not be able to go to meet him and everything points to my having to moulder here until All Saints' Day, which is when M. Haardt will probably arrive

[1] These two essays were completed.
[2] The travellers were able to send some letters through India and Russia, but were still unable to receive any.

and we'll start back for Pekin. Some time before that I have hopes of getting permission to travel around the countryside a little, and do some work, but there's no certainty. So all I shall have is a summer and autumn wasted, far from Pekin, on which I was counting for some essential and exact work at the laboratory.

At first I thought I was paying dearly for what I could get from an expedition to Sinkiang, but in fact I have not too much to complain of. In the first place, to waste weeks on end is the common lot of anyone who adventures into these parts (Hedin knows something about that) ; and secondly I am becoming increasingly aware of how much my geological knowledge has profited by this journey, brief though its useful part may have been.

Thanks to the friendship and boldness of Victor Point, Père Teilhard was one of those selected to go with four tracked vehicles to meet M. Haardt. They travelled as far as some 700 miles west of Urumchi, four days from Kashgar. There they waited, for Haardt had already left Kashgar ; but they had thus been able to cross nearly the whole of Sinkiang, following the southern slope of the Tien-Shan, which was a valuable completion of Père Teilhard's earlier geological observations.

Aksu, 24 September, 1931

A fortnight's journey—no automobile had ever been along that route, which would be impossible for wheeled vehicles. The caterpillars took us over the rocky passes, marshes, rivers and sands.

The Tien-Shan grows in majesty. At Aksu it rises to over 21,000 feet in height, and to the south the vast depression of the Tarim stands out in unforgettable wildness. Human life—one might almost simply say life—is confined to the string of oases lying between the Tarim marshes and the enormous gravel folds running down the mountains.

The vegetation, unfortunately, is monotonous : willows, poplars and tamarisk. There are no Chinese any more apart from the administrators and a few merchants. The men bearded and turbanned, trotting on their asses ; the women strictly and becomingly veiled ; bazaars chock-a-block with carpets ; the loud chant of the muezzins calling to evening prayer at every corner of the little villages. You begin to see Afghans, Persians and Hindus ; it's no longer the Far East. After all, am I not just halfway between Pekin and Paris ?

I am writing to you in a very pretty garden belonging to a big Aksu trader, under a pergola from which hang mighty bunches of grapes, with peach and apple trees to one side, weighed down with fruit ; the sky an unchanging blue, with just a trace of cloud ; the heat of summer's last days. All this is most agreeable and restful, very different from Urumchi, north of the mountains, where just before I left we had a pronounced impression in many ways of autumn in Auvergne.

[. . .] I have drawn up a memorandum on the first part of the journey, which gives me a more precise idea of the problems to watch for on the way back.

La Prière dans la durée is almost finished in my head. But I have also quite definitely taken a step forward in my awareness of being now on the downward slope of life.

When we join up with the Pamir party, as we soon shall, the nature of the expedition is bound to change ; there will be much more formality but at the same time much greater intellectual resources. [. . .] From another angle, the junction with M. Haardt means the beginning of the return journey. Nobody can yet quite see how we are going to manage it with equipment that has had over 3,000 miles' wear, in very difficult country and in political conditions that aren't exactly serene. Making Suchow is the crux of the problem ; for only there can we get supplies and spares for the vehicles. I don't doubt that we shall manage, but we shan't be in Pekin before the end of December. Incidentally, it's at Suchow that we hope to find our mail.

When the Pamir party finally arrived, the expedition took up winter quarters in Urumchi, in heated houses or comfortable yourts.

I myself am sharing a comfortable room with Hackin and Commandant Pecqueur, and we are making it into delightful living quarters. Things are easier with the Governor, who has become very affable. The Shantus have just made peace with Khami, putting an end to the revolt which had made our entry into Sinkiang so dramatic and was threatening to close our best return route.

In these new conditions, we are mixing more with local 'society' and getting to know it better : Russians, Danes and also the curious 'Princess Palta', a Mongolian who has become Parisian to her finger-tips, and with whom some of the Expedition had danced in Paris and Pekin. Parties make a gay interlude in the preparation of furs and overhauling of equipment and stores for the journey back to Pekin. The other day it was an evening party given by the Swedish expedition (which is just off) at which I thought the Russian dances charming. It has been a real joy to me to meet Norin here again, Sven Hedin's geologist, who has been working in the country for the last four years. The two of us spent hours on end building up the geology of Central Asia, and had the rare pleasure of discussing the vast expanses we both know and love.

Norin is leaving for Kashgar and India. I would very much like to follow him, but my future is obviously tied up with M. Haardt for some months still. The new arrivals, most of all M. Hackin, director of the Guimet Museum, and Le Fèvre, the historian of the expedition, whom you know perhaps from his book on Russia, have brought a change of atmosphere. But what a Noah's ark ! [. . .] The essential thing for me is that I am now able to incorporate Central Asia in my own geological reconstructions—and that's worth a year, even at the age of fifty.

It was only after protracted negotiation with the Marshal-President King that Haardt was able to obtain authorisation for the expedition to start on the return journey. The route lay through the unmapped wastes of the Gobi desert. The cold was so severe (– 20° to – 30° Centigrade) that they had to choose between the risk of frozen radiators if they stopped at night, and of running short of fuel if they kept the engines running. It was decided to keep going.

'At this stage we were running for twenty hours out of the twenty-four,' wrote Le Fèvre. ' Fatigue gradually made us all feel the cold more cruelly, and we all succumbed to a dangerous lethargy. The enforced immobility meant that we were petrified with cold. It paralysed our curiosity and plunged us into an odd insensibility. We sat there inert, dozing in snatches, while the red-eyed mechanics struggled on, with hardly a couple of hours' sleep at night, crouched over the wheel. Twice a day, however, we stopped for a meal in the open. Speed was essential or the boiling hot soup ladled into mess-tins would be ice before we could drink it. We took it greedily, standing up ; and at night, silent, muffled in furs that made any movement impossible, and without knowing who was who, we stood in a group round the mess-vehicle, outlandish dummies with shadows distorted by the glare of the headlamps. The thermometer fell to –33° Centigrade.' [1]

Even so, Père Teilhard found the country rich in material,

[1] *La Croisière jaune, pp. 292-3.*

for the ground was littered with prehistoric tools. ' *His sharp eyes picked out the smallest palæolith whose red stood out against the grey bareness of the wind-swept ground. He would stop his vehicle, get down and pick up one stone after another : traces not of a centre of palæolithic culture: but of the southern limit of a vastly ancient human wave that set out from Siberia.*' [1]

Suchow, Kansu Province, 21 December, 1931

At last we have got out of Sinkiang, though not without difficulty, and now I am more or less on the slope that runs down to Pekin. But new delays, political or mechanical in origin, keep cropping up, and I have little hope of being back before the end of January. It's very difficult to do any work during this journey ; the risk of the engines freezing up entails long night stages, which are quite useless for me. [2]

Breuil must have gone through Pekin at the end of October, just in time to appraise and criticise the finds of tools (which I started last April) : and to think that I was not there to receive my old friend after I had induced him to come!

Looking back on the whole expedition, Père Teilhard was not dissatisfied with the results.

We are on our way back. The fascinating crests of the Tien-Shan are behind us and we are slowly making our way east in bitterly cold but clear weather. [. . .] These last nine months will remain among the hardest and most rewarding of my career.

[1] *La Croisière jaune*, pp. 292-3.
[2] Père Teilhard had a similarly tantalising experience in Abyssinia. He was with Père Lamare in a little train that was puffing its way laboriously to Addis Ababa, and was itching to get out and use his hammer. ' If only we could have a break-down ', he said, and sure enough, a break-down came. Père Teilhard took advantage of it. When they set off again, ' For pity's sake, ' begged Lamare, ' no more miracles! '

We missed many opportunities ; we were too much at the mercy of our machines ; but what a compensation for me that I have now seen with my own eyes the vast zone that lies between Kashgar and Tsitsikar.

And when he was back in Pekin he wrote to his brother :

Climbing on to the caterpillars as though I were mounting a camel, I asked only one thing of the expedition : to take me across Asia. [. . .] So far as that goes, I have had what I asked for. I often strained at the bit when I was unable to follow up the marvellous opportunities that presented themselves. But, as someone truly said, the drawbacks of a thing are part of the thing itself. In the end I had nearly doubled my store of information about Asia. For that, ten months of life, even at the age of fifty, is not too much to pay.

Pao-Teo, 30 January, 1932

We are now back at Pao-Teo, the end of the railway line from Pekin and the end, too, of our adventures and misadventures. [. . .] Two days before we arrived here, we were passing through a small village when a group of soldiers, half bandits, suddenly opened a heavy fire at point-blank range on our convoy, which at the moment was rather scattered.

The vehicle in front of mine was hit in a dozen or more places, mostly on the trailer. No-one fired from mine, but our party replied with such vigour that a white flag was hoisted by the ' enemy ', who then said that a mistake had been made. Nobody, fortunately, was hit : just a boost for the publicity the Expedition is going to receive.

Georges Le Fèvre gave a more dramatic account of the incident.

190

' *The head of the convoy was coming up to a little village called Pa-Tse-Koulin. We had hardly entered the village when some fellows came out from a farmyard and covering us with their rifles made signs to us to halt. Larger groups of soldiers were concealed by the sloping bank on either side of the road and were ready to open fire. If we stopped it was doubtful if we could get away again; so the convoy continued to advance. But suddenly there were violent reports. We stopped. A volley had been fired at Audouin-Dubreuil's vehicle; he got out, rifle in hand, and everyone did the same. Vehicle No. 3 also came under rifle fire. We could see figures moving in the fields. They came nearer, and it looked as though the convoy was going to be surrounded. Bullets whistled by, but our machine-gun had the last word, loosing off two belts in sharp bursts.*

' *A flag of truce was hoisted on the other side, and the faces of three soldiers appeared.*

' " *We thought you were bandits,*" *they said.*

' " *Have you ever seen bandits in cars flying the French flag?*"

' *Apologies and bows : just a slight misunderstanding.* " *Perhaps you'd take a cup of tea with the General and accept his card?*" *The card read,* " *General of the Independent Horse*". *In China the honorific formula is everything.*'[1]

Pao-Teo *is the terminus of the line from Pekin and Père Teilhard was tempted to take the train, but there was still another 60 miles he wished to investigate and in any case he preferred to stay with the Expedition till the end. Once back in Pekin, moreover, he would have to leave them. M. Hackin was asking him to accompany him to Japan in the spring, and M. Haardt was anxious for him to go to Indo-China, but he felt that the latter journey might be chiefly for publicity.* ' *I believe I have no place in the expedition once it has ceased to be hard going : I can't have it said that I took advantage of it to enjoy myself.*'

[1] *La Croisière jaune*, pp. 329-30.

The travellers were fêted in Pekin, but plans for the future were upset by the death of Haardt in Hongkong after a few days' illness.

Pekin, 18 March, 1932

We have only today learnt of the sudden death of M. Haardt, who succumbed, I presume, to a fresh attack of something akin to the pneumonia he contracted on arriving in Pekin. I imagine that had Haardt been able to foresee his end, he would have appreciated that there was something fine in being struck down by death in the full vigour of activity. The desert would have been a nobler tomb for him, not that Hongkong hasn't its own beauty. To me, personally, the sudden loss of a man whose generosity and warmth of heart had captivated me is a real grief, deepened by my regret at not having been able to be with him in his last moments. From what I knew of him, he would have turned to me for support and I am sure that I could have eased his passing. It is a real sorrow to me.[1]

Summing up the scientific results of the expedition, Père Teilhard wrote :

The Central Asian Expedition could do no more than skim the

[1] On getting back to Pekin, Père Teilhard learnt also of his father's death (11 February, 1932). He was deeply moved by a series of family bereavements during his exile in China, two of his brothers, his mother and his sister. (He was never able to get home, even though he knew the end was near. He never undertook a journey, even one necessitated by his scientific career, without the authorisation of his superiors.) Père Teilhard owed to his father, who had guided his sons' early studies before they went to school, ' an enormous number of things : certain clearly envisaged ambitions, no doubt, but still more a certain fundamental balance on which everything else was built '. Living for the greater part of the year in the country, Emmanuel Teilhard had given his sons a taste for natural history which, in the case of Pierre, was the germ of a vocation to science.

surface of the study of these majestic entities that make up the present contours of Upper Asia. What it achieved cannot compare with the extensive and exact results obtained at the same time by our rivals and friends in Sven Hedin's party. But the little that it did bring back was worth a great deal. It enabled us to establish the intimate connection between the geology of the Gobi and that of Sinkiang, and so distinguish and follow out more clearly, under secondary modifications, various basic features of the internal structure and external appearance of the great continent. (Père Teilhard's appendix to *La Croisière jaune*, p. 357.)

Less than two months after the return of the Expedition, Père Teilhard found that his researches demanded another journey to Shansi.]

Taiyuan, Shansi Province, 11 July, 1932

We have been on the road since July 4th : back again to long days on mule back, filthy inns, flies. [. . .] At first I found this something of a test for my morale. I don't know why I felt so low at the end of June ; partly physical fatigue, turning to a sort of revulsion of the spirit. But with the interest of my researches to help me, I think the journey will go off well. I had a sort of conviction that it was my duty to make this fresh effort, to show my fidelity to what God asks of me ; but I have an idea too that this is the last time I shall be off on this sort of expedition. I can see new vistas opening before me, probably of a different sort, more suited to my age and the type of work I can now contribute.[1] In any event, I feel that I am reaching a turning point in my life, and it is precisely in order not to miss the turning that I

---

[1] Père Teilhard continued to be an indefatigable traveller, but his methods of travelling were to be considerably altered. In the expeditions organised by various scientific institutions in which he took part, the automobile took the place of the mule and physical conditions were greatly improved.

have accepted the present journey. We are now on the edge of the great Taiyuan plain, but this evening we shall be plunging into a labyrinth of country ravaged by erosion, through which the tracks wind in the oddest way. Our plan is to go down as far as the Hwang-Ho and thence join the Pekin railway line.

1932-1934

*Père Teilhard returned to France for a short visit, from September,
1932 to the end of January, 1933. He travelled in the 'Porthos',
returning in the 'Aramis'.*

[Travel Notes.] A magnificent all-white liner. A Basque bar
or inn (in memory of Aramis ?) and a cleverly-decorated saloon—
a Trojan horse for the children to play with. But the whole ship
practically empty. The second class is principally taken up by
missionaries or officers joining their ships. The first class rather
smarter—one of the young Citroëns, and a young Rothschild ;
Doumergue and his wife, with whom I have renewed my
acquaintance. But Breuil and Lejay,[1] of course, are my mainstay.
Their presence by itself is enough to people our floating wilderness
for me.

(To Max Bégouën). *On board the 'Aramis', 6 March, 1933*

My dear Max,

Tomorrow we reach Saigon. So now is the time to get to
work on a letter with some news for you and for my dear Simone.
The first ten days of the passage were greatly cheered for me by

[1] Père Lejay, s.j., the geophysician, later (since 1947) a member of the
Académie des Sciences.

the presence of Breuil,[1] who was at the top of his form ; and I felt a great gap when he left to enjoy, with Vernet, the hospitality of Monfreid, who came alongside the *Aramis* in his dhow, with his Somalis, to the great delight of the passengers. I hope indeed that it will be good hunting for Breuil.

The Indian Ocean, smooth and sleek as a lake ; Ceylon, Penang, Singapore, under their domes of flamboyants in full bloom, each a burst of radiance in the hot night. In the end, of course, I hardly notice these scenes, but I still vividly feel their presence around me. There are not many passengers, but such as there are are interesting or unusual : as far as Port Said we had Doumergue and Madame D., friendly and communicative ; as far as Djibouti an Abyssinian minister and his progeny ; as far as Singapore, a party of Parisians on a pleasure ' trip ' to Java, among whom I made a number of good friends. Saigon will leave us reduced to the minimum, but there will still be Admiral Berthelot's family, some delightful Belgians and lastly a fat Chinese extremist politician, Honourable X ; one can only wonder why he is going back to China.

Since all these smart folk are in the first class, which I enter only with a certain amount of discretion, I have had time to work in my cabin, which is cool and roomy and which I have had to myself all the time. I have taken advantage of this to define in a few pages under the title ' La Structure de l' Esprit ' a number of ideas that seem to me to have emerged from conversations I had last autumn. [. . .] I am now beginning to turn my eyes towards Pekin with some curiosity. How shall I find things there after the ominous fall of Jehol and of the American dollar ? Will it still be possible to get some work done ? Now is the time to ' stick ' to one's destiny, or, if you prefer to put it so, to the hand of God, and so make sure of not being found wanting when things claim us.

[1] On his way to Abyssinia.

6 March, 1933

We are still sailing over a completely calm sea—the deep blue waters of the Indian Ocean, the jade green of the Strait of Malacca —through scenes so familiar that I now hardly look at them, though I enjoy them deeply. We arrived at Penang late in the afternoon, under a stormy sky, copper and inky black. It's the first time I've had an opportunity to have a good look at this scenic paradise. Lejay and I and two Belgian friends drove out in a car, rolling smoothly over the fine red roads, among forests of coconut palms, with huts built on piles, and great umbrella-like trees with a finer profusion of purple flowers than you'd find even in a flower-bed. Night came all too soon for us.

Yesterday we put in at Singapore and made a pilgrimage to the Botanical Gardens, brilliant with colour, and a home for monkeys living in complete freedom. The fall of Jehol and the other fall—that of the American dollar—may well, I fear, profoundly modify all my plans for the future. But I have faith in destiny!

10 March

[. . .] Tomorrow morning we leave Saigon. This evening, dinner with Pasquier, the Governor-General, and a lecture to the Saigonese with Lejay—which I could well do without. It's beginning to get hot, but I am never able to resist the appeal of flowers, and here there are such quantities of them!

Pekin, 26 March, 1933

I'm back in Pekin at last, since the day before yesterday. The last part of the voyage was not very entertaining : an empty ship, and going back to the cold. I did what I could not to drag it out : two days at Shanghai and two at Tientsin. And here I feel that I'm at my journey's end. What can one say about the general situation ? Politically the country seems cowed and still divided. There is no apparent change in Pekin, except martial law, which obliges people to be home before eleven in the evening (which suits me perfectly). But fear, probably unjustified, that the Japanese may forcibly occupy the city is making the institutes panic. The Museum collections have been packed up and sent off to the concessions in Shanghai.

24 April, 1933

We are still living here in profound tranquillity, though we expect every morning to wake up and find ourselves annexed by Manchukuo, under the sceptre of the puppet-ruler P'u Yi. There appears to be fighting—for form's sake—100 miles or so from here. But the most serious thing, so far as I am concerned, is that the Survey, as a political and administrative rather than a military precaution, has removed part of its books and collections. Fortunately, this material has not followed the ' *curios* ' from the Imperial Museum to Shanghai, but is still housed here at the Rockefeller Foundation under the care of my friend Black ; so that it's only a partial mishap. Moreover, work on publications still goes on, so that I have no business to complain. All the same it has given me something of a shock these last days to meet ' my ' furniture and drawers being carried by coolies through the city.

10 June, 1933

Pekin has been through a pretty feverish week, with the Chinese leaving the city *en masse* at the approach of the Japanese. Then everything became quiet again, and now, although the exact

nature of the agreements reached is not known, life is back to
normal, and the cases of books are coming back to the Survey.
II benefited from this easing of tension while on a ' *trip* ' to Shans
ast week with an American friend. We found the trains runningi
to time and no longer crowded. Splendid weather. Our headquarters were a Protestant industrial school south of Taynan.
The missionaries were most hospitable and helpful. I visited a
most beautiful mountain where the Chinese have managed to
erect temples clinging to the dizziest heights. Exceptionally,
and largely because of the presence of the temples, the forests
have been preserved (in particular a fine wood composed almost
entirely of silver-barked firs) : we were transported straight into
the scene of a Chinese painting.

I'm now getting ready to leave for Washington. I expect to
leave Pekin on the 22nd and Shanghai on the 27th. There's the
Congress from the 20th to the 30th July, and then a trip to the
American West. I expect to sail again on September 15th from
San Francisco. This new journey doesn't thrill me particularly,
for it seems to me to be so much time taken from my own
researches (which time, with increasing age, I grudge the more),
but it may open up new horizons and lead to unforeseen contacts :
so that I can't let the opportunity slip by.

Père Teilhard found many old friends at the Museum in New York,
where he was asked to examine fossils from China and Mongolia.
He delivered his book on Fossil Man in China in Washington,
read a paper and moved on to San Francisco, where he took part
in a geological expedition in the Sierra Nevada and Grand Canyon.

In California, 12 September, 1933

On top of the Sierra Nevada excursion, I made a three-day trip
(about 1000 miles!) in the south, as far as Santa Barbara, with
Camp—an American colleague—and three of his pupils. The

geology is absorbingly interesting and the country fascinating. I am exceedingly fond of these wild sun-drenched mountains, covered with ilex and laurel, or with cactus and yucca. And then, life's so simple, so ' *un-conventional* '! You sleep in the open ; eat whenever you feel inclined, at a bar, perched on high stools ; nobody bothers about you if you want to be alone. After being here only a month, I felt really at home in California.

(To Max and Simone Bégouën)

My stay in America has interested me from every sort of angle. I met many old and new friends at the Congress, and both in Washington and California (where I stayed a month) I initiated a series of undertakings that may considerably extend my scientific field. Moreover, I obtained close personal experience of the geology of the Pacific coast (which was my chief purpose in going) in a wonderful setting of light and contour (in itself no small consideration). I savoured the fragrance of sequioa forests, and ' nosed out ' the last traces of the Sierra Nevada ' *gold rush* '. America is a country of freshness and expansiveness, and in it I certainly breathed an atmosphere that France lacks. I wasn't able to form any clear views on the Roosevelt experiment, except the power and cunning of the methods used to get it across to the public. I brought away the impression of a fine attempt with a good chance of success. Something, at any rate, in the way of a common effort is getting under way in the United States. Work is picking up again. And in January there'll be wine to drink. Meanwhile there is no more amusing sight than the half-resentful, half-laughing air of free Yankees realising they're living under a dictatorship.

(*Back in Pekin*), *11 November, 1933*

Clearing up [at Chou-Kou-Tien] has brought to light an adjoining cave, also completely filled, but of a much later period, and with abundant traces of an upper palæolithic culture (= the reindeer age in France)—two human skulls, stone and bone implements, necklaces of pierced teeth, and a variety of extinct fauna. Lower down, on the other hand, we find proof that before being inhabited by Sinanthropus the rocks had been the home of baboons. This is becoming interesting and complicated. I am still largely responsible for interpreting the facts disclosed.

In March 1934, the sudden death of Dr. Black,[1] director of the Geological Service, was a personal loss for Père Teilhard, and brought him (until Dr. Black's successor should be appointed by the Rockefeller Foundation) the supervision of all the excavations in addition to that of the laboratories.

(To the Abbé Breuil)   *Pekin, 19 March, 1934*

My very dear friend,

I have just had your letter of 4 February. Thank you. I wrote to you only a few days ago, but I must begin again in order to give you some details about a misfortune you will have read about in the papers. Davidson Black died suddenly in the evening of the day before yesterday (*heart failure*). His heart had been giving trouble for some time, and five weeks ago we had a warning of what might happen. We were hoping that he was pulling round, but then the end came suddenly. Black was feeling better (or seemed to be) ; he had just been talking briskly with some

---

[1] Père Teilhard had been working in close collaboration with him for over ten years.

friends and was full of plans, as usual. A moment later he was found dead, by this table, in this Lab. you know so well, between the Sinanthropus and the skull from the Upper Cave. A fine death, in the full force of activity. But he leaves a great gap. We shall have to close our ranks to get on with the work.

[. . .] But what an absurd thing life is, looked at superficially : so absurd that you feel yourself forced back on a stubborn, desperate, faith in the reality and survival of the spirit. Otherwise —were there no such thing as the spirit, I mean—we should have to be idiots not to call off the whole human effort.[1]

(To the Bégouëns)   *Nankin, 10 April, 1934*

Just how far these events will influence my future, I can't yet estimate ; but I have the feeling of being faced by an exact and hallowed task in the sphere of the ' human effort '. From time to time, and perhaps more than ever, I shall always need to renew contact with Europe ; but, as things are, I can't see how I can finally leave China for a long time yet. [. . .] Black was the companion of my mind and my heart, and it was with him that I envisaged my work. But there is more in it than that. I mean a sharp and concrete ' realisation ' of the utter vanity of ' human effort ' unless there is a both natural and supernatural emergence of the universe towards some immortal consciousness. In my distress following Black's death, and in the stifling atmosphere of ' agnostic ' condolences that surrounded it, I swore to myself, on the body of my dead friend, to fight more vigorously than ever to give hope to man's work and inquiry.

Père Teilhard could never give up field-work for long. His

[1] He refers to Black's death again, on the 18th June : ' I miss Black greatly : it's like a shadow continually lying over me. At any rate, I still have your friendship.'

American friend Barbour took him to Nanking and the Yangtse.
They were accompanied by his colleague Wong and two Chinese
geologists. ' I have learnt and understood a great deal : mountains
whose peaks look down on great lakes and ricefields ; pine-woods,
pagodas, bamboos, hills covered with azaleas in flower. The
green vegetation and the colours give a fresh look to the austerity
of northern China.'

6 May, 1934

Hardly was I back in Pekin (by the Hankow-Pekin line) than I
went to spend two days at Tientsin. The day after tomorrow I
leave for Chou-Kou-Tien and then on the 13th I'm off again for
Hankow, where we are proposing, Barbour and I, to complete
the ascent of the Yangtse as far as Szechwan (Chungking). We
are a little too late in the season but mean to make the attempt
all the same ; it's a matter of two or three weeks at the most.
Finally, to fill up the rest of Barbour's stay, we shall go to the west
of the Yellow River. I don't quite know what we shall have to
show for all this, but one thing is certain, that this summer I'll
never be for long in the same place. The autumn looks like being
quieter, but plans are rather vague. Nothing has yet been decided
about appointing Black's successor and the continuation of his
work at the Rockefeller Foundation. I feel that I cannot leave
China until the situation is cleared up and the work going
smoothly.

Chungking, 30 May, 1934

We arrived here yesterday, after a splendid journey through the
gorges ; they have certainly not been over-rated, especially from
the geologist's point of view. For more than 60 miles the
powerful waters force their way between high walls of cliff with
frequent rapids, where you can read almost the whole geological

story of China. Once through the gorges, you enter Szechwan, a rich green country in which every moment showed me a China more Chinese than the north. The pagodas are more brilliant and more mannered, hats are wider and more pointed, the whole countryside more like the China we know in books.

3 July, 1934

As things worked out well, I decided to push on from Chungking to Chengtu and a little beyond, as far as the first foothills of Tibet—about 300 miles by a good motor-road. The journey taught me a great deal : and it gave me a chance to meet again my excellent friend Béchamp who for the last six years has been combining the functions of consul and head of the medical mission. We had a pleasant time together, in a very agreeable house, most artistically decorated. In the evening we could hear music and talks from Paris as clearly as though it came from the next room. From Chengtu I returned to Chungking, then to Ichang, with several stops in the bush.

There followed a four or five weeks' tour in Honan, which for twenty years it had been impossible to travel in. They took advantage of a period of calm to visit a district still unknown to geologists, crossing the eastern end of the Tsingling range from north to south, and obtaining information which enabled them to determine the connection between the Tertiary (and later) forma-tions of the north and south of China. ' Our hopes were exceeded.'

In January a new expedition to the south was organised. ' Three of us are going with Wong, our inseparable companion, and Pei, the official excavator at Chou-Kou-Tien. Pei is a delightful fellow, full of enthusiasm ; he has never been in a boat, and it will be entertaining to initiate him into a new field of work. Itinerary : Shong-Kai, Canton ; thence we leave for the Kwansi—

Travelling in China with the Abbé Breuil in 1935

country completely new to me, in which I am hoping to see and learn a great deal. The province is said to be quiet, and the roads good. We return through Nanning, very close to Indo-China. I am expecting the trip to give me the link I want between Northern and Southern China.'

23 September, 1934

I have sketched out a draft of an essay that M. B. de S.[1] has been asking me for for a long time. I am calling it 'Comment je crois' ('*Why and How*'). [. . .] Thinking this out forces me to analyse and synthesise my own self more fully. I am determined to persevere until I have finished it and with all the sincerity that I can achieve. [. . .] I am studying the successive developments of an adherence which, proceeding from faith to faith, rejoins the Christian current (or *phylum*) by convergence : faith in the world, faith in the spirit in the world, faith in the immortality of the spirit in the world, faith in the ever-growing personality of the world. I feel that I have a better grasp than I had a year ago of concepts which enable me really to have confidence in my thesis.

The Abbé Breuil had just arrived in Pekin, where Père Teilhard showed him over the deposits at Chou-Kou-Tien. At the beginning of May, they left together by the Trans-Siberian railway for Europe. Père Teilhard spent only some three months in France. It was about this time that he wrote to a friend in distress : ' Never give up : try to attack it from another angle, the correct angle—where success is in proportion not to the extension of the individual but to constancy in the effort to make the world around HIM *less harsh and more human. If the pressure of events can induce you to make the mental sacrifice of every personal ambition in favour of a higher duty, I am convinced that you can reach a degree of emancipation and clearness of vision in relation to the external world,*

[1] Mgr Bruno de Solages, rector of the Institut Catholique in Toulouse.

far greater than you imagine. One must contrive to preserve a real appetite for life and action whilst at the same time renouncing any desire for personal happiness. Therein lies the secret—and not the illusion—of living in the " Milieu divin ".'

The winter was spent in supervising the work at Chou-Kou-Tien and the laboratories, which gave Père Tielhard little leisure from ' the notes I have to draw up and revise. Still, the work is interesting: since it allows me to impose a homogeneity of thought on everything produced from my department.'

His religious work was still unpublished. The ' Milieu divin' had been under consideration at Rome for a long time. Meanwhile Père Teilhard was at work on another essay, ' Christologie et évolution', ' strictly limited in intention to some intimate friends in my own profession.'

' I have written this with all my love for Christ, as a token of the worship I cannot keep shut up within me. Père Maréchal, of Louvain, has done me the honour of writing to me in answer to a short paper on " the place of man in nature " which was printed here last year in the " Bulletin des étudiants de Pékin " : " There is no-one today who has such a grasp as you have of all the material bearing on the problem of evolution—theological, philosophical and scientific. . . ." Surely it should be to the Church's interest to make use of my acknowledged reputation, even if it's not justified ? '

And a few days later he writes : ' I still can see only one answer : to keep pressing on, in ever-increasing faith. May the Lord only preserve in me a passionate taste for the world, and a great gentleness ; and may He help me persevere to the end in the fullness of humanity.'

1935-1936

After three months in France, Père Teilhard returned to the East,
this time to northern India. He sailed for Bombay on 6 September.

    He had been invited from America to join a small scientific
expedition to Kashmir. 'They want (and quite rightly) a geo-
logist with knowledge of China. I know the leader, de Terra,
personally. I am not greatly excited about the idea of going to
India, but I look on it as my strict duty to do my best to make the
trip.'

    During the voyage he was considering what his own attitude
should be in the future to the scientific work he was engaged in,
and was trying to clarify some views on ' the discovery of the past '
by putting them on paper.[1]

On board the ' Cathay ', 8 September, 1935

It is almost as though, for reasons arising from the progress of
my own science, the past and its discovery had ceased to interest
me. *The past has revealed to me how the future is built* [2] and preoccupation with the future tends to sweep everything else aside.
It is precisely that I may be able to speak with authority about
the future that it is essential for me to establish myself more

---

   [1] ' La Découverte du passé ', *Études*, 1935.
   [2] Italicised by the French editor as being a cardinal expression of Père
Teilhard's thought.

firmly than before as a specialist on the past. But isn't it an odd thing that the very object of my work should fade into the background as it yields me its fruits ? and that I should attribute less value to the discoveries I may make because henceforward their interest for me has been superseded ? Now that the fundamental discovery has been made, that we are carried along by an advancing wave of consciousness, does anything of importance remain to be disclosed in what has been left behind us ? Certain rhythms or impulses, perhaps, that are still hidden from us by the slenderness of our knowledge at this actual moment. It is along these lines that I wish to do my thinking, and so save, if possible, the passion for geology for my old age. Even so, what a difference there is, in the object of my ambitions, between this voyage and the 1923 one! I hope I am right in looking on it as an advance.

After a too-brief reunion with his family in Auvergne, Père Teilhard writes to his brother Joseph :

On board the ' Cathay ', 14 September, 1935

So here I am, back again to my vagabond existence. My enthusiasm has lost the freshness it had of old ; but what I like to do is to follow my destiny and trust myself to it, though never, indeed, have I known less where it was leading me : probably to nothing but a new series of moves until I end my days by the roadside. Even that, too, may have its significance.

At the moment we are coming to the end of our third and last day in one of the hottest passages through the Red Sea that I have known. At this time of the year and travelling in this direction the breeze is behind us. At last we are passing the volcanic islets at the entrance to the Bab-el-Mandeb. The sea is smooth, our wake enlivened by schools of dolphins leaping like trout or disporting themselves by swimming in single file in the swell the ship raises. On the whole it is being a pleasant voyage. After a week, faces begin to emerge as individuals. There are a great many officers on board, red-faced with moustaches, the typical picture of the Englishman ; a certain number of civilians, too, bound for Bombay, Lahore and even Assam, whose company and conversation is entertaining.

He wrote to Max and Simone Bégouën on the same day :

In this mixed society you hear every sort of comment, from black to white, on the Abyssinian question : and I'm annoyed within myself as I realise my difficulty in finding a good reason for adopting any particular attitude. It's clear that we must tend towards a moral and biological organisation of the earth ; but what should be the attitudes of human groups in relation to one another, seeing that their social values and capabilities differ so greatly ? [. . .] The more I see of the East, the more I distrust the demagogue in international matters.

I saw few traces of Italian preparations during our journey : no more than a small transport-vessel at Port Said, loaded with troops. Poor devils, just think how they must be suffering from the heat.

Meanwhile I have written a short article on ' the discovery of the past ', which I am thinking of sending to your father for his birthday book. But I am not sure whether what I say may not shock my friends in prehistory. In the end I come to the conclusion that there is only one real method of discovering (as we learn from historical research) ; it is to build the future. It's perfectly simple, but there are still so many people who behave as though the past was interesting in itself, and treat it as only the future deserves to be treated.

So there you are. Never lose your radiance or your smile— there are more people around you both who live by them than you imagine. Keep, too, the assurance of my ever-increasing affection.

Père Teilhard landed at Bombay on 20 September.

Bombay, 23 September, 1935

Bombay is a big, white and rather commonplace city, surrounded by sea. The spur of the headland is occupied by luxurious Anglo-Hindu buildings. Over the rest sprawls the huddle of the native town, a teeming medley of dark Hindu and Semitic types. What I like best is the great bushy trees with red and yellow flowers, through which from time to time you see the flight of flocks of green parrots. The monsoon is just over but it is still humid and already hot. It will be better in the north.

I had a very kind welcome here from the Spanish Fathers at St. Xavier's College ; and I have met an old Toulousian whom I knew by name and reputation. He and I have many friends in common and we have chatted together for hours. However, I have no desire to hang around here for ever. Time is short between now and January.

[. . .] I have finished my business in Bombay and am taking the train for the north this evening—the ' frontier mail ' which should get me tomorrow evening to Rawalpindi (Punjab) where I shall be met by Patterson, the Englishman. From there we leave together the next day to join de Terra in Srinagar (Kashmir).

(To the Abbé Breuil)   *Rawalpindi, Punjab, 8 October, 1935*

My dear friend,

Tomorrow we are leaving, de Terra and I, for a fortnight's expedition to the Salt Range. [. . .] Since my arrival in these parts, then, I have spent a week in Kashmir, a fantastic super-

Alpine country, becoming acquainted with the Himalayan glacial series, and another week in the sub-Himalayan hills of the Punjab visiting the alluvial terraces that correspond to the glacial formations.

[. . .] Yesterday we were on the Indus, in a country of impressive wildness, the formations magnificently defined. [. . .] Some fine mammal deposits at bedrock—we shall open them up next week. The upper gravel beds contain enormous erratic blocks ; any that are smooth and weathered are covered with hammered or pricked drawings. The drawings very much weathered. Date probably late oeneolithic. But the whole would interest you intensely, in comparison with Spain. You can recognise riders and even a zebu with its hump. An odd thing : these drawings had been noted by an English commissioner in the Punjab, but no archæologist has yet mentioned them. Patterson is taking casts of the most interesting ones and copying the others. But a full study of them would be a long job.

Chakri, Punjab, 16 October, 1935

On September 25 I arrived at Rawalpindi (a two day's journey by a good train, without changing our carriage), where young Patterson from Cambridge, a friend of Breuil's and Miss Garrod's [1] etc. was waiting for me. On the 26th we took a car and drove by a good road that follows the Jhelum gorges, to join de Terra on a houseboat in Srinagar.

Connections with China are becoming more frequent and there are traces here of one and probably two prehistoric periods which no-one has yet really drawn attention to.

Kashmir is a ' super-Alpine ' valley, full of rice-fields, poplars, nuts, enormous sycamores, ringed with pine-forests, dominated to the south by Pic Panjal (15,000 feet) and to the north

[1] Dr. Garrod, of Oxford.

by the High Himalayas. You can imagine what it looked like under a fine autumn sky. We spent a week up there studying the Himalayan glacial system. Then back to Rawalpindi, which we left ten days ago, de Terra and I, and since then we have been wandering about the Salt Range, sometimes by camel, sometimes by car, sometimes under canvas, and sometimes (as today) in one of the comfortable bungalows that the British government has put at frequent intervals for the convenience of travelling sahibs. You arrive ; the caretaker opens the bungalow and you move in and instal yourself with your kit and your boys. My boy is called Simon ; he has a big turban, a formidable moustache and makes an excellent 'housemaid'. A very convenient arrangement.

It's picturesque country, but three-parts desert, cracked and stony. There are moments when I might be back in Egypt or Abyssinia. All the plants and trees are thorny. I am extremely well and surprised to find myself ' so young '. Every day we are on foot nearly all day long and I feel no tiredness at all. Not a cloud in the sky : we wear nothing but slacks and a shirt—very convenient.

(To the Abbé Breuil)   *Rawalpindi, 21 October, 1935*

Since the beginning of October I have been working with my friend de Terra on the Tertiary and Quaternary formations of the Punjab : a vast cone of dejection from the folding (a process probably still going on) of the Himalayas. A very healthy life, and one that I haven't found in the least tiring—rather the contrary—even though we are on our feet for seven or eight hours every day. It's semi-desert country in which all the plants are thorny, mimosas and jujubes, and even the grasses in seed. In every direction the ground is furrowed by erosion, and the fields the people cultivate are poor and stony. But it's a countryside of wonderful luminosity—not too hot, at the moment. The population is entirely Moslem. I should like you to see the women here so that you could appreciate what our western civilisation has succeeded in winning for their sisters in Europe. The poor creatures here are prematurely lined, buried in their veils, and permanently cowed. All this has got to be swept away, and before very long too.

I am yielding to the exotic charm of the place, with less enthusiasm than before, to be sure, but still just as fully ; and I never tire of the pleasure of seeing the charming little chipmunks coming to nibble tit-bits at my door, or the flocks of parrots bickering in the trees—these parrots fly at a surprising speed and whether in the air or among the branches they never stop their chatter. We are staying in Rawalpindi for a few more days, using it as a centre for drives into the countryside. I am proposing to go farther east in November, towards Simla. In December, it'll be Calcutta.

(To Max and Simone Bégouën)   *Rawalpindi, 5 November, 1935*

My last letter to you was written from Bombay. Since that time I've been very much on the move, though always in the same corner of India. First a week in the magnificent setting of Kashmir, as an introduction under de Terra's guidance to the Himalayan glacial formations : huge snow-covered masses, with a border of pine-forest overlooking a valley rich in green vegetation ; on the roads I could see the still perfectly fresh tracks of Haardt's caterpillars. Grey mud villages in which the turbanned and moustached peasants live and say their prayers in the mosques, with their women-folk, always cowed-looking and generally ragged, with a ring in the left nostril. Camels, cows and buffaloes are perpetually across the road and you have to look out for them : overhead, a dazzling light and a permanently cloudless sky. Now that the weather's not so hot, it's ideal country for the geologist.

On the whole I'm well pleased with our work. For the Pliocene and Pleistocene in Asia, I couldn't imagine a grander complement to China, and de Terra is the perfect guide. (He has already done the Pamirs and Karakorum twice.) Fossils are difficult to find, although we have come across a fine early Pleistocene deposit near the Indus. Anthropoids are rare (one good jawbone fragment). The pick of de Terra's finds this year is certainly a rich palæolithic industry whose existence was hardly suspected and which, most important of all, had not yet been dated. There are two main levels, one, rich in palæoliths (the stones worked in a very special way), lies at the base of a ' loess ' (pretty early Pleistocene)—more or less corresponding to our Mousterian. The other, more difficult to date but apparently more ancient, contains some fine bifacial implements, generally rounded. I have an idea that our work may lay the foundations of Hindu prehistory, which has been rather a Cinderella so far.

Rawalpindi, 15 November, 1935

I'm now really beginning to acquire personal knowledge of the district. As I wrote to a friend recently, I believe that once again Providence will be found to have brought me to a critical point in my scientific life, and at just the psychological moment. This countryside is indeed a vast field in which you follow the operation, at the very height of the Quaternary age, of far-reaching geological movements. Yesterday, for example, some hundred miles south of here, we were busy looking for fossils in the crevasses that gape in the middle of a real fold of consolidated mud in which are buried the remains of buffaloes and elephants. To the south lay an endless expanse : the great alluvial plain running down to Lahore that is still biding its time to heave itself up into undulations. To the north and east, a series of crests, some lofty, some rather lower ; other folds, like solidified waves, and finally the white barrier of the Panjal, the youngest of the Himalayan chains, floating in the blue sky, higher than Mont Blanc. All this fascinates me, particularly the golden light that plays on the mimosas and the dry grasses and jungle of the Punjab ; and my whole being is agreeably filled with this serene grandeur, which still delights and heartens, even though it no longer overwhelms me.

(To the Abbé Breuil)   *Rawalpindi, 15 November, 1935*

[. . .] For the last three weeks there has not been much change in my life in India : long days, full of interest, spent in the sub-Himalayan hills—millions of yards of consolidated mud and gravel creased like crêpe paper. We're beginning to see our way to clarifying our findings. A week in the neighbourhood of the Indus brought us a respectable pile of cases of fossils found in a new district. On the whole I feel that we have done well. Once again Providence will be found to have led me to a critical point at just the psychological moment. I do indeed believe that it is the work in which I'm now sharing that will lay the first serious foundation for the prehistory of India. The weather at present is marvellous. Yesterday in particular, when we were working in the jagged ravines of a minor mountain range south of here, the setting was tremendous. In the foreground, deep crevasses exposing under the mimosa growth the striped mass (yellow, violet, pink) of regularly curved Pleistocene formations ; in the middle distance, much further back, the violet mass of Pliocene and Miocene mud almost forming one with the great chains ; and finally floating in the blue sky on the horizon the white barrier of the Pic Panjal, the last corner of the Himalayan peaks ;

and lying over the whole scene a golden light playing on the dry, bleached grasses.

Last week we went to Sind, towards Baluchistan ; there we found astounding palæolithic and neolithic workshops in a plateau rising up from the alluvial basin of the Indus—impossible, unfortunately, to work out the stratigraphy properly. It's picturesque country in which the sun, the sands, the fertile alluvium and the forests of date-palms reminded me vividly of Egypt. We went out of our way to look at the famous excavations at Mohendjo-Daro (one of the centres of the 'Indus civilisation'). In the middle of the tamarisk bush you find a red-brick town, partially exposed since 1922, with its houses, drains, streets, wells and water system. . . . More than 3000 years before our era, people were living there who played with dice like our own, fished with hooks like ours, and wrote in characters we can't yet read. We live surrounded by ideas and objects infinitely more ancient than we imagine ; and yet at the same time everything is in motion. The universe is a vast thing in which we should be lost if it did not converge upon the Person.

19 December, 1935

There are, in fact, human groups that differ biologically and physically, and they can be 'converted' only by first transforming them within the human plane. I believe such convergence to be possible. So far as I have been able to form an opinion of them, the Hindus have been a disappointment to me. In them, too, the creative power seems in a pretty poor way, and you have to go to India to realise the numbing and deadening effect of a religion obsessed by material forms and ritualism.

Finally they explored central India, on the sacred Narbada river.

216

The real peninsular India : soft summer weather (21 December) ;
golden light ; a countryside thickly shaded with mangos and
banyans, fine bushy trees like ancient oaks ; tall ridges covered
with thick forests (tiger jungle) ; peacocks in the jungle ; crocodiles in the river ; parrots in the gardens ; at every corner
frolicking bands of big black-faced monkeys with white ruffs ;
very gentle, even gracious, people living in big, beautifully clean
huts ; the women red-veiled, the men in white.

(To the Abbé Breuil)   *Calcutta, 18 December, 1935*

I ended my stay in India with a most interesting fortnight in the
celebrated basin of the Narbada (Central India).

The Narbada is taken as the classic of Indian Pleistocene, and
a palæolithic tool was noted there *in situ* about 1850, but nothing
had been done about it in the last eighty years. Great was our
surprise to find deposits extremely rich in ancient industry. You
will find that the material collected by our little expedition may
supply a fundamental basis for Indian prehistory.

Near a little town called Hoshangabad we looked at the celebrated paintings described by Mitra [1] and reproduced more than
once since then. ('Memoirs of the Archæological Survey of
India, 1932' (?) ; *Illustrated London News*, 1935.) The paintings
are in black and red on quartzite walls (the jungle must be full of
them!). My impression is that they have been very poorly
analysed by such writers as I have been able to read. You would
find dozens of things to note in them.

The work had been attributed to the ninth or tenth centuries A.D.
*Père Teilhard believed them to be much more ancient, possibly
going back to the arrival of the Aryans in India. 'It is a fact that*

[1] Raja Rajadralal Mitra (1825–91), the most learned Hindu scholar of
his time, who rendered great services to archæology.

some of the inhabitants of the jungle still use bows, and produce fire by friction.'

De Terra may well be pleased with the outcome of his expedition. We parted from one another with some regrets, on December 15, he going to Bombay (for America), and I to Calcutta.

On the 22nd he left for Batavia, at the invitation of the Dutch scientist, von Koenigswald, to study the latter's finds on the spot.

(To Joseph Teilhard de Chardin)
>   *On board the 'Tjinagara', 21 January, 1936 (in passage from*
>   *Java for China, by Hongkong)*

I left Batavia six days ago ; and yet, thanks to a contrary monsoon, this elegant Dutch steamer which bears my fortunes (and those of a number of planters bound for America) has not yet managed to reach the lost islands that some romantic traveller has called ' Paracelsus '. Meanwhile I am impatient to see the peak of Hongkong again, and still more the mud of Wangpu, so that I can judge what Japanese intrigue has left of my ' office ' in Pekin. It would be no joke to shuttle, like the Ambassadors, between Pekin and Nanking ; it's enough, as it is, to have to keep going to and fro, as I do, between Paris and China.

[. . .] As you no doubt broadly know, my journey, which I undertook with some hesitancy, has been most interesting and fruitful. . . . In brief, both in India with de Terra and in Java with Koenigswald, I pitched most opportunely on two of the hottest sectors in the prehistory front—and just at the very moment to take part in decisive offensives. This is proving a great addition to my experience and another valuable plank in my platform. But fundamentally it gives me only moderate satisfaction. As a purpose in life, my science (to which I owe so much) seems to me to be less and less worthwhile. For a long time now, my chief interest in life has lain in some sort of effort towards a plainer disclosing of God in the world. It's a more killing task but it's my only true vocation and nothing can turn me from it.

I was delighted with India. I was living chiefly in the grimmer parts of the country, so often featured in English literature : the famous ' Hills ' (or their neighbourhood, at any rate) where nameless tribes still swarm which, it is generally believed, would be a serious threat to the Peninsula if they should ever come to a common understanding. I was there for the best time of the year ; dry, cool in the morning, with never a cloud to be seen : semi-desert, thorny country. A transition from Central Asia to Africa, through Arabia. To end up with, a wonderful fortnight in Central India, in a setting of jungle and heavy green growth, in a countryside teeming with life since there is hardly anything a Hindu will kill. At every turn in the road you find large monkeys installed, black-faced with white ruffs, sitting in the middle of the fields and eating great handfuls of green corn. And then the cows—cows everywhere : the Hindu neither eats them nor controls their increase. ' Philip, there are too many bulls in India,' said de Terra to his impassive boy. ' Yes, sir,' answered Philip, without turning a hair. Most annoying for cars. At Srinagar, three years' in gaol for killing a cow—result, the ' bus ' runs into a tree rather than hurt the lord of the roads, the cow.

The people (in Central India) are very gentle. In Lahore and Calcutta I saw something of the Hindu upper classes (highly civilised, the women in dazzling costumes, their beauty set off by a red spot on the forehead, and sometimes by a precious stone in the left nostril). As individuals, Indians are charming, but taken as a whole the country seems to be just as incapable of self-government as China or Malaya. Unfortunately, dislike of the English is general among the ' natives '. They want complete independence at all costs, even if it means death to the country. The English allow them as much rope as they can, but they don't let go : and I imagine they're quite right. The more I get around the world, the more I fear that Geneva (of which I am in my heart a great supporter), numbers of liberal Catholics, and especially my colleagues the ' Missiologues ', are making a grave mistake in recognising the equality of races in the face of all the biological evidence. ' Universalism ' is not democracy (=egalitarianism).

Java I liked greatly. I saw it in the rainy season, but under very favourable conditions. Koenigswald (young and brilliant) has friends everywhere among the Javanese. We shared the life of the kampongs (villages), slept in the chief's hut : the whole population helped in our search. For refreshment we drank from coconuts. Every time I experience it again I become the more convinced that I was made for life in the tropics. I am intensely fond of the rich vegetation, the heavy vegetal scents, and even the thick clouds which after the daily downpour drift away from the mountain sides. Java, as you know, is on the whole overpopulated. The plains are simply one huge village, which is hidden, however, under a forest of palms. Bandoeng, where I stayed with V. K., is right in the mountains among the tea and cinchona plantations. Central Java shows more definite conformations : a series of symmetrical volcanoes, like so many Vesuviuses or Fuji-Yamas, rising up from a vast expanse of rice-fields and coconut palms.

. . . Even so, I shall be glad to see brooding old China again : so many of my friends and interests are there now.

Between Hongkong and Shanghai, 24 January, 1936

I left Calcutta for Java on the 22 December, in a small English steamer which brought me to Rangoon : a fine tropical city, not too buried in the mud of the Irrawaddy, and crowned by fine pagodas with shining gilded domes. You would have to go to

Russia to find so romantic a scene, and in Burma the sun and the palms have a quality that is all their own. I was there for Christmas. As elsewhere, except in Calcutta and Singapore, no-one knew who I was and I was lucky to chance on a little church where a small and colourful congregation of half-breeds and rich Burmese had gathered for an early Mass (everything happens early in this country). A pleasant-looking group of 'low-caste' mammas with their restless offspring thronged the porch, behind the congregation.

I stayed three days in Singapore, very kindly received by the Foreign Missions, where I found some old friends. I sailed in a small Dutch liner, the *Ophir*, among booming Netherlanders with their plump blonde wives and daughters. And so, for the first time, I crossed the line. At Batavia, the young and brilliant Koenigswald was waiting for me on the quay : a jolly fellow with whom I was immediately on the most friendly terms. He took me straight to Bandoeng (the administrative centre of the Dutch East Indies) and installed me in his bungalow. His young wife was in Batavia, recovering from typhoid, but the Malay boy and his wife, Bibi, looked after us. The greater part of my stay was taken up with excursions in the south and centre of the island, where V. K. had just made some extraordinary finds which he wanted to clarify with me : in particular a magnificent Chellean industry that no-one had even suspected. I thought myself back in India, on the Narbada. After the last finds with de Terra, it seems somehow providential that I should arrive in Java just at the right time to give my opinion on and to some extent place definitely what V. K. has unearthed. I am sometimes a little disturbed when I think of the uninterrupted succession of such strokes of luck that runs through my life. What does it mean, and what is God expecting of me ?

I didn't have time in Java to see any of the things that ' you mustn't miss ' : neither Bali, nor the temple of Bara-Budin, nor any volcanic craters. On the other hand, I lived in the Javanese kampongs among the gentle and graceful natives, and I fairly revelled in the exoticism of this marvellous country. Java is over-populated : apart from the high peaks and some remnants of jungle, it is nothing but one immense village ; but the huts are so small, so scattered and so lost in the vast sea of green, that all you see is a forest of palms enclosing rice-fields, the whole dominated by a series of volcanoes, each as big as Etna.

I have taken advantage of this long voyage to get down my travel-notes and write a number of letters aimed at passing on to discreetly-chosen quarters what I saw and what is not even suspected by any prehistorian in Europe.

Père Teilhard made use also of the voyage to ' re-concentrate myself upon God, and reap the fruits of action.

' I do indeed believe that I have never before seen my vocation so clearly and stripped of non-essentials—to personalise the world in God.' He developed this theme in his essay, ' Un Univers per-sonnel ', in which he examined in turn : the significance of the person ; the extension of the person (the ' sur-human ') ; the consummation of the person (in God) ; the energy of personalisa-tion (love, the cosmic sense, the sense of the human) ; the religion of the person (Christianity). He insists throughout that his attitude is ' supremely Christian '.

Shortly after his arrival in Pekin he learnt of the death of his mother (7 February, 1936) : ' the dear and holy mother ' to whom ' I owe all that is best in my soul '.

The situation in Pekin had changed considerably. The Japanese occupation of northern China had cut the country in two. Nanking was now the capital, to which some of the public services, in particular the Geological Survey, had retired.

20 February, 1936

Here it is like being marooned in a wilderness. Four or five of us wander about the buildings that used to be so full of life. Hardly any of the books or collections are still here [. . .] I have rarely lived in such an unstable atmosphere.

26 April, 1936

My friend Bardac invites me to lunch with any interesting people who are passing through. Quite a number of tourists. Before Easter we had Chaliapin, whom I went to hear. A fine tall white-haired old man, most moving in the decline of his power. Some days Pekin is like a little Paris. Meanwhile, with a rather mournful gaiety, it is succumbing to the Japanese infiltration: khaki uniforms, hobnailed boots and narcotics. It is impossible to imagine such serenely immoral brutality. In return the Chinese, incapable of resisting by force, seem to be pulling themselves together and forming an elastic but stubborn *bloc* which Japan is going to find very difficult either to dissolve or assimilate. There's a very good chance that the Chinese may have the last word.

(To the Abbé Breuil)   *Pekin, April 1936*

[. . .] No news to speak of: during Easter week I went over to Chou-Kou-Tien for the resumption of the digging. A rather unpleasant spring as so often in China: north winds battling with south winds, each in turn bringing eddies of dust; and under the dust, pink apricot- and peach-trees flowering miraculously in a desert of grey.

Politically, under the smiles it's all confusion.

A little later :

[. . .] So I went to western Shantung, down the peninsula that runs out towards Japan : a real Brittany, granitic, but with higher mountains and no gorse bushes nor heather. Interesting results from the point of view of structural geology, but rather hard going, for the roads had been washed away by the rains. I renewed my acquaintance with the horrors of Chinese inns and Chinese carts. But a spell of field-work was just what I needed to get back into form.

In Pekin, Père Teilhard was busy again with the publication of details of the recent finds at Chou-Kou-Tien, among them a new ' good' Sinanthropus jaw-bone which confirmed and emphasised the information that had already been obtained about fossil man in China. He received invitations, too, to take part in two conferences during 1937 : one in March in Philadelphia, to which he was asked to contribute a paper on early man ; the second, in Moscow in July, he was unable to attend.

I have been going out a good deal these days, in French, American and even Russian circles (white Russians of the old regime). I often see the new Ambassador, Nagiar, when he's not in Nanking—tourists, too. At the moment there's something a little uneasy about the Japs and they seem a little less sure of themselves.

On the international political situation, Père Teilhard comments : ' I can hardly stand the turmoil of humanity any longer, and many of my friends feel the same. It distresses me to see so many men allowing the pressure of events to force them back into old-style conservatism. It seems to me the time has come to make a clean break with the old stuff. Fascism, Communism, democracy, have ceased to have any real meaning. My own dream would be to see the best of humanity re-grouped on a spiritual basis determined by the following three aims : Universalism, Futurism and Personalism, and co-operating in whatever political and economic movement should prove technically most able to safeguard those three aims. Something on those lines really needs saying : I feel it and I know it.'

While superintending the work of the Geological Survey, Père Teilhard was keeping in touch with European thought. He was deeply concerned with the needs of his own age and anxious to lead the contemporary world to ' the discovery of God '.

1936-1937

13 June, 1936

Today human activity as a whole is faced by the problem of God ; it is a problem that can be approached only by the total effort of human research and experience. It is not only that God gives lasting value to the human effort, but also that His revelation is a response to the sum total of that effort.

During the summer of 1936 Père Teilhard suffered a fresh bereavement by the death on 17 August of his sister Marguérite-Marie. For many years an invalid and often bedridden, she had borne her suffering with admirable courage.[1]

' Her disappearance has created a sort of universal wilderness around me ; it affects every element of an interior world of which I had gradually made her a partner. The two of us thought together in everything that makes up spiritual activity and the interior life. I shall miss her physical presence terribly ; on the other hand I think that her power of inspiring and watching over me has strengthened.'

[1] For the past ten years Marguerite-Marie Teilhard de Chardin had been president of the Catholic Association for the Sick. Cf. the memorial volume edited by Monique Givelet to which her brother contributed a preface, *M.-M. Teilhard de Chardin, l'énergie spirituelle et la souffrance.* (ed. du Seuil.)

(To J. T. de C.)   *Tientsin, 5 September, 1936*

The blow of Guite's death was softened for me by the fact that it was expected and that I had had no direct news from her for some months. But I feel that a great void has opened up in my life—or rather in the world around me—a great void of which I shall become increasingly aware. [. . .] The only way of making life bearable again is to love and adore that which, beneath everything, animates and directs it.

Referring to his participation in the Philadelphia Conference on Early Man, arranged for March 1937 :

From the narrowly personal point of view, 1937 looks like being a laborious and complicated year, and my own life in general an unending pilgrimage. But I can see quite clearly that it would be a betrayal on my part not to take up my staff again and accept the routine of perpetual separations.

The acceptance of ' what happens ' had for Père Teilhard the force of religion. ' To believe, to be in communication with the future : my only strength, my whole strength, lies and will ever lie, in never turning aside from that.' The threat of events in France and Europe was constantly in his mind at this period.

Pekin, 23 October, 1936

In spite of everything my real concern and interest is still the present and the future of mankind. From that point of view I often regret that I am tucked away in the Far East while the game is being played out in the West. What strikes me is how events disclose what lies at the bottom of the heart : there isn't a single one of my correspondents whose letters don't show me quite clearly in what direction, backwards or forwards, they lean. They have made their choice. I feel that I must be doing something, and so I am trying to put down just what I feel in an essay I shall send to *Études*. It seems to me that on a higher level than the confused currents of moribund democracy and nascent Communist and Fascism—and of an ageing Christianity, too, that no longer informs the material world—there should be some way of grouping the ' elect ' who have made up their minds to build the earth on the three ' columns ' of Universalism, Futurism and Personalism : which would bring together the warring fragments of religion. In the light of the present conflict, one could profitably look into the problem of the technical means best adapted to the end we seek. Such a reformation may seem utopian. But it seems at the same time to be a *sine qua non* for human survival. And I do not think that humanity can perish.

> *This idea was embodied in the essay ' Sauvons l'humanité '* [1] *which called for the formation of a ' Human Front ' : What must be believed (the future of humanity), what must be seen (the convergence of humanity), what must be done (the Human Front).*
>
> *In February 1937, Père Teilhard left for the Philadelphia Conference on palæontology.*
>
> *He travelled by Shanghai and Honolulu and landed in America at Seattle. He arrived in Paris on 15 April.*

(To J. T. de C.)   *On board the ' Empress of
                                          Japan ', 12 March, 1937*

[. . .] We are just approaching the American coast, and the day after tomorrow, in the evening, I hope to be installed in a Pullman for the three-day journey from Seattle to Chicago ; then I must get to Philadelphia as quickly as possible. [. . .] So far

---

[1] Published in *Études*, 20 October, 1937, under the title ' La Crise présente '.

it has been a very quiet and interesting journey. In Tokyo I was received like a friend at the American Embassy (I baptised their little daughter in Pekin, in January). Then the *Empress of Japan*, a very fine ship in which I was economically travelling ' *tourist-class* '. Even so I met plenty of interesting passengers in the first class at an unending series of cocktail parties : fat Americans and Canadians taking a cruise (several of whom I had met in Pekin). I paid discreet attentions to the Ranee (= the wife of the Rajah of Sarawak), with the idea that the future might well take me to her dominions in Borneo. She is English ; so is the Rajah, the son of an Englishman whom an odd fate transformed into a Rajah during the last century.

At Philadelphia I am to meet, under the aegis of the Carnegie Institute, a group of people interested in the study of human origins. (The idea is to set up a systematic plan for investigations that may take me again next year to India and north of the Himalayas.) [1] There I shall meet again de Terra, von Koenigswald (Java), Miss Garrod (England). As usual, I shall be the only Frenchman. At the beginning of April I shall go on to New York.

After a stay in Paris in the early summer, Père Teilhard returned to China. The last part of the journey proved awkward.

(To J. T. de C.)   *On board the ' d'Artagnan ',*
10 August, 1937

Cholera in Hongkong, war in Shanghai. I am proposing to push on to Kobe (Japan) in the hope of finding a Japanese ship for Tientsin. Shanghai is at present a trap which it's difficult to get out of. Large tricolour signs have just been painted on our upper decks in the hope of preventing a ' mistake ' on the part of enthusiastic pilots.

[1] In fact it was Burma, which Père Teilhard visited with de Terra in 1938.

(To J. T. de C.)   *Tientsin, 18 September, 1937*

This is to let you know that yesterday I arrived safely in Tientsin from Kobe : six weeks by sea from Marseilles, but without any hold-up on the way. After Hongkong, everywhere was in a state of war : large tricolours painted on the *d'Artagnan*, but for all that materialised it might have been large-scale manœuvres, for China has practically nothing at sea or in the air to set up against the valiant Nips. We were moored for twenty-four hours at the entrance to the river at Shanghai, where the scene was almost as impressive : a large number of transports, vessels and warships, fires and bombs exploding in the suburbs of Shanghai, but that was all. A French cruiser came to escort us and take off passengers. Life at Shanghai, particularly business life, is very disorganised but there is practically no danger for foreign nationals in the Concessions. All the damage in the first days had been done by inept Chinese pilots who scored a record number of hits on masses of refugees. Japan is very worked up. The ports are under military control. About 300 troopships are running a shuttle service [. . .] Meanwhile the occupation of northern China is proceeding in stages, at a pace that may considerably hasten the anticipated defections of Shansi and Shantung. It's difficult to tell you more, and I only hope this letter will reach you. There's nothing more to add about the journey, except that we arrived two days after a typhoon had beached eighteen steamers (including the famous *Conte Verde*, a Japanese vessel of the same size, and a large Dutch one), and that we ourselves were caught by a typhoon as we arrived at the opportune shelter of Kobe : in one hour the barometer fell from 760 to 732 millimetres. Because of the cholera in Hongkong we had to cruise about for a day before being allowed to enter the harbour, where the Japanese public health authorities received us without turning a hair with methods which might have come straight out of the first chapter of Daudet's *Morticoles*.

Since the outbreak of war between Japan and China in July, the situation in China was becoming increasingly confused. Pekin was quiet, but the surrounding country was infested with isolated groups of combatants and bandits, so that it was impossible to leave the city. Although there were no tourists, there was an unusually large population of foreigners resident in Pekin.

30 September, 1937

[. . .] I have found most of my friends here. The Survey is almost at full strength, and work is going on as usual (there have been many interesting acquisitions since I left). But in all this we're really just free-wheeling. Nobody can foresee what will happen to our undertakings here when the war is over. We have only too good reason to fear that Pekin may be administratively separated from Nanking : and then what ? I have plenty to do for several months, what with geology and my own essays.

During the voyage from Marseilles to Saigon, Père Teilhard had written a new essay on 'L'Énergie humaine', whose conclusion was to be a chapter on the Love of God. In this he distinguishes the true character of what he called 'the Christian Phenomenon'.

' Christ's essential message is wholly contained in the proclamation of a divine Fatherhood : put it another way—in the assertion that God, personal Being, is to man the term of a personal union. Many times already (and especially in the dawn of the Christian era) man's religious gropings have felt their way towards this idea that God-Spirit can be attained only by the spirit ; but it is only in Christianity that the movement is definitively realised. The gift of the heart instead of the prostration of the body, communion transcending sacrifice, and God-Love finally attained only through

231

Love : therein lie the psychological revelation and the secret of Christian love.'

(To Max Bégouën)   *Pekin, 26 September, 1937*

I finished ' L'Energie humaine ' as I arrived in Shanghai, and I'll send it to you as soon as it's typed. Fairly long. I believe I have come close to putting my meaning into words. In the last few days I've had the idea of adding a very short appendix on what I shall call ' the principle of conservation of personality ' ; and then I think I shall be able to get on quietly with preliminary work on *Man.*[1] [. . .]

It's difficult to tell you much about the war, partly because ' Anastasia '[2] has become so cantankerous, and partly because the situation in itself is so confused. On the whole it would appear that as far as Nanking is concerned, from now on the north is definitely lost. But won't Nanking try to keep up a long and desperate resistance in the south and west ? That would be by no means impossible.

The Japanese occupation of northern China was a serious hindrance to geological work.

(To Max Bégouën)   *Pekin, 21 October, 1937*

We're not clear of our difficulties yet, or rather we're only just reaching the tricky moment where we shall have to re-adjust our organisation to the change of regime in Pekin. Nothing is certain so far, and we are having to keep up a friendly struggle against our headquarters in the south, who are inclined to withdraw their troops—geological troops, I mean—prematurely. Still, I hope we shall manage to reach an understanding without abandoning our positions. For me personally, the most serious

---

[1] Finally entitled *The Phenomenon of Man.*
[2] i.e. the censorship.

aspect is that all my colleagues, Chinese and foreign, are unanimous in agreeing that my place, '*for the time being*', is here and not in Burma, where de Terra expects me at the beginning of December. And it would have been so important for me to go to Burma! I shall wait a little while longer before I finally decide ; but I am very much afraid that it will soon be impossible to be in two minds about where my duty lies : I must stay here.

Pekin is fairly empty, but a good nucleus of friends remains, Lucile Swan for a start.[1] She has just been working with Weidenreich [2] on the restoration of the front of the Sinanthropus : we had nearly all the materials but they had not been fitted together in place. The reconstructed individual (a complete head including the mandible) is a female : we call her Nelly, and I don't doubt you'll see her before long.

[1] The American sculptress.
[2] The new director of the Geological Service.

1938-1939

Difficulties arose about the Burmese journey. Père Teilhard was suffering from the after-effects of a severe bout of malaria that had been wrongly diagnosed during his last stay in Paris, and the Pekin doctors were against his leaving for Burma.

He did not, however, abandon the idea, the more so that the situation in northern China was becoming more difficult. Nanking was gradually evacuating the north and withdrawing Teilhard's Chinese colleagues. Père Teilhard was left almost alone to look after the scientific institutes, but was afraid that he too might be ordered back. Meanwhile he thought it best to hang on, even if it meant giving up Burma; and he took advantage of his enforced leisure to write his long-planned ' Phenomenon of Man '.

In December, however, he was released by the arrival of a Chinese colleague, and decided to join de Terra in Burma.

On board the ' Anhui ', on the way to Singapore, 16 December, 1937

I left Tientsin in a small cargo ship bound for Hongkong (no easy matter just now, embarking at Tientsin—ice and mud) and yesterday I had the luck to find another at Swatow, carrying Chinese emigrants to Malaya. This will take me in four days to Singapore, and there I have a good chance of getting a steamer fairly soon for Rangoon, where I am sure to find instructions from de Terra. So that's that. I find it most odd to be transported suddenly into the tropics, when ten days ago I was resigning myself to a winter in Pekin.

(To J. T. de C.) *On board the ' Anhui '*,
17 December, 1937 (on the way to Singapore)

Travelling comfortably by myself in a small steamer carrying Chinese emigrants, I am back again after three months on the blue expanse of the Malayan seas, not a little surprised at no longer freezing in the icy weather of Pekin.

I came on board with some difficulty at ice-bound Tangkou, and had the good luck to find in Swatow, before we reached Hongkong, a small cargo vessel bound for Singapore. If I have any luck at Singapore, I can be in Rangoon before 13th January. I hardly hoped it would go so well. If everything works out as it should, I expect to return to Pekin about the beginning of March, after spending the winter in the warm and with the satisfaction of my duty accomplished.

It's difficult to give you any definite news about the situation in the Far East. There is talk of a Japanese landing south of Canton, very close to Indo-China. All this may well turn out badly, and the Japs seem to be giving increasing evidence of their complete ignorance of psychology. It's difficult to understand how they can persist in trying to ingratiate themselves with the Chinese by dealing them blow after blow ; in fact, if they had made up their minds to get themselves detested, they couldn't have chosen a better way of doing so. Meanwhile the occupied territory, except for the big cities like Pekin and Tientsin, is in an indescribable state of confusion. Japanese troops are posted in little groups along the railway lines. But as soon as you leave them, the whole countryside is infested with disbanded Chinese troops or bandits. What it amounts to is that China was attacked before she could collect her strength and is defending herself by crumbling into dust ; and how the invaders can bind the dust together is impossible to imagine.

Père Teilhard arrived in Rangoon on 28 December, and joined de Terra on the 31st at Mogok in the Shan plateau. They then made their way down to the plains and worked in the terraces of the Irrawaddy or the slopes of the Arakan-Yoma (the chain separating the Irrawaddy from the Bay of Bengal). There were five of them in the party and they were living under canvas or in British Government bungalows.

Pagan, Burma, under canvas, 28 January, 1938

The bungalow at Pagan (built for George V when he was Prince of Wales) is exceptionally attractive. From where I am on the verandah I overlook the Irrawaddy, fringed by low mountains and held in a ribbon of green, exactly like the Nile in Upper Egypt. Pagan, the former capital of Burma, is now only a picturesque bazaar, lost among the palms and mimosa, but the surroundings are simply one great forest of pagodas, some of them dilapidated red brick, some a vivid white or even gilded, like the dome of the Invalides. The population is very much of a mixture. First the Burmese, all grace and beaming smiles, their hair worn in a bun by both men and women, and dressed in dazzling colours, with an extraordinary proportion of orange-robed monks. Towards the Arakan-Yoma you meet the ' Chins ', small men, with moustaches, almost Mongol. To the east the black-turbanned Shans and a chequer-board of small groups of strange ethnic types. But all these people occupy only an insignificant part of the country itself. Outside the delta the jungle is master—very beautiful towards Mogok, with its forests of bamboo and huge teak-trees that are rafted down the Irrawaddy. Marvellous weather. The midday sun is trying, but the nights are cool and the sky permanently cloudless. Such are the advan-

tages of the dry season, which lasts until April. No wonder I
feel so well : it's as though I had found a new youth. I can
walk indefinitely without getting tired, just as I did in India.

(To J. T. de C.) *Chauk, Burma,*
13 February, 1938

Our work progresses well in an extraordinarily picturesque setting.
At the moment we are camped near an oil-centre : a forest of
' *derricks* ' on ashy hills fortunately doesn't succeed in spoiling
the charm of the Irrawaddy. A few days ago we were at Pagan,
the ancient capital (before Mandalay) of the Burmese kings.
Now it is simply a village lost in palms, banyans, mangoes and
mimosa, but surrounded by over a hundred pagodas, some of
them in ruins that may well date back to the twelfth century.
Nothing really artistic or grand (all brick-built) but about the
whole, particularly when the sun is setting, there is something
most fantastic and unreal. I am becoming very fond of this
radiant country, three-quarters covered with bush or jungle, in
which the most insignificant inhabitant is as graceful and colourful as a flower.

For the last month and more we have been taking advantage
of the dryness and the cool weather to work in the low-lying
country of Upper Burma. Results—geological and archæological
—have been satisfactory. We have succeeded in sorting out the
Irrawaddy formations, where we are collecting abundant evidence
of ' old palæolithic ' industry that is completely new. [. . .]
This spell in the field has given me new youth. I am as brisk as
I was in India two years ago. The only thing I regret is that the
lack of good roads makes it impossible to cover the whole
country. For example, for the last three weeks we have been
skirting the Arakan-Yoma range, between the Irrawaddy and
the Bay of Bengal, without being able to enter it. It's a lofty

range covered with elephant-grass and you can only get about by bullock cart—10 miles a day! [. . .] You would like jungle travel as much as I do. At the moment it has a rather unusual appearance : some of the trees are beginning to produce pink or yellow blossom, yet the intense dryness has already caused a large-scale shedding of leaves, just as in Auvergne at the end of September. [. . .]

You see, then, how I am spending in the calm of ancient nature the hours that are so full of tension for China and Europe ; and you may well imagine that I am not too pleased at being a deserter. Still, I am biding my time—should it ever come—and I am working patiently to clarify my 'message' (?) and strengthen my platform. It seems to me more important to create a new concept of human activity than to plunge into the feverish intoxication of a political drive which already has its leaders and will never lack followers. At the same time I am watching with great anxiety the strange transmutations we are undergoing but fail to understand. The emancipation of the Far East disturbs me because I have no confidence in the human qualities of the Japanese : they will turn out, I fear, to be false shepherds.

(To Max and Simone Bégouën)   *Lashio (Burma),*
                                               28 February, 1938

We left the Irrawaddy some days ago and are now working in the grandeur of the High Shan plateau : dense forests over which spring is scattering patches of cream, pink and flame—an odd country in which I don't know how many Shan tribes rub shoulders—including ' head-hunters '. Some miles from here there has been forcible mobilisation, and thousands of coolies are working feverishly on a road which will take arms from Lashio (here) into Yunnan.

(To Max and Simone Bégouën) *Java, 5 April*

My stay in Burma came to a satisfactory conclusion, and we are
going home with a good collection of results. When we arrived
here we were able to determine that there is a striking resemblance
between our new old-palæolithic industry from the Irrawaddy
(which was completely unknown five weeks ago) and that of
Java. I have a lot to tell you, and I have greatly enlarged my
geological knowledge—my indispensable platform! Here, I am
close to some new Pithecanthropus remains, remarkably similar
to the Sinanthropus.

We are going to look at the key sites of central and eastern
Java in an attempt to determine more exactly the Pleistocene
stratigraphy and physiography.

(To J. T. de C.) *Bandoeng (Java), 5 April, 1938*

We arrived at Batavia the day before yesterday, and I am staying,
just as I did two years ago, with my friend von Koenigswald in
Bandoeng. It was he who six months ago had the good fortune
to find the second Pithecanthropus skull. The rains are nearly
over and in consequence I can see the fine ring of volcanoes
standing out against a clearer sky than in 1936. [. . .] I leave
Batavia on the 16th and travel by the excellent Messageries
(Félix Roussel) which should bring me on the 25th to Shanghai.

Our stay in Burma ended satisfactorily. Plenty of interesting
results—ancient prehistory and geology. I was sorry to leave
the country—I had 'adopted' it immediately. The forests on
the Shan plateau are magnificent. I left them in a purple mantle
of flowering Bauhinia. Animals were very difficult to see. But
the population is an extraordinary mixture of different types,
Shans, Kachins, Wans, etc., some mongoloid, others almost

negroid and completely wild : extremely graceful people, making a colourful and picturesque whole. We pushed on as far as the Salween, which flows in a dizzy cutting through thick jungle. We could see Yunnan a few miles away. Caravans from China on all the roads, the men and their mules exactly like those by the Hwang-Ho. There was a lot of talk of hastening the construction of a Burma–China road for six-tonners. There's no doubt that a ' European' front is being built up here against Japan.

Java is really an ideal country. I am just back from an expedition to an active volcano whose summit (crater) can be reached by car. The summit is covered with virgin forest, the lower slopes with tea and cinchona : luxury hotels along the road, bungalows with swimming pools. I prefer the real jungle— still, there's something very pleasant about this artificial beauty.

Père Teilhard had just learnt, he writes to his brother, that he had been offered an appointment in the Sorbonne's Palæontological Laboratory. His superiors in Rome had given their consent, and in future he would be dividing his time between Pekin and Paris.

On arriving in Pekin, he found that the Japanese occupation was making excavations impossible and that Chou-Kou-Tien was now a no-man's-land.

On the social side, the European colony was greatly reduced. ' We are closing our ranks to preserve the traditions and spirit of the old gaiety of Pekin. It must have been much the same with the " ci-devants " on the eve of the French Revolution.' The Japanese censorship made it necessary to be discreet in sending any political news to Europe, to which Père Teilhard was expecting to return in the autumn.

(To Max Bégouën) *Pekin, 23 May, 1938*

The situation here is essentially the same as it was when I left in December. [. . .] Thanks to the Rockefeller Foundation we are managing to retain a reasonable measure of independence, but it's obvious that things are going to become increasingly difficult. Meanwhile we are living from day to day. It's impossible to work at the digs, for they're in ' *no-man's-land* '. Socially, the people of Pekin are putting up a fine defence against annihilation. [. . .] So, everything is going not too badly, in spite of an oppressive atmosphere of uncertainty, even of uneasiness. No-one can foresee how the trouble will end ; Japan is making it increasingly obvious that she has no intention of stopping until she has destroyed the Kuomintang : and the latter, in the reaction against the way things are going, is becoming more and more absorbed into the very blood of China. Then what ?

[. . .] I am making progress with the preliminary notes of my big work on Man.

(To J. T. de C.) *Pekin, 6 June, 1938*

I found poor old Pekin rather deflated, and more and more Japanese. In some districts you see as many brilliant geisha girls as elegant Chinese ladies : an odd mixture of Tokyo and Pekin. A less attractive sight is the Jap ' *trucks* ' hurtling through the rickshaws like thunderbolts. The normal routine of life continues at the Lab. but with a reduced staff. We are managing to get some useful work done, even in this oppressive and yet rarefied atmosphere. But it's impossible to do any digging at Chou-Kou-Tien, which is caught between the Japanese troops in the plain and the ' red ' regulars based on the mountains.

Socially speaking, Pekin is not beaten yet. The increasingly narrow circle of friends closes its ranks. I often see Bardac still, and the friends he sees.

I have just learnt that at its final meeting the Commission of Higher Studies has just accepted my nomination, practically unanimously—which is not very surprising since mine was the only name put forward ; but what has touched me more is that three institutions (the Trocadéro, the Museum and the Monaco Institute) wanted to have me. I must obviously choose Boule's place. So that, I think, is settled. All that is now needed is the Minister's signature. I expect, then, to be back in France for some time during the autumn, but without, of course, abandoning China ; for here, where my real field of work lies, I have still many commitments. So my normal routine will still be an alternation between France and Asia, but how it works out in detail will depend on quite unforeseeable political developments.

Père Teilhard writes to tell the Abbé Breuil that the Hwang-Ho-Paiho Museum at Tientsin is taking on a new lease of life. Its founder and director, Père Licent, had just been recalled to France, and Père Teilhard had every hope that the Museum would be modernised and develop into an institute of biological research for the continent of Asia, with a new and younger staff. His own long experience made him the inspiration behind the plan.

In Pekin, geological work had been brought almost to a stand-still by the political situation. It was impossible to continue without an understanding with the Japanese ' intruders ', and no form of compromise with the occupying forces was acceptable to the Chinese.

He congratulates his friend on his election to the Institute, ' where prehistory needed a representative '.

He expects to embark on 14 September for America, spend several weeks there, and then leave for France, where he should arrive at the beginning of November and stay until the summer.

(To J. T. de C.) *Pekin, 25 July, 1938*

Forgive my typing this letter—it's so hot and sticky that I don't want to use a pen. People are off on leave for sea bathing. The city is particularly empty just now. And, what's more, last week it suffered one of the worst downpours I've ever seen here. The principal streets were transformed into torrents and the rickshaws were steering their way with the water halfway up their wheels. Everywhere you could see, the mud walls and houses were collapsing.

On the 4th and 14th of July, the presence of Admiral Le Bigot was the occasion for magnificent celebrations. I saw the Admiral several times : a fine, heart-warming figure. At the moment it is very much France—for various reasons probably not of her government's seeking—that is gaining face in the Far East. The ancient spirit of dignity and independence automatically reappears in moments of crisis. The Admiral was the centre of a splendid and friendly collection of representatives from the diplomatic corps.

Pekin, 5 August, 1938

No news here. The monotony of one day after another is almost stupefying. [. . .] This enforced leisure has given me the opportunity to finish two palæontological memoranda, which I hope to have seen through the press by the time I embark about the middle of September. I took a great deal of trouble and even found the work interesting ; but I find it difficult not to smile when I see myself so absorbed in describing a fossil bone.

It's odd how in the course of one's life the light falls from different angles, and yet changes of angle are inevitable ; but it is always the same light, increasingly clear.

I am working steadily on the first chapter of *Man*, a page or two a day. For the last ten months I have been thinking about it a great deal and it seemed to me that plan and inspiration had reached maturity. So far I have come up against no ' fault ' as the structure develops.

Apart from all this, the date of my departure is getting closer, though I can still hardly believe it's true. I take the *Empress of Japan* from Kobe on 21 September, and go by America, so that I shall be in Paris in the first week of November.

Père Teilhard left Paris again for America in the ' Champlain' on his way back to China across the Pacific. He arrived in New York on 30 June. He describes his stay in New York to his brother; much of his time was spent in the Natural History Museum; he met Malvina Hofman, who modelled a bust of him;[1] *he had a quick look at the World Fair; stayed in Chicago with his friend Field; arrived in San Francisco, where a Geological Congress was being held at Berkeley, and met a great many friends again.*

(To J. T. de C.) *25 July, 1939*

A delightful reception at the Exhibition. It's much smaller than at New York but more compact and more of a fairyland : on an island in the bay, overshadowed by a vast façade, and in one corner you can see the startling snout-like noses of ' transpacific clippers '. I went on from Berkeley to Vancouver by train—a slow journey, two nights and a day—but magnificent landscapes of pine forests and great snow-capped volcanoes (the Cascades range), [. . .] and now once again I can see deep blue sea and flying fish. I am very conscious of how far, since 1923, my interests have been extended beyond the exotic externalities and crust of the earth. I'll send you my impressions as soon as I get to China. I hope you have a good holiday and that things don't blow up in Europe.

[1] Now in the Paris Museum of Modern Art.

1939-1946

As a result of the Second World War, Père Teilhard was to be stuck in Pekin for seven years. Against the background of his work at the Geological Survey, his scientific studies, and the completing of his book, ' The Phenomenon of Man ', can be seen his constant anxieties about France, and his friends and relations.

Pekin,
24 September, 1939

I arrived safely in Pekin on August 30th. There were some physical inconveniences towards the end (a night on the floor at Tangku and eight hours in a crowded boat from Tangku to Tientsin) ; but that is no more than any traveller must expect as things are at present. I didn't stop at Tientsin, wisely as it turned out, for I could only have gone to the Hautes Études[1] by boat (!), they'd have had some difficulty in putting me up (the house being full of refugees) and there was nothing I could have done. So force of circumstances brought me straight back to Shilhutung, our well-known house in north Pekin, where I was very well received.

The town, particularly the laboratories, is very empty. How-

[1] The Jesuit house of higher studies at Tientsin, where Père Teilhard had first lived before moving to Pekin.

ever, there are some people about, and I have more work in hand than I can deal with. [. . .]

Seen from here, the war has begun and is developing like something quite unreal. The declaration of war, in fact, made no appreciable difference for any of us, for hardly any are liable to be called up. Social relations in the town are still going on, with their odd international character. This war in Europe is only something one reads about in the papers, and it's quite impossible to get from them any real impression of what is happening. We feel quite out of touch ; even the advantage of being at a distance doesn't help much to see things in their true perspective. [. . .]

There must be something that I can and should do during this crisis. Is it just to go on with my work, like my Chinese friends ? My plans for the future are a blank. For the moment I can do no more than see to the running of the laboratory at Pekin (fortunately Pei is there). From time to time I expect I shall have to go to Tientsin, where the Museum has suffered some damage from the floods ; the director, too, may be called up in December. That's how it is : nothing very exciting, but this is hardly the time for anyone to complain.

I've had no news from France since September 4th : not surprising, but still rather distressing. Where are you ? and what can you do ? Help me to feel what is happening, and to bring it into my life.

(To J. T. de C.) *Pekin,*
24 September, 1939

I am sending you this letter on the off chance, for I can't be sure how or where it will reach you. Are you in Paris ? or called up ? [. . .] Here, apart from the official news, we are still quite in the dark about things in Europe, and it's very difficult to get the feel of what is happening. In any event, you may be sure that you—all of you—are seldom absent from my thoughts. At such a distance all these events seem to have something unreal about them, a sort of dream one can't understand. Just one of the countless inconveniences of being so far away.

[. . .] For the moment I'm carrying on with the routine work in the laboratory, where there's still quite a lot to do, and I have other things on hand to keep me busy. But what a humiliating position mine is, while your life—all your lives—is probably completely altered, and engulfed in the immediacy of the conflict. Am I missing my chance, this time ? On the other hand, had I been in France, what use could I have been ?

[. . .] Over here, the declaration of war has made hardly any noticeable impact. Japan is still neutral ; practically nobody has yet been called up ; international relations between members of the colony are hardly affected ; so that, to all outward appearances, life goes on in much the same way in our little Pekin oasis. This seclusion makes me wish I could appreciate better the atmosphere at home. In such circumstances it is not good to live in another world, particularly if it's that world that has the less vital existence.

I am naturally very eager for news of you and of Gabriel ; [1] but I can hardly expect to hear before the middle of October.

Be of good heart ; and God keep you all.

(To the Abbé Breuil)   *Pekin, 5 November, 1939*

How are things going with you, and how, do you imagine, with me ? I have left you too long without news, partly because I was waiting to get a better idea of what is going on, and partly in the mistaken hope of receiving news from France, which comes, in fact, with shocking slowness. We're worse off, in this matter,

---

[1] The elder of his two brothers.

than any other nationals. At this distance it is hard to get a clear picture of the way things are going or of the general feeling and conditions of life in France. All one gets is the impression that things are very different from 1914 and that both sides are rather holding back and fighting with some reluctance. Is that so ?

So the days go by. As things are, my plans for the future are rather in the air. Should I do better to go back to France ? On the one hand I wonder whether I am not cutting myself off from the real life of my generation by not taking part in what is going on ; on the other hand I cannot quite see what I could do in Europe. I'm too old for any active service. And I find it hard to work up any enthusiasm for this war, no doubt because I'm out of touch with the general atmosphere in Europe. I must wait till I can see things more clearly.

Pekin, 12 November, 1939

I have just had your letter of 16 September (it took 2 months to come!). At the moment your plans, I suppose, have been modified by the unexpected way things have turned out (in an American ' *cartoon* ' yesterday I saw it represented by two tortoises facing one another, each carefully withdrawn into its shell). So far everything is so different from what was foreseen—especially for us living here quite unable, in spite of all the radios in the world, to appreciate the real atmosphere of the conflict in Europe. No-one here, of any nationality, has yet been called up. We still carry on the same unreal existence, with hardly more than a few slight modifications (and those purely conventional) in international relations. The civil invasion of Pekin [1] continues without interruption under our eyes, and makes much more impact than the ' western front '. In fact what strikes one in this new war is

[1] By the Japanese.

248

a certain vagueness, and even a certain ambiguity, in the aims of both sides. [. . .]

Lost in this sort of mental uncertainty I still find plenty to do while waiting for something better. I am going ahead patiently with my essay on *Man* which may come at the right moment when people again have time and inclination to listen. I often fear that by taking no part in the happenings in France I may lose contact with the whole ' front ' of life in the West. Shouldn't we always position ourselves in the living heart of events ? But what could I do in Europe, ' *just now* ', that would be any more use than here, where I can help a fine thing [1] to survive ? Tell me, if you know the answer.

We are in the cold limpid beauty of early winter. Life is a little ' *dull* ' in this exactly ordered establishment here, where the rule of the house is unusually strict,[2] and I am too far from my laboratory. Raphael is back, and so is Bardac. We're gathering a circle of friends again. No news still of Gabriel or Joseph—or of the Bégouëns, and all our friends in Paris, in the *Études* or elsewhere. It's hard to bear this complete absence of news. Tell me how things are with you. Tell me too, I beg you again, whether you think I could do anything in France.

Tientsin, 3 December, 1939

I am writing to you just after finishing the retreat which I dutifully came here to make. Rather an austere time, but one feels the need of it more as one gets older in an increasingly disturbed world. Let us hope that this stock-taking may have brought me

---

[1] The scientific establishments at Pekin to which ne had contributed valuable assistance for more than twenty years.

[2] The Jesuit house, which was too far from the centre of Pekin. The conventual time-table did not fit in with his working hours in the laboratories at the Chinese University of which he was more or less in charge, nor with his social commitments.

back to the central axis, closer to the Unique, which increasingly seems to me to be the only Necessary.

A few days before leaving Pekin I at last received your letter of 30 October (by air mail), which had taken only three weeks to come. It's a pity that, from this end, the air route is so unreliable. At the moment I'm still as much in the dark about most of my friends as I was at the beginning of September ; I don't even know what's happening to Gabriel or Joseph—and Olivier! [1]

[. . .] I'm still wondering, of course, whether there's nothing better for me to do than, provisionally, to stay in China. But I still don't see the answer. If you have any ideas, do please help me to see my way. One thing is certain : we are advancing towards new situations which will call for new solutions and a new spirit. God grant that I may find the right thing to do and the right means to accomplish it.

(To J. T. de C.) *Pekin, 11 December, 1939*

Yesterday, to my great joy, I received your letter of 18 October (the last I wrote to you was dated in September). This is the first news I've had of the family since I left, and the first real news from home. It helps me to understand and appreciate the situation ; and for the first time, as I read your letter, I felt—as distinct from working it out in my mind—that I was missing something by not being in France during this great crisis ; for the situation in the Far East is still as paradoxical as it was on the very first day, for westerners exiled by the Pacific. Nobody has yet been called up ; and the disconcerting slowness of development in the war, combined with the vastness of scale, has the effect of giving events a deceptive air of unreality. People here —starting with the officials—end up by closing their eyes to the

---

[1] His nephew, his brother Joseph's son.

conflict in Europe, as to the Sino-Japanese 'incident'. And yet they are both things that really matter! As you already so wisely wrote in October, the great danger lies in the awakening of Russia. What happened in Finland—with Rumania perhaps still to come—fully bears out what you say. It is unlikely that the Russians will be content to go back to their pre-1914 boundaries, and I should be very much surprised if they were not as concerned to strengthen their position at Vladivostock, i.e. in Manchuria, as to consolidate on the Baltic. In that light, their understanding with the Japanese seems as precarious as that with the Germans. On any assumption, it is difficult to see any way out without a complete recasting of the whole existing international system. Some new solution will have to be found for the problem of world organisation, but that can hardly be envisaged without a common ideal. That is what makes the Russian schism fundamentally so formidable, combined with a certain excessive conservatism in England. You seem convinced that we shall not have to go through a phase of total war. If only changes in the present balance of power may spare us that extremity! I still have hopes ; and meanwhile I can understand how heavily the situation must weigh on you, and your anxiety for Olivier. God keep you!

[. . .] As I must have told you before, I'm too old now for my old job in the medical corps or for any active service ; so perhaps it's better to work, and conserve my energies for a greater effort when the post-war period comes—which will be another sort of war, in men's minds and hearts. The danger of staying here is that I risk losing contact with the *real* movement of humanity, like those who never knew the front in the 1914–18 war. From that point of view it might be well for me to go to the 'European front'. If you have any ideas about this, let me know.

[. . .] In the north, outside the towns, there is still no respite from the incessant guerilla activities. Here we have the dramatic spectacle of a systematic invasion : the Japanese mass pushing back the equally dense but less resistant Chinese mass. One plenum forcing its way into another. Pekin will soon be another Mukden. At Tientsin, where I went a fortnight ago to make my retreat, the blockade of the foreign concessions is becoming permanent, which is extremely trying. You can only get coal in small quantities. People queue for days to get through the barriers. Lorries have to be unloaded, cases of eggs emptied by the hundreds. It's all aimed at wearing down the English. You'll find a good account of the situation in an article on Tientsin which came out in *Études* at the end of September (or the beginning of October) under the name ' Maurice de Monchiennes '. Except that the blockade is described as ' moral ' rather than ' real '—which is inaccurate (the author left too early)—it's a completely true account, and will enable you to understand just what is going on. January is expected to bring the next turning-point, when the renewal of the Japanese–American trade treaty comes up.

(To the Abbé Breuil)   *Pekin, 16 December, 1939*

I hope you received my October letter safely. The posts are terribly slow at present. But this last month we have at last been beginning to receive some news. I hope that you're managing to get some work done in spite of the present state of affairs, or rather that you can make good use of enforced leisure.

There's no change in my routine here. And as it has turned out I have a great deal more to do than I can get through.

First of all, at the laboratory. Your essay is safely at the binders', and would already have been issued but for a mistake on the cover. Pei's essay on the Upper Cave (Archæology) is in the press, and also a new number of the *Bulletin*, devoted entirely to the palæontology of vertebrates : full of interest. And now I have started a new essay (site 18, Villafranchian). There must be still enough there for more than two years' work, at least. Let's hope that they're now going on again with the dig.

In the end we found that the floods at Tientsin had done a great deal of damage to many specimens (jaws of proboscidea, and antlers of cervidæ).[1] We hope to save the essentials, but this has not yet been done. And, with the shortage of coal, everything in the big galleries is frozen and uninhabitable. Here we have great schemes for rearranging and recasting the whole idea of the institution, but I shall have to wait till later to tell you about that. Finally, I am working every day at my book on Man, first sketched out in my mind two years ago. It makes steady progress and I think I can see its final shape. It is this, in fact, that occupies the greater part of my real activity and makes me feel too, in a way, that I am not abandoning the good cause by staying, provisionally, in China.

All these interests help me to pass days that otherwise would be pretty dismal. My remote position in the north of the town, the regularity of community life and the cold, all combine to make me give up any ' evening party ' ; I regret this a little for the sake of the influence I might exert and of the good cause, but it has some advantages too. A good nucleus of friends stay faithfully at their post. We often speak of you.

In such circumstances, my plans for the future are of the vaguest, depending largely on how the war develops here and in Europe, two problems that may well coalesce into one. I may perhaps make a trip to Yunnan this winter to renew my contacts. I might, I think, be able to do something to preserve continuity between my past and my future researches in China. After all it is a job like any other. I don't see what good I could

[1] At the Natural History Museum, Hwang ho pai ho.

do in France at the moment—except (which is indeed a consideration) take my part in the experience. Here there is still no-one called up on either side. Tell me what you think.

The last mails we have had are helping me to understand a little better how things are going in France and the state of people's minds. In the end, it is Russia that is becoming public enemy no. 1. According to a recent conversation I had with a person well placed to judge, the danger in that quarter would appear no longer to be Marxism and the Third International (which, but for the jargon, is completely dead) ; it is the formation of a national group, hostile, watertight, completely ignorant of what lies outside itself, and so incapable of being included in the far-reaching combination of mankind we need. I am rather frightened when I feel that I can read between the lines of Allied literature the objective of a dismembered Germany or of some sort of return to a pre-Napoleonic Europe. What we must envisage is something quite different. And I hope that the inexorable natural pressure of facts will automatically create what we cannot at this stage give expression to ourselves.

When you have the chance, give my most friendly greetings to Gaudefroy,[1] Le Roy [2] (where are his sons ?) etc. I feel terribly badly about not having written yet to Boule.

I have just heard from V. Koenigswald. He has just found in the deepest beds of the Trinil (again at Sangiran) a big fragment of the mandible of a large anthropoid (anterior pre-molar with two roots, but small canine) which he is inclined to link with the Australopithecus. But the description he gives is not full enough for me to form my own opinion about it. In any case it's an important find.

A happy new year, in spite of everything ; and God keep you.

[1] L'Abbé Gaudefroy, professor at the Institut Catholique in Paris.
[2] Édouard Le Roy, professor at the Collège de France.

Pekin, 25 January, 1940

As you see, and in spite of my prognostications, I am still writing to you from the cold of Pekin ; the reason being that, at the laboratory, there has been so marked a repugnance to my Yunnan journey that I have been obliged to put it off *sine die.* I am really very much put out, for the trip seemed to me just the thing to do, in the Lab's own interests. But I fear that for the present I can only give way.

So there is nothing really new to tell you about my existence here ; it goes on in the same routine, and with the same exemplary regularity.[1] I must admit that thought is the gainer up to a certain point, and the interior life too. In fact, particularly since my last retreat, I have a kind of feeling of being closer to Our Lord. It seems to me so simple, and so simplifying, to look for Him by 'communicating' with the becoming of things— their motions, their repressions, their rhythm, their personal soul and above all with Him. Thus I can get back a little more into the *milieu divin.* [. . .] This interior reinforcement means a great deal to me at a time when the course of events and probably increasing age are dimming for me life's radiance.

In this general monotony, the only variety comes from occasional gatherings of friends (on the 9th we copiously celebrated the seventieth birthday of my old friend Dr. Grabau, with me as the ' *toast-master* ' of the occasion!) and, more particularly, from the progress of various tasks which I have in hand. [. . .] On the other and most important side, I am just half-way through my new draft of *Man,* which means that my next chapter will deal with Man himself. What I have done, I think, represents by far the largest part, for the material to come falls into place of its own accord and along familiar lines that are already almost

---

[1] Referring to his ' monastery ' : see the letter of 3 December, 1939.

completely drawn. At the same time, it took me nearly six months to write the second part. There are still two (Thought and Survival). Anyway, page by page, the end will finally come in sight. I long so much to finish, and finish well!

Politically, things drag on here, even more perhaps than they do with you in the west. The Chinese question is not simply a matter of determining the frontiers and declaring peace, but of finding out how two hostile intermixed populations are going to reach a state of equilibrium. Here the invasion and consolidation continue all the time. At the same time food supplies for the people are very badly looked after in the towns ; in the country, where the organisation has broken down, it means unspeakable misery. And on top of all this, there's the cold. If there were a recorder of human suffering all over the face of the world (a very real conception, after all) what would we not have to read at this very moment!

Unable to receive any news of his friends: Max and Simone Bégouën, Père Teilhard tried to get a first letter through to them. Gradually they managed to establish a correspondence, at long intervals, until the beginning of 1941, when the mails ceased to arrive. At last a letter reached him.

(To Max and Simone Bégouën)   *Pekin, 8 February, 1940*

I cannot tell you the great joy your long Christmas letter gave me. It put me in living touch with all of you, and with France. All that you say has given me strength and life. And it is such a pleasure to read of your courage and energy. More particularly, your advising me provisionally to do what I am in fact doing makes me feel easier in my mind and able to think more clearly. In fact what could I do other than what physical necessity obliges me to do ? I should have told you that I was thinking of making a (very necessary) trip to Yunnan. I have had to give up this jaunt which would have renewed my contact with friends in the south and (what I am beginning to need badly) with field work. For various imperative internal reasons, I can't leave the laboratory just now. For some weeks I hesitated ; and then I had to accept the facts. So life is pretty monotonous in a general atmosphere of social impoverishment. My lot is much the same as that of people in France, except that there you must have the awareness of living in an organism which is defending itself and growing ; while here in Pekin (I can't speak for the south) we are living through an end—the end in particular of the old European influence. In this liquidation we have to try to discern the potentiality, the germ of the future. The most useful work I can do is to help in reshaping (and, it seems, in transferring here) the Licent foundation ; in its new form, it might well become an ' ark ' to preserve from the flood the materials and intellectual values that have been collected here in the north during the last twenty years. [. . .]

So I continue to follow the routine of my two laboratories [. . .] The continental geology of China is gradually being sketched in ; and *The Phenomenon of Man* progresses at the rate of a page or two a day. I am beyond the half-way mark in the draft. What its value will be I don't know. But I long so much to finish it properly. I feel that I have seldom worked so entirely for God alone. I am sure that He will give me the light and the strength to complete as it should be completed what I wish to say *only for Him*.

Apart from that, as I said before, there's nothing new. The end of January has gone by with its great cold, heavy with doom, made less disagreeable by a beautiful sky. Just two falls of snow, beautiful dry snow that disappears without bringing mud (though whether this is good for the fields is another matter).

It is the Chinese New Year today, whose celebration (as opposed to the solar new year) the new masters of the country are encouraging again, as part of their general policy that the more Chinese a Chinaman is the better. Here again it is basically a war of one mentality against another ; but in any case the fireworks go off, the children wave their red lanterns, and everyone guzzles as much as they can afford : splendid people, so appealing in the way they enjoy the little they have. How easy it would be to make them happy, at least to begin with.

There is little to look forward to except the coming of the fine weather. We would like to believe that spring will bring some sign of peace on our side of the world, but in fact the situation seems as hopelessly confused as ever. And then we tell ourselves that with orientals the most unexpected is not necessarily the most unlikely ; and we go on waiting.

(To the Abbé Breuil)   *Pekin, 16 February, 1940*

In your December letter to Pei you say that you haven't yet heard from me. I hope, judging by the time taken by a letter to Max which took two months to get to Paris, that the news I sent you (at about the same time, the end of October) will finally have reached you. We are not too sorry for ourselves : after all we are at war. [. . .] I am still in my monastery, to the north of Fujen,[1] very pleasantly settled now in my community but still rather lost geographically. I spend the mornings at Ping-Ma-Ssu[2] (though I have not been as faithful as I might during the recent great cold) ; the afternoons at Lockart Hall ; [3] and I end with a visit to Mrs. Hempel Gowan's, and tea at Lucile S's.[4] And then, muffled up against the half-hour rickshaw ride in the darkness, I

[1] Fujen, the large Catholic University founded by the American Benedictines in 1928.

[2] The street in which lay the palæontological laboratory where Père Teilhard was working.

[3] An offshoot of the Pekin Union Medical College.

[4] Lucile Swan, the American sculptor.

go up through the forbidden city again,[1] past Coal-Hill, lose myself in the paddy-fields and hutungs,[2] and finally get home to my little Chinese room. Out of consideration for the house I no longer even try to go out in the evening (I have done so only once since my return, for Grabau's seventieth birthday). I am basically well enough, both intellectually and spiritually ; but all the same I am anxious not to lose ground in influence and social contacts.

With peace and leisure I can of course work more methodically than I did in Paris. We have just brought out a number of the *Bulletin* entirely written (or re-written) by me, mainly palæontological, except for the last article on the Meso- or Neo-lithic, which will interest you. I am at the moment engaged on other papers and also in sketching out a more ambitious work : a continental geology of China ;[3] not to mention the book on Man, which takes up the greater part of my time and thoughts.

Combined with looking after the Cainozoic Lab [4] I have also on my hands the remodelling of the Licent Museum (don't say anything about it to him yet if you see him) which I may have already mentioned to you. It's all practically decided. Except for the public museum, which is provisionally left at Race Course Road everything here will be changed—for the time being in rented buildings (rather cramped), ultimately in buildings to be put up on a fine site close at hand. My idea is to see a new institution come into being on this new site : no longer just a museum, but a research centre in a very definite, though wide,

[1] The former palace of the Emperors of China, in the centre of the town.
[2] Chinese for the alleyways characteristic of the town of Pekin.
[3] Among the purely scientific works Père Teilhard was to write during this period we may mention : *Early Man in China* (1941), *Chinese fossil mammals* (1942), *Le Néolithique de la Chine* (1944), *Les Félidés de Chine* (1945), *Les Mustélidés de Chine* (1945), not to mention numerous reports in the *Bulletin of the Geological Survey of China*.
[4] The name given by American geologists to the period covering the end of the Tertiary and beginning of the Quaternary periods.

field. This calls for a specialised team : shall we be able to organise it ? I have hopes, but it is not easy ; the more so as I am careful not to form part of the working staff ; I ask nothing better than to inspire its work, but it must be able to function without me. However things turn out, the spring will probably see us installed in new premises, which will be the end incidentally of my monastic life. After that, shall I be going back to Paris ? My return cannot be delayed for very long. But what plans can one make with this war ?

On the whole I am fairly well. But since I got back I often have to fight against a slight depression, mostly nervous, I think. It makes one live by finding more room for, giving more reality to, God—which is a good thing.

Pekin, 7 March, 1940

Not much news from France for some time ; except for two nice letters from Joseph and Gabriel. The latter, I think, would be better at home in his own part of the country than flying barrage balloons round Tours.[1] I am surprised to see how many men of his age, or even younger, are just carrying on with their peace-time jobs. Who is in the war, then, except the youngsters ? [. . .] Here, in the east, the conflict drags on interminably ; and the propaganda, combined with the censorship, is so shameless that it's practically impossible to find out just what is going on. Meanwhile we are still in a state of being invaded, and the invader is a leech whose only function so far seems to be to suck the country dry. The result is a monetary and food crisis which is now beginning to become alarming. Everything is upside down, even the Yellow River, which is apparently refusing to return to its own bed and threatens to make its way to join the Yangtse, at the risk of silting up Shanghai. As usual foreigners

[1] Père Teilhard's brother had been called up in the balloon service.

have so far been spectators rather than victims of the state of affairs. Even so, for the Tientsin ' *businessmen* ', who are under a continual blockade, the situation must soon become intolerable.

But with all these troubles spring is beginning its imperturbable advance, the cold has gone, though the skies have not lightened, and we expect soon to see the first peach trees in flower. Ten days ago, I went for a picnic with some American friends to one of the temples which are still accessible in the hills to the west. Everything was enchantingly grey in the pure light. Eating mutton grilled in the Mongol fashion, I thought how agreeable it would be to take my hammer and get about the place as I used to in the good old days. But when will that be possible again ?

[. . .] *Man* continues its more or less unhurried progress—but still, it progresses. By Easter, I don't doubt, I shall be not far from three-quarters of the way through ; and the further I go now, the more I find a field already prepared and worked out, in which progress is easy. At the same time the whole interest and point of the book is concentrated towards the end, which must be particularly lucid and carefully done. I hope that the Lord will help me, since it is entirely as an attempt to make His countenance seen and loved that I am taking such pains, which sometimes I could well be spared.

In the next letter Père Teilhard explains to his brother the transfer of the Museum from Tientsin to Pekin.

(To J. T. de C.)   *Pekin, 6 May, 1940*

My scheme is to build up a real continental research centre, less cumbersome and more active.[1] At the moment it's something of a gamble ; provisionally, we are moving into a building let to the army, right in the Legation grounds, 3 rue Labrousse. Immediately facing it is a big empty site, rented for a song by the

[1] In comparison with the Tientsin Museum.

Embassy, where it will be a matter of building as quickly as possible ; and that's the snag, with the fantastic cost of materials and the fall of the piastre.[1]

Theoretically it is no concern of mine, since I don't officially belong to the '*staff*' of the institute, but in fact I bear most of the responsibility.

And all this in a horribly oppressive political atmosphere. It's quite clear that the situation between east and west is hardening more and more. The whole sky is clouding over, and it is difficult to see how any country, including America, can fail to be overtaken by the storm before the weather clears [. . .] But in the end we may not perhaps be sorry that fate should have brought us into existence at this particular moment when there is so great a duty to forget self, and give.

(To Max and Simone Bégouën)   *Pekin, 9 May, 1940*

If I have not sent an earlier answer to Max's long and treasured letter of 4 March, it is because I have been thinking of you as being in Morocco, and rejoicing at this rest and relaxation for both of you. I hope I haven't waited too long and that this letter won't seem to you to be too slow in coming. [. . .]

You must send me your news after your journey. My brother Joseph in Paris is lamenting having to run his factories at Rouen and the estate and everything, with a skeleton staff. I wonder how la Capp[2] is managing. Here, I have been continuing all the time with exactly the same life. It is a long time since I have had such a regular and unruffled existence. So much so that I begin to wonder where I shall ever again be able to live otherwise. Everything is going on normally. And now my

---

[1] The Embassy and the Foreign Office were giving Père Teilhard's projects their backing.
[2] The venture in Morocco, directed by M. Bégouën.

book has an excellent chance of being finished before July. In fact, since I'm just up to the last half-chapter, I almost feel that I've finished it. But when I really have put in the last full stop, then I shall indeed feel that a weight has been lifted from me. It has given me some bad moments, this winter. I rather wonder what effect it will have if it ever gets published—as I hope it will. I shall have the pure scientists against me as well as the experts in pure metaphysics ; but as I shall say in my conclusion, I do not see what else you could say if once you try to work out to its conclusion a coherent place for man in this universe of ours. [. . .]

I imagine you must at last have received my short notes on the war (*L'Heure de choisir*).[1] Just in case, I am sending you another copy (a better text than the other, in fact, and to be preferred should there be any question of a choice). A copy of *Études* arrived just after d'Ouince's [2] regretted departure. Père Jalabert has given me his own reaction—very favourable. But so far, nothing has come out, I don't know why. As it happens, the latest war developments only strengthen me in my opinion, which must seem the obvious one to all.

Against us stands a religion of plain, brute force ; and on our own side, there does not always seem to be a sufficiently clear vision of the ideal we are seeking to vindicate. A force of conservation against a force of conquest : it is an unequal struggle.

With the affairs of his friends, news of whom reached him only after a considerable delay, always in his mind, Père Teilhard wrote to me about an illness whose seriousness had been magnified in his eyes by distance.

---

[1] A plan for an article in the review *Études*, in Paris.
[2] Père d'Ouince, editor of *Études*, had been called up.

Pekin, 9 May, 1940

I do hope that you are easier in your mind and really feeling better. ' This is the last straw ', one might be tempted to say, if one did not cling to what is, what must be true. In any case you must have had some bad moments ; but are not such moments necessary to accustom us to that gesture, essential not only in death but in life, which consists in allowing ourselves to rest, as upon an invisible support, on Him who sustains and upholds us right outside all the tangible things to which we feel so strong an instinct to cling. It is undoubtedly by becoming accustomed in this way that we shall finally be released from speculation and give to God—as the saints do—His true value of reality. I do not feel very strong or very proud of myself. I am sure in the end it is Guiguite who was right, when she prayed for the grievously sick that they might be able to renounce everything, even the satisfaction of feeling capable of having sufficient trust. But this renunciation being itself an excess of trust. [. . .]

Pekin, 12 July, 1940

Where are you ? What are you up to ? How are you ? I have had no news of you since Easter. And then came the cataclysm which we have followed from a distance without being able to understand it. And now the Vichy ' government ' (!) which we understand still less. Things are evidently moving fast at this very moment and seen from a distance they look ugly for France. Unless, of course, we are misunderstanding the position. [. . .]

The latest developments must have caused many to lose faith in a Providence which failed to meet the expectations of an elect people. I think that they may more reasonably serve to force us out of our petty dimensions, our petty egoism, and throw us back on the ocean of the Unique Necessary.

Père Teilhard then explains that work is going on in the setting of the new geo-biological institute recently established in the European legation quarter of Pekin, ' a really pleasant, warm setting. A new feeling of having a home of one's own and of not being able to go out without running into friends on the pavement.' His friend, Père Leroy, who was also his assistant at the laboratory, was sharing his studious life—eased now by his freer relations with university circles and diplomatic society in Pekin. In this group Père Teilhard was exercising a powerful moral influence and felt himself to be in a wholly sympathetic atmosphere.

There was a considerable time-lag, after the German invasion, before news came from France.

(To J. T. de C.) *Pekin, 26 July, 1940*

Where are you, and what are you up to ? I am told that the Siberian mail with France is still working—in this direction at least. At any rate, I am taking a chance.

Out here in the Far East it is absolutely impossible to appreciate what has happened, and still less what is now happening, in France. All these events, which we know only from propaganda news services, have overwhelmed us like an inexplicable avalanche. I fervently hope that your morale stands firm, and I pray that you are able to find the right line to follow or encourage. I refrain, of course, from any judgment, but I am anxious to know on what elements of reconstruction one can count. We are obviously no more than half-way yet in the development of the crisis.

Try to get some definite news through to me. No-one here knows anything or has had any letter since the armistice. And I fear that the silence may not be broken.

I still wonder what useful purpose I could serve at this moment. There must be something to do. [. . .] I am just going to send a line to Gabriel. God keep you.

Pekin, 3 September, 1940

My letter of 12 July just crossed yours written from Pau (or thereabouts) at the end of May. Yesterday I had a letter from Gabriel sent from Tours on the 16 June : and that's all I know since the collapse [. . .] At this distance there are some things we can see more clearly than you can in France, but there are many others which we cannot understand at all. So I shall refrain from expressing any judgments that might be imprudent on more grounds than one : except that one would give a great deal to feel that there was at home anything resembling a real spirit or driving force!

I still feel sure that a flame is blazing up without our being able to see it from here.

No news here. These weeks, which have brought to an end or scarred for ever the lives of so many Frenchmen, have passed in an oppressive but calm atmosphere—constant uncertainty that ends by becoming a habit. You get accustomed to waiting, to knowing nothing and to foreseeing nothing of the future.

(To Max and Simone Bégouën)   *Pekin, 20 September, 1940*

Have you had my letter of 28 July ? I very much fear that you have not. For my part, I am beginning to receive some news of my family, still intact and together in Auvergne—but fragmentary news. Everyone seems to know only just what is happening in his immediate circle. And I have no information about many dear friends—you, Ida, the *Études* people, Breuil

etc. I am most anxious to know, first of all for their sakes and
secondly in order to sketch out plans for reconstruction. I know
that at your end you are doing all you can to get through to me.
Where are you ? And how are things at Bréhat [1] itself ?

Of one thing I am certain : that you are reacting with all
your strength to the defeat and are trying to find a way that will
lead to a renaissance which will not be a bourgeois 'Restoration'.
From this distance, it is the spectre of such a 'Restoration' that
most disturbs me. Vichy's copy-book maxims for good children
seem to me entirely to lack the fire which alone can bring out
the virtues so rightly advocated.

I hold on to the firm hope that in the end the word we are
waiting for will be found and that we shall finally achieve not
a reaction but a creation. A year ago there were in France
too many seeds of good for a return to Christianity not to
mean ultimately a resurgence of an expanding and progressive
humanity. Otherwise it is Marxist materialism that lies in wait
for us.

What I sadly miss here is being in the ' atmosphere ' of France.
I can well understand now what happens to émigrés ; you jump
the points and get on the wrong track. Do what you can to
keep me on the right one. The only advantage of being so far
away is that there are some things, external to France, which we
can see better than you can. And from this point of view it
seems to me that your press is ridiculously petty (or servile)
in its anti-English attitude. It is not by arousing further
antipathies that we'll bring about any improvement in the
West. [. . .]

The epoch of this war has gone for good, like that of peace
conceived as a repose. Peace is not the opposite of war. It is
war carried above and beyond itself in the conquest of the

---

[1] The island of Bréhat, in which his friends might have been cut off by the
German invasion.

trans-human.[1] Always the same solution, so simple, so radically dependent on synthesis, for the problems that ravage us.

In an article which, by a striking coincidence, appeared on the eve of war (in ' Études', 5 July 1939) Père Teilhard examined ' Les Unités humaines naturelles, Essai d'une biologie et d'une morale des races'. He showed that the complementary character of biology and moral culture called for a synthesis of the two in the light of the common future of humanity. And this conclusion was a reversal, in the ' human kingdom' of the law of vital competition.

' As a palæontologist I cannot preserve any illusion about the fact and the inexorable forms of biological competition. But, in the same capacity, I absolutely reject a crude transference of the mechanical laws of selection to the domain of man. For if nature teaches us plainly that there is a universal struggle for life, she teaches us no less categorically that in passing from one level of existence to another living properties can subsist only by being transformed or transposed. Mutual exploitation and destruction may be the necessary condition between infra-human groups since they live by continually supplanting one another and breaking away from one another. The case of the human 'bundle' is quite opposite. If, following our theory,[2] it can progress only by converging, hostile competition must be replaced within man by a brotherly emulation, and war becomes meaningless except in relation to dangers and conquests external to mankind as a whole.'' [3]

---

[1] A higher state of humanity, which it will reach if it makes effective use of all the material, moral and spiritual forces it will develop. There is no notion, it should be noted, of automatic progress. The ascent depends on human wills working together in harmony in a common effort.

[2] Cf. *La Convergence humaine.*

[3] Cf. *La Vision du passé*, ch. 14.

Pekin, 18 October, 1940

I have just received your letter of 14 August (the still longer one of 20 August has also reached me). Thank you for helping me to get my bearings in the atmosphere of things in France, so difficult to understand at a distance. On the Vichy side, such discretion is rather astonishing and one would like to be sure that their conversion has its roots in the people—and still more to feel that there is some fire beneath the discretion, a will to march forward into something new beneath the repentance. But that, no doubt, is too much to expect immediately, while the country is still dazed and split in two. Shall we in the end see the figure emerge and hear the word that we have been waiting for so long ? I hope so. Never, perhaps, for two thousand years has the earth had greater need for a new faith or been more released from older forms to receive it. [. . .] Christianity must show itself, with all its resources for renewal, now or never : God, the Christ, presenting Himself as the focus of salvation—not simply individual and ' super-natural ' salvation, but collective and earth-embracing too ; and a new concept, consequently, of charity (incorporating and preserving the sense of the earth) ; and all this summed up and made concrete in the figure of the universal Christ.[1] I see no other issue to the problems and aspirations of the moment, and I shall never tire of saying or trying to say so. An odd situation ; on all sides the battle rages unchecked ; but the closer you look at it, if you get back to the source of the conflict, the more clearly you realise that the root of the evil is not in the apparent conflicts but very far away from them, it seems, in the inner fact that men have despaired of God's personality![2]

[1] Père Teilhard had a deep and ardent faith in the risen Christ, the universal Christ, in whom, as St. Paul teaches, all things have their being.

[2] A surprising remark at first reading. In more than one passage Père Teilhard has expressed the concept that the world has a centre, and men fight

Here the same routine, pleasant enough, continues in our new house. But now things seem to be deteriorating in the Pacific. On the whole, people here don't anticipate a conflict with America, and they are wondering whether the Americans will really evacuate China—which they certainly don't want to do! [. . .] Apart from occasional news, we know nothing about France. Nothing about the Bégouëns, and nothing about so many others. Père d'Ouince is a prisoner, which dismays me. Where are the others ?

(To J. T. de C.) *Pekin, 30 October, 1940*

I have only just, but to my great joy, received your letter of 27 July (I wrote to you on the 26th of the same month). I already knew, through Camille,[1] that you had moved your offices to Lezoux![2] There won't be much that we haven't seen, when this war's over. [. . .] Over here it gives me a very odd feeling to read in the papers 'Transocean' dispatches (which are German) or 'Domei' (Japanese) dated from Vichy or Clermont. What a frightful ' *mess* ', as the English would say. [. . .]

On top of the domestic news you give me, I greatly appreciated your note on events in France. The most irksome part here is perhaps not so much the feeling that you are half without a country of your own, as the inability to feel the atmosphere in France. In the Anglo-Saxon circles which have become my second home, and for which I have an unfailing sympathy, it is

one another because they have not yet learnt to recognise in a personal God a love which brings them together in that centre.
    [1] Mlle de Guyadet, a friend of the T. de C. family, who was living in Shanghai.
    [2] A little town in Auvergne, near Clermont, and not far from Joseph Teilhard's property.

especially painful to me to ' swallow ' some of Vichy's attitudes. The more I have always been since 1920 an advocate of a friendly understanding with Germany, the more repugnant to me now is a forced understanding which would entail a sort of betrayal of our real friends. I try to suspend my judgment, since here, I repeat, we have no idea what is really going on in the country. My general impression is that the game is reaching a position of stalemate.

[. . .] Here we are in a state of American–Japanese tension. ' *By order* ' a number of American women and children will be leaving China during the next month. We would like to believe that this is only an administrative measure and that it won't go any further. But it is obvious that the United States wishes to feel its hands completely free if anything should happen at Singapore or Java. Those who are leaving are resigning themselves rather regretfully, and their going will cost me some very good friends. On the other hand the French Embassy is coming back in force, with all its archives.

Pekin, 20 November, 1940

Weeks have gone by and at this distance we are a little sceptical about the reality and depth of the much-advertised changes in the French conscience. This fine discretion still seems to me a sort of top-dressing, and I think that the real soul of tomorrow (in which I have faith) has not yet begun to show itself. In any case it is not a Restoration that we want but a Renaissance—not discretion but a passionate faith in some future. But can we even talk about it so long as there is no peace ?

My own life goes on the same. I am writing various articles, and in particular I am trying to push further my views on ' Noogenesis '. I used to wonder whether my book was not bringing me to the end of what I could see or had the power to say. But now I feel differently, that I can see more clearly, more to the centre, and to a greater distance.[1]

The American evacuation has deprived me of many friends, but we still have a pleasant little circle ; and the personnel of the French Embassy is getting back to strength. M. de Margerie has arrived, but at Shanghai. Last Sunday I was able to crack some stones in the Western Hills [2]—my first experience of ' research on the field ' since Burma.

Keep me posted, my dear friend, and help me to think with France.

Pekin, 11 December, 1940

Your letter of July 6 reached me yesterday! A long time, but everything seems to come in the end. News here is sparse and infrequent. Gabriel wrote me a nice long letter but, now, what worries me most is occupied France (the Bégouëns, Breuil, all my Paris friends . . .) : not a line from them though I have written all over the place.

As for my own concerns, life is still unchanged, somewhat monotonous, but scandalously easy. [. . .] I wrote to Rome ten days ago, to the Vicar-General [3] about my book and its revision. At the same time I told him of my desire to take part in the conference in New York in September 1941 when scientists, philosophers and theologians will meet again in an attempt to reach a common understanding on the foundations of a human credo safeguarding the liberty of the person (and the value of the personal). The first conference (last September), of which I

---

[1] When Père Teilhard came to write *Le Groupe zoologique humain* and later *Les Singularités de l'espèce humaine*, he thought he had achieved a higher degree of precision and a greater richness of expression in his vision of things. Cf. *L'Apparition de l'homme* (1956) and *La Vision du passé* (1957).

[2] Hills to the west of Pekin.

[3] Of his Order.

heard only recently, included seven Nobel prize winners and many other eminent people (at least one Jesuit whom I know). I would like at least to send a paper. Perhaps Rome [1] will let me go in person. [. . .]

' Besides ', the weather is marvellous. The Pekin community has been greatly depleted by the recall of a large number of American women, chiefly wives of American diplomats or servicemen. In this exodus I have lost several very good friends. To make up, the French Embassy has moved in again in a big way. M. de Margerie is still in Shanghai but his wife is coming to spend the New Year here. Paradoxically, in fact, it is France that diplomatically speaking is best represented in China at the moment.

Give me your impressions of what is happening in France—deep down—in people's minds. Looking at it from a distance the danger would seem to lie in failing to distinguish between Renaissance and Restoration : a danger that I hope will be avoided. Everything now depends upon the Anglo-Saxon peoples. This will be England's greatest day. Poor us! [. . .]

Being unable to go to New York as he wished, Père Teilhard drew up a memorandum from which the following is an extract :

'The sense of the Earth, as it unfolds and bursts open upward in the direction of God ; and the sense of God as He thrusts his roots downward in the direction of Earth, and nourishes Himself from below : God, the transcendent personal, and the universe in evolution together forming no longer two antagonistic centres of attraction, but entering into a hierarchical union to raise up the human mass on the crest of a single tide. Such is the astounding transformation which the idea of a spiritual evolution of the universe entitles us to expect in logic, and which is beginning in fact to

[1] For Père Teilhard this means the Jesuit authorities in Rome.

operate on an increasing number of minds, free-thinkers as much as believers. [. . .]

'*In spite of the wave of scepticism which seems to have swept away the hopes—too naïve and materialistic, no doubt—on which the nineteenth century lived, faith in the future is by no means dead in our hearts. But more than that, it is this hope, deepened and purified, that seems destined to be our salvation. Not only, indeed, does it become clearer every day that the idea of a possible awakening of our consciousness to some sort of super-consciousness is well founded on scientific experience, and psychologically necessary if man is to retain his taste for action; but further, this idea pushed to its logical conclusion seems the only one which can pave the way for the great event we await—the discovery of a synthesised act of adoration, in which a passionate desire to conquer the world, and a passionate desire to unite ourselves with God, will join hands and raise one another to the heights. So the vital act, specifically new, will correspond to a new terrestrial age.* [. . .]' (*Sur les bases possibles d'un credo humain. Notes on the recent New York Congress on Science and Religion, 1941. Published in 'L'Avenir de l'homme', 1959.*)

(To J. T. de C.)   *Pekin, 13 December, 1940*

Air mail with ' unoccupied ' France seems to travel slowly but normally. Nothing, on the other hand, seems to get through from occupied France and I am still in the dark about a great many of my friends.

In these conditions, my life has been unchanged since the summer. My days are spent in the same routine. I write notes and papers which we manage to print. On Sundays I go to the Western Hills in a friend's car and am beginning to do a little geological work again.[1]

---

[1] He adds, however, at the end of the letter, ' I have just come on a visit

In the last month I have given three lectures here in very different circles (the Women's Association College, the Protestant Theological Society, Yenching University)—a new experience for me.

If the Pacific is not engulfed in the war, I am wondering whether America may not see me before France. I don't see how I can get back to France nor what to do at the moment. But all this is extremely uncertain and depends entirely on the Anglo-German duel. From here we can feel the external developments of the struggle better, probably, than you can. But it is impossible to form a correct idea of the real atmosphere in France and Europe.

A relative calm still prevails here, troubled only locally by police restrictions at the city gates. It's very difficult to foresee whether the storm will break between Japan and America. Everything will depend on how things turn out in the Mediterranean. We expect some development in Saigon, however.

(To Max and Simone Bégouën)   *Pekin, 11 January, 1941*

What a joy it was the day before yesterday to receive at last your letter of 12 October, which reassured me of your health and spirits. I was sure that you would not weaken. But it has heartened me greatly to have from you the assurance that the fire is not dead but getting ready to burst into flame with greater life and freedom than ever. My own most constant preoccupation at the moment is where to go, and what to do so as best to defend and reawaken faith in the future. It seems obvious to me that the moment has come when mankind is going to be divided (or will have to make the choice) between faith and non-faith in the earth's collective spiritual progress. It's the human front we have

---

to Chou-Kou-Tien, travelling with a strong protective screen of Japanese soldiers. I am here with Captain Takata.'

so often discussed. That is why I feel resolutely determined to devote myself by all possible means to the defence of the idea of the reality of a progress (collective and personalising)[1] against every secular or religious pessimism. It is on this elementary credo that from the four quarters of the earth the ' soldiers of Gideon ' must take their stand together. The objective is simple, clear, perceptible to all minds, passionately contended for.

Inevitably, my plans for the future are still uncertain ; if field work remains impossible, I am attracted by the idea of a visit to America in the coming autumn. While continuing my scientific work, I could make contact there with western thought : I should be within range of France, though I would instinctively hesitate to return there for fear of falling into some trap. I would welcome your advice about that.

Everything seems to be going as well as can be expected with my family, but I have no news of very many friends in occupied France. The last I heard, d'Ouince was in a prisoner of war camp near Baccarat. With such a mass of prisoners, what energy must be running to waste in captivity—unless, of course, it is building up for tomorrow.

Pekin, 12 January, 1941

Your letter of 7 December came the day before yesterday, only a few days after that of 14 October, and taking a little longer than that of 11 November. So nothing gets lost and the Swiss route (Trans-Siberian) is much the shortest (German censorship, of course). It is only through you that I can share a little in what is happening in France.

In this quiet observatory of Pekin I turn over in my mind, as best I can, all the news that comes to us almost impartially. And

---

[1] Cf. the idea frequently expressed by Père Teilhard that ' union personalises '.

everything strengthens my conviction that the future can be forced and led only by a group of men united by a common faith in the spiritual future of the earth. ' Get behind me,' I would make bold to say, ' all Godless pessimists *and* all Christian pessimists.' We must take up again, on a sounder scientific basis and as a more exact philosophical concept, the idea (or, if you prefer it, the ' myth ') of progress. This is the essential setting in which I see the simultaneous rebirth of humanism and Christianity. After many years of thought it seems to me that I have now the scientific, philosophic, and religious equipment to attack this fiercely contested strong-point : the one vital strategic point standing at the fork which commands the whole future of the Noosphere.[1] I feel that at the age of sixty, I have at last found or pinned down my true vocation. Now the question is to find the right platform, the right significant act. You know that, mistakenly perhaps, I do not like to force events. May the Lord help me not to fail the opportunity when it is offered me.

(To J. T. de C.)   *Pekin, Institute of Geo-biology, 20 January, 1941*

[. . .] The situation is still unchanged. The clouds are thickening over the Pacific. In China itself things are still at the same apparent degree of confusion ; the conquered still obstinately evade any real domination or noticeable assimilation by the conquerors. The latter are not so much a leaven in the country as a vast blood-sucking leech. On the whole Pekin continues to appear as a privileged islet on which disturbances are reduced to a minimum, and where we (we foreigners, that is) live in an enclosed microcosm. The only advantage of our position is that it makes a good ' thinking-den ' and observation post. Propaganda from various quarters reaches us with almost complete

[1] The ' thinking ' layer or sphere of the earth (from *nous*, mind). See *The Phenomenon of Man.*

impartiality. The different belligerents continue to be represented here, and my position allows me to maintain friendly relations with the greater number of them. In this oasis of tranquillity I continue, for want of anything better, to draw up memoranda, and more particularly to organise a synthesis of the detailed results I have managed to collect in the last twenty years.

I am giving even more urgency to my attempt at clarifying the scientific and religious lines of thought at which I have been working so long. There will be no real peace, I am sure, until men share a common understanding, at least as a first approximation, on what we should expect and hope for from the world's future.

I feel rather ashamed of my own existence when I think of yours. I hope that you—and Marguerite [1] too—can at least feel that you are paying the price of something fine to come : that, I think, is a belief to which we must cling passionately.

The situation in Pekin had never been more fluid. The new Geo-biological Institute depended entirely on Père Teilhard and Père Leroy, but the future of such institutions in the China of tomorrow was quite uncertain. The rue Labrousse might turn out to be no more than a ' temporary billet '.

Never, says Père Teilhard in the next letter (17 February), had correspondence seemed so slow and infrequent. On the other hand there was a feeling in Pekin that this was ' the end of every-thing '. The Americans were leaving in increasing numbers, and the Cainozoic Laboratory, which was his real reason for being in China and had kept him going for the last twelve years, was threatened with closure.

On 3 March he gave a lecture at the invitation of the French Embassy on ' The Future of Man, as seen by a palæontologist '. He was very busy, too, with various papers in which he was

[1] His sister-in-law, widow of his brother Victor who had died in 1934.

collecting and organising the results obtained since 1920 in the search for a better knowledge of the geology and palæontology of China. But he found it a great drawback to be barred from field-work. He still managed, however, to go out in a friend's car every Sunday and do some practical petrology.

Pekin, 18 March, 1941

It is some weeks since l wrote to you or had a letter from you. The last I received, a fortnight ago, was from Joseph, posted at Limoges and dated 17 October.

No change here, except that the clouds are still gathering over the Pacific. That we should have war there this spring seems to me unlikely, but it was easy to feel the same in Europe in the spring of 1939. Meanwhile the Americans, especially the women, are leaving China one after the other. Pekin—the foreigner's Pekin, I mean—is becoming more and more like a village, for the Japanese tide still rolls over us, and very unpleasant it is too. Without the French diplomatic contingent it would be practically a wilderness.

A diplomat's wife,[1] one of the little French colony at Pekin, has spoken of Père Teilhard's influence on his companions, through his friendship, counsel and example, during those difficult days.

' Every one of our little group admired him, and many, of whom I was one, venerated him. What wonderful Sundays we spent picnicking in the hills and little deserted temples on the outskirts of Pekin! In the course of those long walks Père Teilhard would use the hammer which he never forgot to carry to break fragments of rock and check by observation the estimates he had already made of the age of local rock-formations and strata. He

[1] Laure Dorget, in the Teilhard de Chardin memorial issue of *La Table Ronde*, June, 1956.

would go back three million years in time and, talking away, would pass freely from the field of pure science to the most daring abstract speculations.

'It was a difficult time for all of us, and I owe to him my own spiritual and moral relief. He kept alive in me the flame of hope and faith in real values, he freed me from the petty conventions that teem in a confined and self-contained community.

'The loftiness of his thought raised him constantly to levels where few could follow him [. . .] Sometimes his attitude might seem surprising, but when you knew him well, you realised with absolute certainty that he was not in fact either indifferent or blind to the troubles of mankind and, above all, that he never applied a false scale of values. It was simply the uniqueness of the point of view of a man whose emancipated mind has reached the peak of the great evolutionary process in which he felt that we were all inescapably caught up. Human frailties? Maybe, but in them there is a grandeur, a divine spark, and this he could always discern. What faith there was in him, and what goodness!'

(To his brothers Gabriel and Joseph)   *Pekin, 20 March, 1941*

[. . .] Not much to tell you about my life here. In a Pekin which foreigners are leaving one after another—the Americans, at least, who make up the real core of the colony—and where everything is still being swamped in a by no means agreeable tide of conquest, life becomes more and more slowed down. All activities wait upon the question whether there will or will not be war in the Pacific, and everyone's answer to that depends on his mental make-up. Paradoxically, and particularly since our inevitable capitulation in Indo-China, we French are in a humiliating but relatively secure position. All the same, we don't feel very proud in the presence of the Anglo-Saxons.

[. . .] In this rarefied atmosphere I am continuing to collect the scattered fragments of various scientific institutions, and to prepare matter for publication (one of my papers came out in January). For want of anything better I have also resumed geological work in the Western Hills where (surprisingly) I have found a number of interesting problems in just the limited area which one can visit for a Sunday picnic with friends. These Sunday expeditions have become quite an institution, and it makes me feel young again to do some field-work once a week.

Apart from that (not to say ' most of all ') I am still trying to clarify a number of my more cherished ideas. The manuscript of my book finally went off to Rome a fortnight ago.

[. . .] As it turns out, I am not going to be allowed to go to the New York Congress of which I must have told you (on the relation between Science and Religion) ; but there is no objection to my contributing a paper.

[. . .] Meanwhile, the whole weight of the present lies on shoulders such as yours, people who are keeping things running from day to day. I could easily feel ashamed of myself : but what could I do in France at the moment, even supposing that I could manage to get back ? I am giving myself until the autumn to make up my mind. The situation will then, perhaps, be clearer. A stay in America, within easier reach of Europe than here, would seem to me to be the right answer. But what sort of state will the Atlantic and the Pacific be in in three months' time ?

(To his brothers Gabriel and Joseph)   *Pekin, 5 May, 1941*

My last letter was as long ago as 20 March ! It is high time for me to send you some news ; but it's rather difficult in fact, either because it's hard to put into words, or because there is nothing to say. With the whole world upside down, life here is paradoxically stable apart from a pronounced awareness of a slow transformation gradually modifying the situation and increasing the pressure of events, though you can't quite put your finger on its significance. It's a progressive rise in the surge of totalitarianism in the centre of which the individual and the westerner are gradually losing their footing. As I have told you before, I expect, I am following this dramatic struggle with intense curiosity—as though I were looking down on the earth from Sirius (a luxury we can still treat ourselves to here!). It's the struggle I have so clearly seen coming, between an inevitable collectivisation of the earth,[1] and the values of personalisation which must—again inevitably—emerge and gain stature on their side. I am confident that the solution will be found and that the Church will be able to intervene at the right moment to animate and christen the necessary transformations. But how long will it be before that happens ?

[. . .] We're now in full spring. The pink of the apricot and peach trees, then the white of the apple trees, have gone like a dream, scattered by the dusty wind. Once or twice a week I have still been going to the Western Hills to do some field-work. The day before yesterday we even went as far as the ' Ming tombs ', a famous site which no-one has dared to visit since 1937 but which now seems fairly quiet. I hadn't been back there since an excursion with the Abbé Breuil in 1935. But my companions were insufficiently active, the sand-laden wind too strong, and the sites too unsafe for me to be able to geologise at ease.

And the future is still undecided. If any decision is taken I shall of course let you know.

May heaven help you and bless you all ; every affectionate message to Sarcenat ; I don't forget it in spite of my unforgivable silence.

---

[1] Humanity, Père Teilhard believed, is moving inevitably towards some sort of unification. This was not a sociological, and still less a political, doctrine, but the view of a biologist and philosopher, equally alive to the necessity of preserving the value and the rights of the individual.

Pekin, 19 May, 1941

Vichy's attitude is becoming harder and harder to understand from here—or, rather, we feel that we understand it only too well. The irritating thing for me—intellectually speaking—is that in all this business I can't manage to ' *make up my mind* '. Impulsively speaking, as you may imagine, I am thinking as all Frenchmen now abroad are thinking. But what good is impulse in such matters ? The most heartening thing is still (one might say) the moral and social work in France ; but there again, isn't there more discretion (rather reactionary) than real fire ?

People are still leaving Pekin one by one. It's a sad business really—and would be sadder still, if one could think of oneself just now.

Well, on the first of May I entered my sixties. It's incredible how quickly time goes : my whole spiritual life consists more and more in abandoning myself (actively) to the presence and action of God. To be in communion with Becoming has become the formula of my whole life. Incidentally, the people here marked the occasion most charmingly : delicacies poured in at the rue Labrousse.

His technical work continued : a description of the Chou-Kou-Tien fossils and a work on ' Fossil Man in China ' in which he collected the substance of twenty years' observations. At the same time he was going on with his essays in scientific and religious philosophy.

(To the Abbé Breuil)   *Pekin, 12 July, 1941*

(not received until 5 July, 1945)

At the same time I am continuing to work towards a better presentation, clearer and more succinct, of my ideas on the place of man in the universe. Julian Huxley [1] has just brought out a book, or rather a series of essays, called *The Uniqueness of Man*, in a way so parallel to my own ideas (though without integrating God as the term of the series) that I feel greatly cheered. [. . .] I know that my book has arrived safely in Rome and has been under consideration for three months. I don't dare to hope for favourable news : and yet isn't this just the time for a Catholic to speak openly and as a Christian on lines determined by the best scientific thought of today ? (Works so orientated are coming out from every quarter at this very moment!) It's no longer a matter of speculation. The very upheaval that is going on at this moment raises the question of the future of man on earth. And yet there is nothing being published to give a constructive, dynamically Christian interpretation of what's happening.

But to get back to Pekin. The town is becoming more and more empty, and life is far from gay—not, however, that it is dismal. Among the French my best friends are Jews [. . .] I still hope that some way will be found in France of distinguishing between suspect immigrants of recent date and men like N——, a Lorrainer, whose family has fought for generations in all our armies. That would be too odious and dangerous for the future.

Pekin, 26 August, 1941

I am sending these lines on the off-chance in case you may have given up your plan of going to Paris. In spite of the breakdown in the Siberian route I have just had proof again that the mail has been getting through from unoccupied France these last two months by sea.

[. . .] With the increasing tension in the Pacific it is impos-

---

[1] Père Teilhard and Huxley had not yet met. But they knew one another's work and had a high regard for one another.

sible to make plans for the future. I feel the need to renew contact with the thinking world. But where is it now to be found? Even if it were physically possible I should hesitate before taking the chance of going to France. What gets through to us of the French press seems quite pitiful. You'll tell me that something very different is maturing; no doubt, but surely that can only be in the concentration camps?

This was to be the last letter to arrive until the end of the war: but through diplomatic channels Père Teilhard was still able to keep in touch for a while, though at long intervals, with his brother and even with the Abbé Breuil in South Africa.

A new family loss came to Père Teilhard in his exile: the death after some months' illness of his brother, Gabriel (29 October, 1941).

(To J. T. de C.)   *Pekin, 25 November, 1942*

[. . .] I knew nothing of Gabriel's death, though I had my fears, until I heard of it three days ago from Madame de Guyadet, but with no details, not even the date. A cable from Tangiers, signed Eyry (Jean, presumably)[1] which came in August, told me that all was well with the family, and this gave me for some time a flicker of false hope. Faced with the stupendous changes of today I am at a loss to estimate the significance of this bereavement. At the moment life demands of us that we shall live, that is to say, think and feel, on more than an individual scale. I hope and pray with all my strength that in the peculiarly depressing circumstances—depressing physically and morally—that have held you prisoners for the last three years, you are succeeding in preserving (even indeed in strengthening) a sharp, impassioned view of the sacred. The very value and happiness of existence consists in passing on into something greater than self. From this

[1] Jean Teillard d'Eyry, one of their cousins.

point of view, I do not think that the family has any cause to regret what the two wars have brought it. ' To serve ' is not ' to be sacrificed '.[1] I am sure that Caro [2] will have been equal to her trial. Assure her, of course, of my deep sympathy, and my great affection.

No particular news of my own affairs. I have never, for twenty years, lived so static an existence. In three years (except for a visit to the sea-side this summer, on the Manchukuo border) this Shanghai trip is my first move. Since 1940 I have been living in our little Geo-biological Institute, of which I am to all intents and purposes the father, so different is it from the old Licent Museum. The Pacific war has naturally deprived me of all my American contacts in Pekin so that my whole time is passed in the little house we have just beside the French Embassy, right in the centre, accordingly, of my friends and acquaintances. Field-work is impossible except in the Pekin hills, where I exercise what youth remains to me in climbing the ridges, hammer in hand. I shall never have published so much : five papers and as many notes in three years. I am saying anything of importance that I still have to say so that as soon as the road is open I may be able to go back to France and work at a reconstruction of the ' spirit '.

Life here is, in fact, much less hard than it is for you. It is somewhat irksome, indeed, to feel so cut off from the atmosphere which you in Europe are, perhaps unconsciously, absorbing. The foreign colony has been now cut down to the minimum, but our circle of close friends is still sufficient for us not to feel quite out in the cold. I have got a good deal greyer, but on the whole I feel fitter, even in a way younger, than in 1939.

[1] His brothers, Gonzague and Olivier, were killed in action in the first world war ; his other brother, Victor, had served as an infantry officer and died in 1934 ; Gabriel had fought as an artillery officer. In 1939 he had joined as a staff-officer in the air force.

[2] Gabriel's widow.

Correspondence between Père Teilhard and the Abbé Breuil was apparently interrupted in 1942. In 1943 they were able, through the Red Cross, to exchange messages, of not more than twenty-five words, by air mail. From Johannesburg,[1] Henri Breuil to P. Teilhard de Chardin in Pekin : ' Long stay here. Health, work, first-rate. Your news six months old. Request more. Boule dead.[2] Replaced by Vallois.[3] Love Pei, you, friends.' (27 May, 1943.) And Teilhard answered on 16 December, 1943 : ' Letter received. Envy you. Well in mind and body. Publishing much, but old. Love from Pei. Send address. Affectionately.'

(To J. T. de C.)   *Pekin, 13 November, 1943*

I have safely received your two letters of 18 May and 16 August, 1943, the latter coming yesterday. This route, then, works well and I reproach myself for not having made use of it earlier. None of your other letters has reached me, and you can imagine what a joy it has been to me to be able to form some idea of how things are going with you all.

[. . .] Everything goes well here. As field-work has been impossible since 1939, I have had to content myself with continuing my series of publications. I am adding to the list of my scientific-philosophical-religious manuscripts, still on the same lines, but giving greater depth and simplicity to my views. [. . .] I am working, in fact, with an eye on Paris and tomorrow. I would give a lot to be in the rue Monsieur [4] at this moment. Give my friends there that message—Père Fessard and Père d'Ouince (if, as I hope, he's there) ; and tell them once more

---

[1] The Abbé Breuil had been in South Africa since October, 1942. He returned to France in June, 1945.

[2] Marcellin Boule had died on 4 July, 1942.

[3] M. Vallois, now director of the Musée de l'Homme.

[4] The Paris headquarters of the review *Études*, where Père Teilhard had many friends among his fellow-Jesuits.

that I am with them in heart and spirit—and that they can count on me absolutely. [. . .]

Since my return from Shanghai nearly a year ago, I haven't budged from Pekin except for a splendid fortnight in the hills at my old friend's, Dr. Bussières. He comes from the Combraille and has succeeded in re-creating here a little corner of Auvergne, on granite too, right in the middle of China. And I don't foresee any serious move until the war ends. As almost everywhere else in the world, material life is becoming more and more difficult here. And even so we are among the lucky ones. The French colony is becoming smaller and smaller. My friends the Dorgets have been posted to Tokyo. Raphael died in the spring (an old, advanced affection of the heart) which was a blow to me. Bardac is still faithful to his post, with his charming wife, and they both stuff me with sandwiches once a week. Socially the Embassy is the great resource, with the visitors it attracts from Japan or Shanghai. M. de Margerie is a fairly frequent visitor and we always have heaps to say to one another. I know few men so well informed about a multitude of people and facts and at the same time with such a gift of discussing them clearly and brilliantly. In spite of everything we are still pretty well cut off from every important current of life—plenty of such currents flow by, but without reaching us or bringing us any animating force ; and this entails a gradual and insidious loss of vigour. I have the feeling that though we are spared the horror and tragedy we are ill-placed for getting through the crisis.

[. . .] So that is about all I can tell you today. My health stays good. If only time didn't go so quickly! These are just the years on which I was counting so much, and I see them slip by while I get practically nothing done. 'Everything that happens is adorable', Termier [1] was fond of saying. Properly

[1] Pierre Termier, the geologist, professor at the École des Mines, a scholar and a fine Christian whom Père Teilhard loved and admired.

understood, that idea sums up my whole religion. May God protect you. [. . .]

(To J. T. de C.) *Pekin, 10 December, 1945*

After a delay that I don't know how to excuse but which is accounted for by a series of false starts and hesitancies, I am getting down to sending you some news. As you see, I am still here, although under notice to return at some indeterminate date. This is what has happened. On the last day in September I had word from the ambassador at Chungking—through ' de Gaulle' channels—that I could (should ??) return to France. I very nearly left by air on the spot. But without any information at all about financial arrangements for my journey or any explanation of the urgency of my departure—and on top of that the difficulty of taking only 40 lbs. of luggage to a country where clothing is difficult to obtain—I have been waiting until I can travel by sea. Opportunities to do this are infrequent, however. Meanwhile, since there has been no explanation or repetition of the September message, I have got down to organising the smooth semi-liquidation of our Institute here, or rather its semi-incorporation in the Chinese Geological Service, which is starting up again. I'm still held up like this, somewhat upset in fact at having missed an English ship which I could certainly have caught if I had made up my mind more quickly or had had clearer instructions from France. A good many of us French in Pekin, from the de Margeries downwards, are in much the same position at the moment. Anyway, what it comes to is that I'm still here marking time. But now I mean to embark for France at the first opportunity. I hope Père d'Ouince [1] will be able to put me up, or find me a place nearby. I wrote him at the end of August, asking him

---

[1] At *Études*, 15 rue Monsieur, Paris.

to give you my news : but I don't know whether the letter reached him.

I've had no news of you for over a year, except that I learnt from a Quai d'Orsay telegram (mentioning several families) that in general all was well with you—news that was, again in general, confirmed by a letter from Madame de Guyadet. But that was all rather vague, and I am most anxious to have more details about you and yours, Caro, Marguerite, and particularly yourself. I wonder how you are managing intellectually and spiritually in the new state of affairs. Present conditions may well be heavy with anxieties ; and I hope that your lot may not be too burdensome. [. . .]

(To J. T. de C.) *' S.S. Strathmore ', 5 April, 1946*

A few lines, from Singapore, to confirm what you already doubtless know through Père d'Ouince, to whom I wrote from Hongkong : that, giving up the American plan which would have delayed me too much, I have jumped at the opportunity of travelling in the *Strathmore*, whose arrival at Shanghai coincided with mine. We should arrive somewhere in England at the end of this month, which will bring me to Paris some time early in May. [. . .]

The *Strathmore* is one of the finest P. & O. ships, converted (the lower decks, that is) into a troopship, so that we are living a gregarious existence, sleeping in hammocks. It's not a bad life, with plenty of simple food, but it's practically impossible to work. It will be the first time that I shall see the end of a sea-voyage without regret.

I am eager now to see you again—what a lot of things we'll have to say to one another!

' Strathmore ', 5 April, 1946

Where are you and what are you up to? And will this letter
reach you at the rue de Fleurus? Since the autumn I have been
living in such uncertainty about my plans—always thinking that
I'm on the eve of leaving—that I have hardly written at all ; nor
have I had any letter from France.

We shall be at Singapore the day after tomorrow, where I
shall post this, and in England by the end of the month, which
means Paris at the very beginning of May. These seven years
have made me quite grey, but they have toughened me—not
hardened me, I hope—interiorly. The first war started me on the
ladder.[1] This one has cut clean across my life, but I have a better
grasp of certain distinct central points, and to these I wish to
devote all that is left to me of life.

[1] Père Teilhard considered that the whole basis of his thought, the inception
of his essential ideas on the world and man, dated from the earlier war. They
were formulated or adumbrated in the first essays he then wrote.

1946-1951

Père Teilhard returned to Europe in the first ship to bring repatriates of all nationalities from the Far East. They landed at Southampton, and he arrived in Paris at the beginning of May, 1946. Through the good offices of the Abbé Breuil he was soon offered a new field of research : after Asia, South Africa, the scene of recent discoveries in palæontology. The Abbé Breuil wrote to him from Johannesburg, where he had been since October 1942 and had been responsible for some important work in prehistory. At Breuil's instigation, General Smuts, then Prime Minister of the Union, had sounded Père Teilhard about coming out to give his expert opinion on the rich collection of fossils that had recently been accumulated.

(To the Abbé Breuil)   *15 rue Monsieur, Paris, 7 April, 1947*

One way and another, it's becoming more and more definite that I shall join you in the course of July, and probably by the same route you took yourself. The money is ready and I shall have no difficulty with the necessary permission. Moreover Camp [1] is very kindly accepting me as an independent member of his party. The only point, but an important one, that I have not yet dealt with is making contact with Mr. Van Riet Lowe and Mr. Broom : [2]

[1] An American palæontologist at the University of California.
[2] The two palæontologists he was to meet in South Africa.

we should make them understand quite clearly the spirit in which I am coming—I have no intention of interfering or of teaching them their own business, but of learning and pooling the knowledge and experience I have gained elsewhere. I am rather counting on you to see that there is no misunderstanding about this.

But on the 1st of June, Père Teilhard suffered a sudden heart attack which broke down his robust constitution and necessitated months of rest. The attack fell on an organism overburdened by the incessant activity of both physical and mental effort. Père Teilhard was never a person to spare himself, but even before his illness he admitted that he was feeling the weight of his years. ' In my life, it's now five o'clock in the evening.' Obliged from now on to take things easy, he felt in himself as he worked those ' forces of diminishment' to which one must learn to abandon oneself and to which he refers in ' Le Milieu divin'. During his convalescence he wrote to the Abbé Breuil that cancelling his journey was a bitter disappointment.

(To the Abbé Breuil)   *15 rue Monsieur, 15 July, 1947*

[. . .] I have to call on all the philosophy of my faith to make part of myself and put to constructive use what is in itself heartbreaking. Everything was working out so well and was so close to realisation! But thank you all the same for all you've done for me. At present I'm progressing normally, getting better day by day, but, according to the medical pundits who have seen me, my case—the classic type, apparently—is simply a matter of time ; which means that I shall not be allowed to lead a normal life (with certain precautions even then) before December 1, which will be six months from my attack. It's rather a long time and since I'm told to avoid stairs my choice of residence is limited. I am thinking of starting with a month with the good nuns at

Saint-Germain-en-Laye ; after that we'll see. But I'm not thinking of leaving the neighbourhood of Paris and you can always write to me at *Études*. I don't, in fact, even know the exact name of what I've had (a lesion somewhere round the heart or the coronary arteries). All I have felt has been a sort of rheumatic pain, with attacks of nausea, but no breathlessness. I must have strained myself without realising it, for I had the impression of being in such excellent form. I still can't estimate the extent of the ' disaster ', that is to say how far extensive field-work will still be possible. That we'll see in a few months' time. If the worst comes to the worst I shall concentrate on mental work, which would fit in logically with my present way of life. In any case I have made up my mind to take this shock as a touch of the spur rather than a tug on the bridle—should the Lord give me the strength.

(To the Abbé Breuil) *Saint-Germain-en-Laye, 23 September, 1947*

Your kind letter of the 14th, which gave me great joy, safely received. If I have not written to you more often in the last two months, it is partly because, oddly enough, I have been pretty busy (in between the long hours of rest that are still prescribed) and partly because I'm still so ' sore ' about my cancelled trip that I instinctively avoid anything that brings South Africa too directly to my mind. It was obviously vital for me to go out there ; so let us hope that the day will come, as I am sure it will, when I shall see that it was still more vital for me not to go. [. . .] But this certainly calls for a good deal of faith. [. . .] ' Everything that happens is adorable ', Termier was always saying ; but that necessitates giving to ' Christic energy ' its real meaning and its full reality in the universe. Fundamentally, my real interest in life is moving irresistibly to a more and more intense concentration on this basic question of the relations between Christ and

'Hominisation'.[1] It has become for me a question of 'to be or not to be'.

Père Teilhard's return to health was to allow a renewal of activity. As appears from his correspondence, he was accepting invitations to address small audiences when he felt that he could fruitfully explain his thought as a scientist and a Christian, and especially in non-religious circles, in which his ideas were beginning to carry weight.

On the other hand, many believers informed on the present state of the biological sciences were thinking that they should give serious attention to a philosophy of nature such as that which Père Teilhard was building up.

Mgr Bruno de Solages, Rector of the Institut Catholique at Toulouse, had recently acclaimed the value and opportune appearance of his work [2] : 'Has he not already done magnificent work in correcting the theory of evolution from within, in snatching the weapon from the hand of the materialist and turning it against him, and so offering the theologian a theory of the universe both evolutionary and uncompromisingly spiritual?'

(To Max and Simone Bégouën).   Paris, 29 December, 1947

Max's letter of the 24th, which came this morning, gave me great joy ; except that, reading between the lines, I rather suspect that you have both been very tired. For heaven's sake, do take care of yourselves, and now that you're finally there[3] do 'take it easy'. I'm sorry for Max that it looks as though he'll miss French West Africa this year ; but here, most of all, I think that it's a case where he should take things calmly (I only wish I could do the same

[1] For the sense in which Père Teilhard uses this word, see *The Phenomenon of Man*, and the two later works *L'Apparition de l'homme* and *La Vision du passé*.

[2] *La Pensée chrétienne face à l'évolution* (Toulouse, 1947).

[3] In Morocco.

myself), in the light of the Christian principle that nothing in the world is really of value except what happens in the end, after we have done our best, according to the circumstances of the case, either to make it come about or, as often, to prevent it from doing so. [. . .]

What can I tell you about my life here ? As far as I am concerned personally, everything is going as well as it could ; my health seems excellent, and (apart from the nights, which I am still making as long as possible) I am almost back to a normal existence. For example, last week I gave two lectures without getting tired, one to the student-inspectors of Saint-Cloud, the other at the students' hostel in the rue de Vaugirard, and I have seldom felt so on top of things or that I spoke so clearly.

I still feel at a loose end without any definite objective, and in particular without any precise line of scientific research, which is a little irksome. I am still waiting for an answer from Rome to know whether I may go to America in the spring. The voyage would really put me on my feet again, quite apart from the fact that I could get to South Africa by sea more easily from New York than from Europe (if, that is, I should really decide that it would be quite safe to take a chance—as I think I probably would) ; but all that is still up in the air. Finally, let me say how much I miss you both—but that's hardly news. May the new year be kind to you—that is, brimful of the presence of God. No need to assure you again of all my deep affection.

At the end of the winter of 1948, Père Teilhard was well enough to make the journey to the United States. He stayed in New York, where he was well known in scientific circles from his expeditions with American scientists in China. It was his sixth visit to America ; he had been there before in 1931, 1933, 1937, 1938 and 1939.

(To J. T. de C.)   *New York, 11 March, 1948*

This is to confirm what you already know, that my journey
went off perfectly smoothly and without incident, and that since
then I have been leading a normal existence without, so far, anything of particular note. I am seeing plenty of people, but only
by degrees, and I am still a long way from having made all the
contacts I would wish : and all this without getting much further
in my own affairs, or rather, I should say, without being able to
map out any definite line of action. Now that the door is closed
on China and that in future it's going to be difficult for me to
consider any field-work, I am obviously left rather in the air,
which I find a contrast to my previous visits to America. My
instinct is to try to arouse interest in, and direct myself towards,
a sort of neo-anthropology more awake to present tendencies
and more alive than that generally practised today. I think I
shall find a response. But it's the devil to conceive a practical
plan and put it into action. [. . .]

It is a great joy to find myself again in this great city and
without feeling too lost. As a general rule I go round to the
American Museum every day, but without actually working
there. After that I see some of my New York friends. I spent
last week-end at my ' millionaire ' friend Frick's lovely place on
Long Island. He lives there very simply, spending most of his
time studying the fossils which diggers collect for him every
year in the bays on the West Coast. Through him I hope to
meet two or three people interesting to me and interested in the
same objectives.

Les Moulins, 4 September, 1948

For the moment my chief concern (increasingly so, for a long time now) is not to know what sort of beginning I have made, but how to *end well* : and by that I mean the problem of ending my life in the spontaneous attitude or the gesture and providential circumstance which best bear witness to the sincerity and value of the vision for which I have lived. It is not a matter of saying that death sets the seal upon life ; on that point we must have absolute trust in God, for the ' good end ' depends on Him alone. It is, in fact, on trust that I am going to focus my most earnest thoughts during the ' retreat ' I am taking the opportunity to make here, once I've finished the job—titles of publications and practical work—the Collège de France has given me : complete, all-embracing trust which is absorbed in active abandonment of self in a universe on the road to Christification.

In the autumn of 1948 Père Teilhard paid his first visit to Rome. His purpose was to have an interview with his General on two urgent matters : to obtain permission to stand as a candidate for a Chair at the Collège de France, about which he had been sounded, and for the publication of his ' Phenomenon of Man ' which had been under consideration since 1940.

Borgo San Spirito, Rome, 7 October, 1948

This is to give you my address (as above) and to tell you that I arrived here safely after a perfect journey without incident. I didn't wake up till we got to Brigue ; on the other hand I watched the magnificent descent to Lake Maggiore ; night again, though, after Florence, which leaves a gap in my first experience of Italy. A friend met me on the platform at Rome at midnight, which simplified things. So now I am staying in the mother house itself (but in a special wing reserved for writers) ; new buildings, with a lift, and terraced gardens, five hundred yards from the piazza of St. Peter's—I have only to cross the corridor to see the dome of old ivory that you know so well. I had a very friendly reception.

I have begun to get about the place with friends. The day before yesterday St. Peter's and the Vatican Gardens; yesterday a gathering (a monthly tea) of French priests and monks at Saint-Louis-des-Français (I saw some curious or interesting figures); tomorrow the first reception for French people at the Ambassador's, d'Ormesson.[1] Rome has not given me—nor will it, I know—any æsthetic shock; I feel oddly inoculated against the past—but I do like the southern climate. And then, as I wrote to d'Ouince a moment ago, I seem to feel an awareness of the extraordinary focus of spiritual radiation concentrated by the two thousand years of history these places have witnessed. In these days it is here in Rome that we find the Christic pole of the earth; through Rome, I mean, runs the ascending axis of hominisation.[2]

(To J. T. de C.)   *Borgo San Spirito, Rome, 19 October, 1948*

As I am half-way now, I suppose, through my stay in Rome it is time to send you some impressions and news. I had a very simple journey, but I only just saw the descent from the Simplon to Lake Maggiore (very impressive) and the plain of the Po (almost aggressively fertile, but monotonous). Night overtook us before we went through Tuscany. Fortunately I was met at the station. Since I have been here I am surprised to find myself living as the Romans live, but superficially, and very superficially at that. The city has made no great impact on me; I have been living too long in another world. But I immediately fell in love with the light and the climate and (old memories of Aix and Egypt

[1] i.e. the Ambassador to the Vatican.
[2] The transformation by which man, from his earliest origins, becomes more and more man.

perhaps ?) I feel curiously at home among the umbrella-pines and cypresses in this Mediterranean setting. I haven't yet, I'm afraid, visited any of the museums (I'm quite capable, I know, of skipping them all). On the other hand I go for a stroll every evening before sunset on the Pincio or the Janiculum (just near here) from which you can see the whole city offering the gilded façades of its countless churches to the last rays of the sun.

Only two things have impressed me, St. Peter's and the Gesù (in spite of its orgy of marbles and mouldings), because in them one feels from time to time—in different degrees of course—the security (that's a better word for it than fixity) of a faith that will not be side-tracked. At this moment in history there is no doubt that one of the poles passes through Rome, the prime pole of ascent of what in my jargon I call 'hominisation'. That, I think, will be the 'principal experience' I shall take away from my stay here ; and that alone would make the journey worth while.

My own affairs progress slowly but on the whole well, although I can't prophesy anything definite—about anything, the book, the Collège de France etc. I had a friendly reception. [. . .]

Apart from our own headquarters, I have seen no influential people. The Holy Father is still in the country and the windows of the Vatican are shut.

I haven't told you that our house—very modern—adjoins the piazza of St. Peter's. From the terrace, or from a garden which runs along the almost vertical slopes of the hill we back on to, there is a magnificent view of the basilica and of all Rome, practically at our very feet.

I have met again a young friend of mine, Baron Alberto Blanc, one of the best and most successful pre-historians of Italy. He will be driving me perhaps in two hours' time to the promontory of Circe where in 1938 he found his famous Neanderthal skull lying among the remains of hippopotamuses and hyenas right on the floor of a cave re-opened accidentally by works put in hand by Mussolini.

I caught a glimpse at an over-crowded reception of the Ambassador, d'Ormesson, whom I used to know well through his sister, Madame Arsène Henry, and the de Margeries. I am going to see him again soon.

(To the Abbé Breuil)   *Borgo San Spirito, Rome, 28 October, 1948*

As the Collège de France kindly approached me about a vacant Chair (to be allotted possibly to prehistory) on my return from New York, the Father General decided to have me come here to talk about a number of things at the same time : this question of the Collège de France, the possibility of publishing my book on the *Phenomenon of Man* (written ten years ago), and my general situation (lectures, publications, etc.). Nothing has been decided yet, but meanwhile I have retouched my manuscript to satisfy two final revisions,[1] and I have had several conversations with the authorities in an atmosphere of full confidence and friendship. In a week from today I shall know whether to say yes or no to Faral [2] about my candidature—it comes up in November, so it's becoming urgent. As for the book, I shall no doubt have to wait some time. Where will all this take me ? I have no idea. Being barred from field-work, as I have been for the last year, makes me less keen, of course, to teach prehistory. On the other hand I find the general question of anthropogenesis more and more interesting and absorbing. It would

---

[1] In an earlier letter he was more explicit : ' On reflection, I thought the best way was to satisfy the censor's demands, without any distortion, of course, of my thought, but by going through the text dotting the i's and crossing the t's (in footnotes, and also in the dozen pages, which are now ready, of epilogue, which seems to me useful). I think these re-touchings have improved my original draft, quite apart from a number of pretty important notes I've added for my own satisfaction since I've been here.'

[2] Administrator of the Collège de France.

obviously be a wonderful chance for me to be able, even if only for two years (for that's all it would be)[1], to take advantage of the Collège as a platform. In short, I am feeling quite philosophical about the outcome. I'll keep you posted, of course.[2]

As you know, Rome in October, with its beautiful golden light, is particularly agreeable. I stroll around without any conscientious sight-seeing. The Eternal City has given me no shock, but I have been impressed—and heartened—by Christianity's extraordinary, really imperturbable confidence in the unshakable solidity of its faith and truth. There is a remarkable phenomenon there, unique, in fact, in this world.

Paris, 7 August, 1950

[. . .] *Études* is practically deserted. You feel almost an exile in Paris. [. . .] I have continued to reflect on and note quite a number of things. The last essay of all is now finished—on ' two inverse forms of the spirit '—spirit of identification and spirit of unification.[3] I felt the need to write this in order to have an exact text to give to anyone who raised the matter with me in conversation.

---

[1] By which time he would have reached the age-limit.

[2] On leaving Rome, Père Teilhard was advised not to stand. He accepted the decision ; but the question of the book was still left open.

[3] It was here that Père Teilhard saw the essential difference with pantheism : identification of all being with God, on the one hand ; on the other hand Christian personalism, convergence towards a personal transcendent God, the centre, loving and worthy of being loved. He was fond of recalling St. Paul's words on the ultimate consummation of humanity, when God will be ' all in all '.

About Hindu pantheism, then experiencing a revival of popularity among intellectuals in search of a mystical system, he remarked, ' An odd thing, this fascination with a religious attitude so faintly marked by the love of God.' Without Christianity, he thought, ' the presence of a loving God would disappear from the psychological equipment of the world—darkness and coldness beyond any we could even begin to imagine '.

I've also sent two substantial pages to Torrès Bodet [1] on the subject of UNESCO's definition of the doctrine of the equality of races. Not equality, I told him, in the name of all palæontology and biology, but complementariness (of convergence), which is truer and much finer. [. . .] I shall also have to prepare a lecture for Belgium on the Human and the ultra-Human : a talk, too, for the ' Congrès des Croyants ' on the appetite for life. And I should like to get on a bit with *Le Cœur de la matière* [2] which is progressing, even though slowly, and taking more definite form in my mind. My views, as you know, hardly change, but they simplify themselves and interlock with such an increase of intensity—in the interplay (so wonderfully contrived) of what I call the two lines of curvature (or convergence)—the cosmic (' natural ') and the Christic (' super-natural ').

[1] Director of UNESCO.
[2] Subsequently published in *L'Avenir de l'homme*.

July–November, 1951

Père Teilhard's projected journey to South Africa became possible in 1951 ; his health had improved, and the American Wenner Gren foundation for anthropological research looked after the financial side. With his election the year before to the Académie des Sciences his prestige was increasing at home and abroad, and he was becoming recognised as an international expert in human palæontology.

He was to spend part of the summer (the South African winter) in Johannesburg, using it as a centre for his expeditions throughout the Union. But first he went through London, to embark at Southampton.

Southampton, 11 July, 1951

At midday tomorrow I sail from Southampton in the *Carnarvon Castle*. As it turned out, my stay in London was more pleasant and more fruitful than I had expected. I saw my old friend Hopwood, palæontologist at the Natural History Museum ; Huxley [1] too, and Robinson [2] and Barbour. With these two

---

[1] In an article in *Encounter* (April, 1956) Julian Huxley wrote as follows about *The Phenomenon of Man* (French ed.) : ' The force and purity of Père Teilhard's thought and expression, in fruitful combination with his capacity for loving comprehension of all values, has given the world a picture not only of rare clarity but pregnant with compelling conclusions.' Paying tribute

last, whom I am to meet again at Johannesburg, we have made excellent progress in working out a systematic plan for research on ' *Early Man* ' in South Africa.

Huxley, by whose friendliness I was greatly touched, had arranged a dinner at his house on my way through. There were two representatives of his famous ' group ' of searchers for a humanist ideology, and Dr. Turner, of Yale, the chairman of the editorial board of UNESCO's *Histoire culturelle et scientifique de l'homme.* I found these meetings fruitful and interesting, not so much perhaps for the ideas that were exchanged (I found at least two, though, to remember and reflect on) as for a more precise understanding, ' *forced upon my mind* ', of the path I must follow towards a different objective and with a quite different type of team from Huxley's.

In short, I am setting off with a much more precise idea of my two-fold objective (the Australopithecæ and the ultra-human) and with plenty to think round and about during the voyage. All this is directed towards the search for the ' ever-greater God ', for ultimately it is only the pull towards Him that is sending me on this new—perhaps my last ?—adventure.

Johannesburg, 13 August, 1951

Everything in my trip is going very well on the whole, and developing as I would wish it to. We had a smooth passage

---

to the 'lucid and fearless mind' of Père Teilhard whom he looked on as 'a partner in intellectual and spiritual adventure', Huxley said that, in spite of certain basic differences, Père Teilhard ' often saw further and with keener vision than I ever did'. In a personal letter he wrote : ' He was a wonderful man, and I am grateful to have been his colleague and his friend ' (to Claude Aragonnès, after receiving the *Lettres de voyage*, 26 December, 1956).

² Curator of the Pretoria Museum, department of vertebrate palæontology and physical anthropology.

from Southampton to Capetown, putting in only for an afternoon at Funchal (Madeira). The cloud-capped peaks were hidden and there's nothing particularly interesting in the town, with its masses of identical villas scattered on the slopes of the volcano, apart from some luxuriant gardens and an old Portuguese church which must have seen the passage of countless navigators, conquerors and missionaries. Rather a suburban place, Funchal. It was not noticeably hot as we crossed the equator, and we landed at the Cape under a magnificent blue sky, between two Antarctic gales which briefly dusted the tall peaks with snow. I only spent a day in Capetown, looked after by a local pre-historian (Goodwin). We arrived in the morning and I left again the same evening for Johannesburg in a fairly comfortable train (two nights and a day). The country is rather featureless, a sort of desert steppe with bare rocky ridges and sheep or cattle farms at long intervals : just like Northern China or the Western deserts of America. I spent the night at Kimberley, the diamond town, and arrived at Joh'burg (the gold town) in glorious sunshine which has lasted the whole of the past fortnight. It's cold at night, but not frosty, and almost hot in the daytime ; the fruit-trees are in full flower, with an effect of late February in Pekin.

Joh'burg is about 7000 feet above sea level, but you don't feel the altitude at all. It's an ultra-modern town, with small skyscrapers (it's like being in America), flanked on the north by the residential quarters (villas) with a luxuriance of green vegetation—chiefly eucalyptus—and flowers, and to the south by unending lines of white slag-heaps (not black as at Mons or Charleroi). These are the waste from the gold-mines which run for 90 miles from east to west along the famous quartzitic reef of the Rand. Here I have found my friend Barbour from Cincinnati, and I have quickly become friends with my fellow-prehistorians and geologists. I have already made a first visit to the Australopithecan [1] sites near here ; and I spent last week, with a stop at Pretoria, at another well-known site 180 miles to the north, the Makapan valley, where I saw a number of most interesting specimens. Out there you're in real African bush country. I'd have thought I was in Abyssinia except for the extraordinary profusion of little aloe bushes in full flower.

One way and another, as I was saying, I feel that things are turning out well. I can see the problems more clearly, and I have a pretty good idea of what will be the substance of my report to Fejos.[2] And at the same time as the question of 'pre-man' is taking shape in my mind, my ideas on the other question—that of the 'ultra-human'—continue to make progress. I wrote 15 pages at sea on the 'convergence of the universe', and these, in an English translation, can serve as a basis for working out the assignment that the Viking Fund [3] are financing for me.

(To J. T. de C.)   *Johannesburg, 18 August, 1951*

Thanks for your letter of 24 July, which came safely and quickly. It found me comfortably installed in Joh'burg, where I don't find the altitude (nearly 7,000 feet above sea level) at all exhausting, and where the continual blue skies are a delightful reminder of Pekin. It was cold the night I arrived, with snow on the peaks towards Capetown, but now it's full spring with the fruit-trees bursting into flower.

Nothing worth mentioning in the voyage from Southampton to the Cape : and nothing to see, except Madeira—we put in for a few hours at Funchal (where I thought of Albéric [4]), and

[1] A group of anthropoid primates discovered in South Africa. Père Teilhard had come on purpose to study some important collections of their fossils.

[2] Director of the Wenner Gren Foundation.

[3] The original name of the Wenner Gren Foundation.

[4] His elder brother, a naval officer (he died in 1902) who had put in there.

the Cape Verde Islands. Crossing the line you could hardly say it was hot. The *Carnarvon Castle* was very pleasant, and I was able to read and work in peace. At Capetown (which is a lovely situation) a fellow-prehistorian drove me around the peninsula ; and that same evening I took the train for Johannesburg—two nights and a day in the train. It's a monotonous countryside, but with the impressiveness of desert grandeur. I might have thought myself on the Mongolian border or in the American west.

Joh'burg, of course, is a mushroom city, sprung up in the last sixty years. To the south of the skyscraper district (a miniature Detroit) which has constantly been pulled down and rebuilt, stretches for a good hundred miles the line of vast white slag-heaps, the refuse from the gold-mines which have been sunk in the east–west reef of auriferous conglomerate, and now running below sea level !

[. . .] That's the picturesque side of it. As far as work goes, I am very pleased. Although I can't get about as I used to, I can see and learn, and above all understand, a great deal ; and I hope that I'll be able to take back some useful reports to New York. The local geologists and prehistorians here are charming. In their company, and thanks to their kindness, I have already begun to visit the most interesting of the sites. Last week I was at Makapan, some 180 miles north from here. It was a four-day trip and most rewarding. After Pretoria you're properly in the African bush country ; you find a profusion of all sorts of aloes, and the arborescent cactiform euphorbias begin to appear ; their candelabra, side by side with the round huts of the natives, took me back twenty-two years to the plateaux of the Harrar. The magnificent fauna of this district has disappeared, of course, except for a few springbok ; but there are still the dog-faced baboons and macaque monkeys ; birds, too—guinea-fowl, secretary-birds etc. Next week I am hoping to go right down the

Vaal as far as Kimberley, a bleak monotonous country, I believe.
When that's over I'll be through with the bulk of my inspection.

(To the Abbé Breuil)   *Johannesburg, 20 August, 1951*

This reversal of our situations, by which I have to write to you
from your ' home ', gives me a very odd feeling ; for I've been
in your Africa now for three weeks [. . .] Goodwin met me at
Capetown and took me round the peninsula in radiant sunshine.
At Dr. Drennan's, in the School of Medicine, he showed me some
material with which you're no doubt familiar : a complex of
bone, unevenly fossilised (elephant and ruminant, plus an exceptionally large horse) associated with a mixture of tools, some
ancient, some mid-palæolithic, found in some consolidated dunes
some hundred miles to the north-west of Capetown : a site
which is difficult of access by reason of the sands. Judging from
the photographs the place is obviously worth a detailed study in
order to identify the material in its own setting. It might be a
good spot for finding human bones!

I took the train for Joh'burg the same evening, where I had a
splendid reception from Van Riet Lowe and Dart. Your name
is still on the door of your room at the University. [. . .]

I was greatly impressed in the Australopithecæ in particular
(as you and Koenigswald both noticed), by the contrast they
present between a series with an extraordinarily widely spaced
molariform development (as in the bears or the ailuropus) and a
series with ridiculously reduced canine-incisors. How on earth
did such creatures manage to live and defend themselves ? One
thing is certain, that at that period (Villafranchian ?—I think
Broom dates them *too* early) they must have formed a large and
' extensive ' population, sharply defined and master—(as primates)—of the countryside. This is a very odd business, and the
interest of Southern Africa from the point of view of human

origins has certainly not been exaggerated. But there's nothing I can teach you about that.[1]

Johannesburg, 5 September, 1951

My life here goes on, on much the same general lines. I some-times find it exasperating not to be able to cover the country as I used to and see things that I feel are no distance away. But on the whole I have nothing to complain about. Thanks to the inexhaustible kindness of my colleagues here I manage to see all the essentials. My last important move, at the end of August, was to spend a week round Kimberley, the diamond town, much more humble and slow in growth than the gold town but situated in an interesting area for my purposes. Thanks to the ' *diamond-diggers* ' the old gravel-beds of the Vaal have everywhere been dug up—too much so, indeed, for it means the destruction of the original sites—and their ancient stone implements exposed in the course of the operation. I learnt a great deal in those few days, all under the same magnificent blue sky. This landscape is less picturesque in contour and vegetation than it is towards the Limpopo (Makapan) which I had visited earlier ; but it is never-theless impressive. There are great expanses, with hardly an undulation, of tall yellow grasses and thorny mimosas in which less than a hundred years ago elephants and giraffes still roamed. I think that I shall concentrate more on my immediate sur-roundings—and the collections in Joh'burg and Pretoria. It's beginning to be about time I got quite a number of things tidied up.

---

[1] Cf. Pierre Teilhard de Chardin : ' L'Afrique et les origines humaines ' (*La Vision du passé*, ch. 16).

(To J. T. de C.)   *Langham Hotel, Johannesburg, 6 September, 1951*

[. . .] Life in Joh'burg continues to go as it should. I already feel as if I were a native of this busy city. At the end of August I went to spend a few days in the Kimberley area. It's an important financial centre—the de Beers diamond reserves are there—but a small place, as though its growth had been retarded. The surrounding landscape, though less picturesque than the Limpopo country to the north, is still typically African : great expanses, often as flat as the Beauce, of tall grasses and occasional thorny bush. It's country in which you find ' *pipes* ' of blue rock, and diamond-bearing gravel-beds ; the former are now worked industrially so that the slag-heaps are blueish instead of white as at Joh'burg ; the latter are still turned over by individual ' *placer* ' miners. The whole district belongs to de Beers, who ' open up ' the country to diamond-diggers at their discretion, some parts being set aside as game reserves. It was the gravel-beds in fact that brought me to Kimberley. They run along the edges of the Vaal at different levels and contain a formidable quantity of stone implements, more or less rounded, like a vast Saint-Acheul or Abbeville,[1] the whole exposed by the ' *gravel-diggers* ' in their search for diamonds.

We pushed as far as Taungs on the border of the Kalahari desert, where the first Australopithecus was found, about 1925, in pockets that reminded me greatly of my deposits at Chou-Kou-Tien. South of Taungs advantage has to be taken of the fact that the valley of the Haart lies much lower than that of the Vaal, to initiate a massive irrigation scheme for the Veld, thanks to a diversion of the Vaal dammed not far from here. The poor Vaal!—already pumped to supply Joh'burg and Pretoria. Water

---

[1] A site near Amiens in which the remains of a palæolithic industry were found. Père Teilhard is referring to an ancient deposit similar to this typical one.

is a very serious problem in these parts. On the whole it was an extremely pleasant trip, with the same magnificent weather and blue skies all the time. Three days ago I was taken for a two hours' drive to the south, to a place on the upper Vaal, called Vereeniging, again to see the gravel-beds. Economically, it's an interesting place, if not æsthetically, for in fifty years' time it may well become the Manchester of the Transvaal. There's plenty of coal in practically horizontal beds (the carboniferous deposits have never been disturbed here). Black slag-heaps this time, against a blue sky.

(To J. T. de C.)   *Mount-Nelson Hotel, Capetown,*
                                         13 October, 1951

Thank you for your last long letter, as interesting as they always are. This is to give you my latest news from Africa, which I am expecting to leave on the 18th in a Dutch ship, the *Boissevin* (Holland–Africa line), for Buenos Aires. There, thanks to the *Boissevin's* capricious schedule, I fear I may have to wait more than a week to make a connection with New York : it would be an entertaining prospect if it didn't look like being very expensive, to judge from what I hear of South American prices. While we're at sea, I'll be glad of the opportunity to check a number of recent statements about the ages of the local stone-age industries, which seem to me quite arbitrary and simply based on analogies of shape. Too many well-known prehistorians sadly lack a geological training.

I left the Transvaal, not without regret, nearly a fortnight ago, via Durban and so down the coast by sea. I sailed in the same ship, the *Carnarvon Castle*, which brought me out in July from Southampton. Durban is a beautiful tropical city, which has sprung up like a mushroom in a countryside where the bush is at your back door. I'm told that you can still see toucans in the gardens, and right up to the edge of the town you meet bands of monkeys, very much at home, who don't hesitate (as I've seen myself) to jump onto the bonnet of a parked car, squat comfortably down and stare at you through the windscreen. Unfortunately I could stay only three days in this delightful place, which is also geologically interesting for me. The sea-voyage was rather a bore. There were plenty of stops which allowed one to have a good look at the country, but they were spoilt—at Port Elizabeth by a big storm, which coinciding with a Sunday and endless loading and unloading of cargo, kept us three days in harbour without my being able to take a trip by car which I would have found most interesting. To make up a little, I was able to visit the small local museums. The one at East London proudly displays the extraordinary ' Crossopterygian ' [1] brought back by a fisherman in 1938, which made a sensation at the time among palæontologists—a survivor from the armoured fish from which the amphibian apparently emerged. The last known had been found in the chalk at Dover and was about as big as your hand, but this specimen is over six feet in length. Miss Lattimer herself, the director of the Museum, did me the honours of this Lattimeria, as they call it ; she was responsible for the creature being preserved. No other specimen has since been caught. [2]

In spite of more stormy weather, which too often maintains a persistent cloud cap on Table Mountain (it is just opposite my window—in fact the hotel is already on the slope of the mountain), I found Capetown in full spring : flowers everywhere, and trees in blossom (the ' Kaffir-trees ' are particularly lovely, with their vivid red flowers). Thanks to some prehistorian friends I have been on several day excursions ; they were made exceptionally delightful by the wonderful weather, which brought

---

[1] Crossopterygii : a family of fish whose respiratory system and skeleton ' foreshadow ' the land vertebrates.

[2] Another has since been caught.

out the jagged crests of the tall rocky mountain chains and gave an iridescent brilliance to the masses of yellow and purple flowers —different sorts of compositae and some remarkable heaths— which cover the ground. Particularly interesting to a European eye are the great white arum lilies, just like those in the florists' shops, growing in the meadows and beside the roads like weeds. One trip took me to a place which at the moment is alive with interest for South African prehistory. I saw something really quite new to me, and was able to give some useful advice. On another trip I met, at the university of Stellenbosch, an authentic ' Teillard ' : a fine family which has produced university pro- fessors, high officials and diplomats. They now spell it Tilyaard, but they are all descended from the same Frenchman, a Catholic, who spelt it Taillard ; he (Pierre-Louis) arrived in South Africa about 1750, perhaps from Normandy (Saint-Lô), though that point hasn't been cleared up, apparently. What we do know is that Pierre-Louis started by going straight to prison for trying to grow coffee here against the wishes of the India Company ; and the story goes that he never knuckled under. I wonder if you may be able to throw some light on this. The Stellenbosch Tilyaard, a delightful fellow, is a geology teacher ; he gave me a book of his that I'll show you, full of the most wonderful photographs ; he is eager to ' contact ' his French ancestors.

Talking of the eighteenth century, yesterday I visited a large and magnificent farm-house of the period ; it's now a well- known wine-producing centre and an historic monument. In spite of many differences I was struck by the similarity there must have been in those days between the life of the great land- owners at the Cape and that of the country gentlemen of Auvergne or Virginia. When you decide to travel, you must take in the Cape ; you can't fail to love this country of trees and green vegetation.

Capetown, 15 October, 1951

This, I imagine, will be my last letter from Africa, for the *Boissevin* (a Dutch ship on the Japan–South Africa run) has apparently made up its mind to sail from here on the 18th. [. . .] I left Joh'burg, not without regrets, via Durban and the coast ; and for the last ten days I have been at the Cape again, which is rather too stormy but in the full exuberance of spring. Everywhere you see the dazzling colours of the flowers—not only in the gardens but in the fields and among the rocks. Thanks to some good friends of mine, palæontologists and prehistorians, I have been able to make at least two one-day excursions in the neighbourhood, with the result that I have formed a good idea of the problems that crop up here. I am beginning to be able to make a fresher approach, in my thought and writing, to geology —and about time too. [. . .] At the last moment I heard that there was someone at Buenos Aires (Dr. Menghin) who would give me some interesting information about South America.

(To J. T. de C.)   *On board the ' Uruguay ', 11 November, 1951*

My last letter was dated from Capetown. Tomorrow we stop at Santos (São Paulo) ; the day after it will be Rio ; only one more stop then, at Trinidad, and on November 26 we shall be in New York.

[. . .] The end of my stay at the Cape, with its remarkable vegetation, was interesting ; but the weather was not too good, and I had a coming-to-an-end feeling. So that I was not sorry when after endless delays, the *Boissevin* (a Dutch ship on the Japan–Indonesia–S. Africa route) decided to sail.

It is a smallish ship, under 15,000 tons, but very sea-worthy and uncommonly comfortable : it is partly a passenger liner and partly cargo. A motley crowd of passengers : wealthy Chinese ; a large proportion of Afrikaners making the ' Round-trip ', Dur-ban–America–Durban, for pleasure or relaxation ; emigrants from the Far East ; not to mention two hyenas for the zoo at Buenos Aires. For twelve days we've had good weather nearly all the time, but with absolutely nothing to see except some whales spouting and two pairs of albatrosses who followed us doggedly for nearly a week. At last, one fine afternoon, the gentle slopes of the coast of Uruguay appeared, and then the muddy, apparently boundless flats of the Rio de la Plata. In the end I had only a week to spend at Buenos Aires. I was very comfortable in an excellently situated hotel. In the city the walls were covered with ' Perón ' and ' Evita ' in huge letters, but the general atmosphere was rather subdued because of Evita's illness : her popularity is quite fantastic. Buenos Aires is very lovely in places, but on the whole it is much too cramped in its checker-board of streets—a huge Marseilles ; and I shall leave it without in the end having had even a glimpse of the countryside. Even from the ship you see nothing as you come up the river, for both banks are low-lying and a long way off. I should dearly have loved to have seen something of the pampas. To make up, thanks to a well-known German prehistorian, now emigrated to the Argentine (Dr. Menghin), I have learnt and seen a great deal (in collections) of the recent prehistory of the Argentine—recent, because it does not go back more than ten thousand years, and also because it is only during the last two or three years that it has begun to be understood at all. It's the other terminus of the human expansion, traces of whose origins I had just been looking at in Africa : [1] interesting, therefore, both in itself and by contrast.

Then, the day before yesterday, I went down the Rio de la Plata again in a big American liner on the New York–

[1] Cf. *L'Apparition de l'homme*, ch. 16, ' L'Afrique et les origines humaines '.

Buenos Aires run, and so now here I am on my way back to the U.S.A.

On board the ' Uruguay ', bound for New York,
13 November, 1951

It was a monotonous twelve days' passage from Capetown to Buenos Aires : literally nothing in sight except some whales and albatrosses cruising in our wake. But it was comfortable—in a luxurious little Dutch liner (Malaya–South America) very far-Eastern in atmosphere.

[. . .] I spent a week at Buenos Aires—a huge Marseilles, built to a chess-board pattern on an expanse so flat that I couldn't get even a glimpse of the countryside (let alone the pampas). Beautiful weather : an atmosphere both of tension and gloom because of the coming elections and the illness of ' Saint ' Evita. But it was a rewarding visit all the same, thanks to my meeting with a well-known prehistorian (Professor Menghin, emigrated from Austria) who put me in the picture about the progress, or rather the birth, of South American prehistory during the last three years : the terminus—right to the end of the journey—of a movement of human expansion traces of whose start I had just been looking at in Africa—a richly suggestive contrast which I hope to make good use of.

At the moment I am on board a large American liner—passengers and cargo—which should bring me to New York on the 26th.

Then we'll see what happens. [. . .] I am hoping to be able to stay at *America's* headquarters,[1] which I know so well, and I shall have no difficulty in finding plenty to do for some time.

---

[1] One of the Jesuit houses in New York, the headquarters of the review *America*, roughly corresponding to *Études* in Paris.

(To J. T. de C.)   *980, Park Avenue, New York, 2 December, 1951*

The last stage of my journey went more than comfortably in the *Uruguay* of the Moore-MacCormick Line which handles (in a highly Irish and Catholic atmosphere) cargo and luxury passenger traffic down the eastern coast of South America. It was the slackest part of the off-season for cruises, so that the ship was far from full ; but they still ran the complete service—including a conjuror, a Broadway singer and a pair of dancers of incredible suppleness ; a chaplain, of course, and an altar. Discreetly attentive and cheerful service—you know the sort of thing—all very successful, in short.

Not an eventful voyage ; the weather was excellent. Rio unfortunately was rather foggy and suffering from a drought that threatened to lower the water in the hydro-electric sources to a dangerous level. Even so, I was able to form a good idea of the marvellous anchorage and of the city. The sea-front is occupied by a series of skyscrapers—Rio is squeezed in between the granitic plateau and the sea, which justifies this rather unsightly style of building—glaring new skyscrapers, but much less beautiful and variegated than those of New York. Our most pleasant call was at Trinidad, kept beautifully clean and neat (as you might expect) by the English. It was hot and humid, but the light was wonderful. A two hours' taxi drive gave me a nice trip in the hills around Port of Spain, through the cocoa, coffee and grapefruit plantations. The vegetation is simply astounding. During lunch (to the music of negro guitars) the final touch was given to the terrace by the appearance of a humming-bird, humming away on a hibiscus flower, and then of an iridescent blue Morpho butterfly. The anchorage is extended to the west by a lofty headland which is actually part of Venezuela.

Two days later we had a spell of cold weather, tempered by the warmth of the seaweed-laden Gulf Stream. Then we were back in the New York climate, welcomed by clear, almost spring-like skies.

Since then I have been more or less settling down here, and getting my bearings.

1951-1953

980, Park Avenue, New York, 4 December, 1951

[. . .] Thanks to the good offices of Father Lafarge, I am staying, after all, in what corresponds in New York, not to *Études*, but to the rue de Grenelle—which has the advantage of putting me in the centre of the city, a quarter of an hour from the Natural History Museum, and, more important still, from the Wenner Gren Foundation.

Rome seems favourably inclined to the idea of my prolonging my stay here. [. . .] That being so, I don't think I can do better than accept the cordial offer made to me by Dr. Fejos, director of research at the Wenner Gren Foundation, to join him as a ' *research associate* '. If the American Fathers don't object—and I don't think that they will—it will be 1925 over again, with New York instead of China. The only thing is, I'm seventy. [. . .] Even so, it may be, once more, an intervention of Providence, and the opening up of a new field.

I envisage three levels of activity for my work at the Foundation :

1. To work at organising research on Fossil Man (and the origins of mankind) ;
2. To initiate (and this is a trickier business) a completely new type of research directed towards the scientific discovery

and verification of what I call a ' convergence ' in man of evolution turning in upon itself ; [1]

3. To pursue (as a completely private venture) my effort to re-think Christology and Christianity in terms of a humanity in process of biological convergence.

As you know, it is the second point that seems to me at the moment to be strategically decisive. The concept of human convergence on itself seems to me as revolutionary a step (for all human thought and activity) as ever was that of a ' revolving ' earth or of biological evolution.

While I am here, the Foundation will be able to put me in touch with all sorts of technicians or thinkers in various fields, and I shall try to familiarise people with this idea and to discover a line of experimental approach. I have just sent Julian Huxley some notes on this question for his jubilee volume—purely scientific in tone, like my Sorbonne lectures.

(To the Abbé Breuil)   *New York, 22 January, 1952*

My life is running along more or less smoothly—with just a slight undertone of disquiet from not feeling completely at home here in my Order.[2] Everyone is as kind as possible to me, but even so I can't help appearing rather a bird of passage, or something of a parasite. I don't doubt that this feeling will evaporate of its own accord—like the certain amount of regret I feel for Paris. In fact, I have nothing to complain about. I am well placed in my little ' *office* ' at the Foundation to meet bit by bit

---

[1] An idea that is worked out in the essay : ' L'Humanité se meut-elle biologiquement sur elle-même ? ' (*Revue des questions scientifiques*, Louvain, 20 October, 1949. Also published in *L'Avenir de l'homme*, 1959.)

[2] As Père Teilhard could not be accommodated in *America's* house he was living at 980 Park Avenue ; ' rather more just a billet, but right in the heart of the city, a quarter of an hour from where I have most to do '.

everything that is most interesting in America and even in other countries ; [1] particularly this year, with the June ' *Symposium* ' when seventy anthropologists from practically every part of the world are meeting to draw up a balance sheet of the present state and requirements of anthropology.

I thought I had told you that the discovery of 'a large number' of remains of Sinanthropus is a legend arising from the fact that when two or three teeth were found during some surface excavations last year Pei wrote a short article (of which I have been sent a translation) in which he recalls the earlier finds. Oddly enough, three weeks ago the director of the Museum of Antiquities (?) at Pekin revived the legend that the Sinanthropus material is hidden in the United States. This time the *New York Times* (5 January, 1952) has published an exact account of the events by Colonel Ashurst, the man who was actually in charge of evacuating the two cases which disappeared from the train (or from the docks looted by the Japanese on Pearl Harbour day).

New York, 2 March, 1952

Your letter of February 25 has arrived safely, and I have also had the *Revue de Paris*—not counting two numbers of *Études*, January and February. All this helps me to ' get over the loss of Paris '— where, after all, the spirit breathes more strongly than it does here. I am interested in your relations with G.—with whom I instinctively sympathise, though I have the impression at the same time that he has not yet quite ' taken the step ' (the recognition of the genetic value of the world. The deep and secret working of modern ideology on human material, called into being and fostered by the spectacular economic and political tensions we are

[1] The universality of science, in the immediate post-war years, was nowhere more manifest than in New York, where eminent scientists of all nations were meeting and working together.

subjected to, always seems to me to be the capital event of our day.) [. . .]

Here, I am continuing, so far as I can, to clarify and spread the elements of this new anthropology ; and I am regularly getting more chance of doing so. Last Monday, I gave a talk to the New York Academy of Sciences on the Australopithecæ ; again on the 14th at the Wenner Gren Foundation, on the prehistory of South Africa. Meanwhile I am to go to the Museum of Natural History to take a session of the anthropology seminar ; and into the bargain I have been asked at the last moment to prepare by the end of the month a report on Fossil Man for the June Symposium. [. . .] In spite of several short blizzards which buried the cars parked permanently in the streets, it has not been a particularly cold winter ; or rather I haven't felt the cold, so overheated are the houses here. A fortnight ago I went to Washington, where they very kindly gave a cocktail party for me at the Catholic University. I had very fine weather for the short journey. The woods along the Potomac, though still quite grey, were charming to see.

Solange Lemaître [1] is here at the moment, just back from Guatemala, an astonishing country of orchids, parrots and monkeys ; it convinced her that the analogies between Chinese and Maya art are purely superficial or very late. I was really delighted to see her again and talk about our friends (Grousset, Bacot, Loriot, Georges Salles, etc.).

But all that is simply the external side of my life. Interiorily, the interest of my life is concentrated more and more on the effort to find and if possible to give voice to the final formulation (the last testimony) in which I wish to express the ' soul ' of my

[1] Madame S. Lemaître, the orientalist, who had been sent by René Grousset to Mexico and Guatemala, to organise a pre-Colombian exhibition at the Musée Cernuschi.

two-fold vision of the ' Upward ' and the ' Forward '.[1] [. . .] We must pray for one another, that each of us may end well.[2]

(To J. T. de C.)   *New York, 8 March, 1952*

I'm carrying on here as usual. I think I told you in my last letter about my short visit, in beautiful weather, to Washington. Quite a few interesting or useful meetings, for instance with Grew and his wife, whom I had seen at the Embassy in Tokyo and whose little daughter I actually baptised in Pekin. I am getting used to my office in the Wenner Gren Foundation, and people are getting used to seeing and writing to me there. I am not without hopes of doing some good here. The June Symposium is still the chief preoccupation in the building. At the last moment, my friend Fejos (the director of research) asked me to fill the gap left by a ' defaulter ' and prepare a preliminary report on the present state of the Fossil-Man question ; impossible, of course, to refuse.

A fortnight ago, accordingly, I gave a sort of lecture on the Australopithecæ to the New York Academy of Sciences, and I have another to give on the 14th at the Wenner Gren Foundation, on the state of prehistory in South Africa. Yesterday there was a big dinner at the Waldorf-Astoria for the annual presentation of the medals awarded by the Foundation—rather too much of a mob. All the same, in the crowd I met several friends I was looking out for. Wenner Gren himself had come up from Mexico for the occasion : a fine Nordic figure, rather an enigmatic personality, but one who, like Rockefeller and Haardt and so many others, has decided that the most interesting thing to do

[1] The two movements, human progress ' Forward ' and the spiritual impulse ' Upward ', which must find their transfiguration and realisation in God, sum up Père Teilhard's view of the world in evolution.

[2] This preoccupation with his end becomes increasingly marked in the correspondence. He went so far as to say that since his heart attack in 1947 he felt ' half in life and half in death '.

Pierre Teilhard de Chardin

with money—more interesting even than power—is to pursue some 'idealistic' aim. At least, that's a plausible explanation of his attitude. [. . .]

Last week I saw my friend Solange Lemaître as she was passing through on her way back from Guatemala, where, besides Maya art, she seems to have seen a great many orchids, parrots and monkeys. If July and August were not the rainy season, I think I should have accepted an invitation from the Minister (Coiffard) to spend some time at his Legation. The Consul here (Seydoux, a friend of mine) has been promoted to Counsellor at Washington (which I regret for my own sake), and has been replaced by the Consul at San Francisco (Lagarde or de Lagarde) with whom I should have some friends in common.[1] Yesterday, I went to see a Madame B. (a Belgian), the moving force behind the U.C.M.[2] in the United States, of whom Monique Givelet had spoken to me. She wants to have Guiguite's life translated. Madame B. lives on the 29th storey of the Astoria, in an extraordinary apartment, a sort of tower, from which you get a view of New York on all four sides : skyscrapers, sea, the Hudson, the East River, all at once. A finer view, possibly, than that from the Rainbow room at the Rockefeller Institute.

(To J. T. de C.) *New York, Good Friday,*[3] *1952*

[. . .] Last week I went to stay the night (following an old custom dating back to 1930) with my friend Frick, at his magnificent place on Long Island (Roslyn) ; and there I had the pleasure of meeting, also down for the ' *weekend* ', Fairfield Osborn (a son of the great Osborn) who is now director of the big New York Bronx Zoo and president of the soil conservation Com-

---

[1] As it happened, they found that they were cousins, Madame de Lagarde (née de Féligonde) being connected with the Teilhards.

[2] Union Catholique des Malades.

[3] 11 April.

mittee. We had a great deal of talk, like three old friends, in a series of enormous rooms packed with flowers (Mrs. Frick looks after the greenhouses) in the company of five long-haired, soulful-eyed basset-hounds (one of them, Suzy, was just back from boarding at Princeton, no less, where a special establishment had seen to her education!). Frick still runs three or four digging sites in the West : Mammalia, Miocene and Pliocene ; and he is collecting, preparing and having drawings made of an interesting body of material from which we may learn a great deal (when it's properly studied by ' *the right person* ') about the structure of what zoologists and palæontologists call a ' phylum ', a whole *bundle* of divergent or interwoven strands. As a sideline he is going on with his collection of conifers (he acclimatises species from almost everywhere) ; he has just added to it several specimens already two feet high, of the famous *Metasequoia* found at Szechuan about 1943, previously thought to have been extinct since the Cretaceous system. In Frick's grounds last week, we had to admire this *Metasequoia* entirely on trust, for since it sheds all its spines in the winter (like a bald cypress) it looks exactly like a dead branch stuck into the ground. You'd get on admirably with Frick and Frick would be completely ' *at home* ' at Les Moulins.[1]

Apart from that, I am still working on a number of papers. I've finished the one on Fossil-Man which Fejos asked me for at such short notice. I hope it won't clash too much with the other papers written for the same occasion (the June Symposium). I'm not thinking of moving before Easter ; but in May I have to go to Boston (to Harvard). The weather is improving and the magnolias in Central Park are in flower, but the trees, except that some of the sycamores are beginning to redden, are still quite black.

[1] Joseph Teilhard de Chardin's place in Auvergne.

(To J. T. de C.)   *New York, 11 May, 1952*

It's already some time since I had your card of the 19th telling me of your Easter visit to Les Moulins. I hope everything is still going reasonably well with you all.

Here too, life still follows its regular course under skies that are now—except today, when it's raining—definitely spring-like. Last Sunday I went to see some friends on the outskirts of New York (Scarsdale) which gave me the chance to see for the first time a fine show of ' *dogwoods* ' in full flower. They're a little bit like white or pink apple-trees, but each flower is as big as a petunia ; it really had an effect of fairyland. I'm hoping to see the climax of this firework display during the short journey to Yale University (New Haven) at the end of this week. The week after, I'm to go to Cambridge (to Harvard University). By then it will be practically June, which brings the anthropology Symposium. Time passes more and more quickly when you get to my age.

I find plenty to do from day to day ; but I do wish that some main objective would present itself (like my African trip last year). No doubt the Symposium will produce what I want, perhaps in the form of something that needs to be written. What I lack, obviously, is the chance to develop and bring out into the open, either orally or in writing, a number of key ideas.[1]

I had a conversation last Friday with Jules Moch, of the Institut Français here, about the position of Communism in the world. It confirmed my impression of the general admiration for France. What a welcome breath of fresh air that was ! Moch seems to be really getting down to it with the Russians at the

[1] Père Teilhard confesses his nostalgia for the ' spiritual climate ' of Paris and for the intellectual life of France in general. Frenchmen passing through New York were made a great fuss of, as leading lights in every field—arts, letters, the theatre, politics.

disarmament committee. I talked to him about you as we shook hands, and he hasn't forgotten you. At the same time I met Georges Picot, whom I hadn't seen since Pekin. He's now with the League of Nations.[1]

(To J. T. de C.)   *New York, 29 May, 1952*

[. . .] I have just met some old Pekin friends again, the Hoppenots [2] and the Lacostes, and Lacoste invited me to an epicurean dinner—foie gras straight from Périgord, which is where Madame Lacoste comes from. The guests were all ex-China or ex-Japan, one of them (equally so qualified) being Malik (from Moscow), whom I met in the lift coming up and then sat almost next to at table. He was very jolly, and much easier to get on with as a man than I had imagined. He drank, of course, ' to peace'. I couldn't help saying that, as an impartial observer, I couldn't understand why tension should persist so long between peoples so naturally fitted to understand one another as the Russians and the Americans. But that they'll never be able to do until the Russians stop telling lies (give up their ' morality of deception '), which is the root of the matter.

Like most New Yorkers in the summer, Père Teilhard was anxious to get away from the extreme heat of the city. He travelled in the western and northern states, always with some definite scientific objective or to meet fellow-scientists.

Berkeley, California, 15 July, 1952

This is a long overdue answer to your letter of June 21st. On July 3rd, I left for California, stopping at Chicago, where I spent only a few hours on the eve of the Republican convention—you

[1] i.e. the United Nations.
[2] French delegate to the United Nations.

can imagine the excitement ; at Albuquerque, New Mexico, right in the middle of the Rocky deserts, I spent two days with my friend Simpson, the palæontologist, on the borders of a forest that skirts the ' bad lands ' ; and finally at Los Angeles, where the director of the local museum is Delacourt, the owner of the zoological park at Clère,[1] who has had a long experience of the Far East. And now I am installed for three or four weeks just at the gates of the University of California, where I have found quite a band of old friends. [. . .] This makes me feel rather more at home, but still I have a curious feeling of a profound change both within and outside of my own self. It's the same setting as before 1940, but now ' the Golden Gate ' is closed to me —no more China ; and from now on geology has been un-mistakably replaced for me by the human and the ultra-human. I'm nevertheless still busy here with the study of fossils, and I am learning a great deal that is useful to me. But the ' neo-anthro-pology ' of which I dream has now first place in my thought and conversation. Meanwhile I am turning over various schemes of work. First, some notes for the June Symposium ; then—but for rather later—an essay on the ' Christic ', a sort of new edition of the Milieu divin. [. . .] All this keeps me pretty well occupied, and I continue to progress in a direction which seems to me more and more to lead towards ' my Lord and my God '. I have absolute trust in Him, whose greatest possible exaltation is my only care.

(To J. T. de C.)   *Berkeley (Calif.), 28 July, 1952*

I left New York on the 3rd for the west—stopped a few hours at Chicago, on the eve of the Republican convention : actually in the hotel where Ike had his headquarters. Great excitement already, with huge favours in everyone's buttonholes.

---

[1] In Normandy.

[. . .] The day after leaving Chicago, I left the train at Albuquerque and took a bus which brought me, after a two-and-a-half-hour ride, nine miles from the place where my friend Simpson, the palæontologist, lives ; he's about 7,500 feet up, on the edge of San Pedro Mountains national park, right in the middle of the San Juan Basin (one of the fine Secondary-Tertiary series of the southern Rockies). A very nice house built in the local style, full of Indian rugs and even Indian pictures—the Indians are developing a most interesting talent for painting. I slept in a comfortable tent. Plenty of the ' *bad lands* '—red and white furrows gouged across the landscape—an expanse as wide as the view from Les Moulins, but with nothing like a ' village ' in sight.[1] But I didn't see the real desert. Almost everywhere you find woods of thuja trees (which they call cedars here), and in the mountain country there's an impressive display of *pinus ponderosa*. The local flora is very individual, mostly with brilliant red flowers and small cactuses. I saw nothing of the fauna, though deer (Odocoilus) are said to be plentiful. Simpson told me that during the snow this winter, wild turkeys came to feed at his place ; he showed me photographs taken from his window.

After Albuquerque my next stop was at Los Angeles, where I went to the local museum to see the director, who turned out to be Delacourt, the ornithologist, the creator of the zoological park at Clère in Normandy, an old Indo-China man. I have never met him before, and we both enjoyed seeing one another.

Now (from the 10th of July to the 8th of August) I'm at my familiar old Berkeley, right at the gates of the University. From my windows I can see San Francisco, the Bay, and the ' Golden Gate ' with its famous bridge. It gives me an odd sensation to

[1] From his brother's place in Auvergne you can see the whole chain of the Dôme unfolding before you.

see the Pacific without embarking for Honolulu and Kobe. [. . .]
I am meeting again a group of dear friends in palæontology, and
I am renewing my contacts with a science that these last years in
Paris have made me neglect a little. The University of California is very much on the spot in scientific research : incidentally, the campus, shaded by eucalyptus and rich in flowers, is a
delightful sight. After a few days, I was allowed, thanks to my
special contacts, to visit the nuclear energy research centre in the
hills above the University and see the group of cyclotrons in
operation or under construction. As I wrote to a friend at
Études, you really have the feeling in such places of being out of
your depth in this new human thing ; in the complexity and
power of one machine—mathematical speculation, laboratory
research, the wide scope of industrial enterprises, military ambition, medical hopes of therapy—and even the secret hope of
finding the ultimate explanation of things [. . .] There's a whole
population, of course, of engineers and physicists to work the
monsters. It's an extraordinary business. The first chance I
get, I must make the acquaintance of the great computers at
Harvard—the last word in systematisation after the last word in
energy.

I found some dear old Pekin friends here, at the Bank of
Indochina, the Bardacs, and so I've had some delightful luncheons
with them. San Francisco is quickly reached from here by a
fine bridge, and it's easy to go and spend the evening there.
Chinatown is just a quarter of Canton or Shanghai, and in spite
of my lack of enthusiasm for Chinese cooking I must admit that
the excellence of their dishes quite comes up to the standard of
Pekin restaurants. Yesterday, my friends took me to a Hun-
garian concert in an expensive college near here (Mill's College,
for Californian girls), and I was surprised to find several Frenchmen : a young teacher from the University of Lyons (Anglès,
who comes from Aveyron), and Darius Milhaud himself, who

is working at his music here for a year. I was rather surprised that they both knew who I was.

I am proposing to leave this enchanting place on August 8th, and go back to New York, by way of the Glacier Park (Montana) where I would like to look at some 'pre-Cambrian' formations which interest me in comparison with China and South Africa.

New York, 18 September, 1952

[. . .] I am back now at the W.G. Foundation, where a sort of future (?) seems to be unfolding for me in the sense that, yielding to my gentle pressure (and that of circumstances), Fejos, back from Sweden and other places, now seems to have made up his mind to direct the main energies of the Foundation towards the question of human origins in Africa, and to take me on as his second in command in the assignment. In fact, the only work which this involves, for this year at least, is long-distance research and organisation. But if only I were ten years younger! [. . .]

It appears that on the occasion of the centenary of Laval University (Montreal) the Catholics are going to hold a congress on Evolution. I would very much like to know whether Piveteau [1] will be going (he's been invited) and, still more, whether, if he is, he will come here on his way. [2] The Duchess [3] sent me a

[1] M. Jean Piveteau, Professor at the Sorbonne.

[2] In a later letter (13 December) to the Abbé Breuil, he writes : ' I haven't been able to find out what was said at Quebec, at the Catholic congress on Evolution at the end of September [. . .] Some eminent agnostic palæontologists were invited : Stensio from Stockholm, my friend Simpson from New York. But not a word, of course, to me, not even an announcement. In his letter of acceptance, Simpson expressed surprise that *he* had been invited and not I. In fact, however, I prefer to have been left out of it.'

[3] Duchesse de la Rochefoucauld : in her *Rencontres avec le Père Teilhard de Chardin* she recalls the meetings at her house which brought together Père Teilhard de Chardin, Paul Valéry and such eminent scientists as Maurice de Broglie, M. Leprince-Ringuet, Dr. Rivet and others.

kind little note on the occasion of the death of our dear Grousset ;[1] she will not be going through New York on her way to Montreal, for which I'm sorry.

[. . .] You're quite right. The writers are in chaos, and, for the sake of publicity, they seem to be adopting a fashion of provoking chaos. Thank you for sending the *Revue de Paris*, which I read eagerly—at least the meaty parts, of which there always seem to be plenty.

New York, 29 October, 1952

Met the other day, and had quite an intimate conversation with, a certain M. Gary (a Frenchman at the League of Nations)[2] who told me that he was a writer.[3] Do you know him in this capacity? Talking of the French, the French colony here is eagerly awaiting the arrival of the Jean-Louis Barrault company, which is coming to a New York theatre. There was an interesting talk on the company the day before yesterday at the Alliance Française. I went to it, because at the end de Lagarde presented the Legion of Honour to my friend Malvina Hofman, the sculptor, a pupil of Rodin's.

[1] René Grousset, the orientalist and historian, curator of the Guimet and Cernuschi Museums, was a friend of Père Teilhard's. They had much to bring them together—a parallel effort towards the scientific exploration of Asia, the one through natural history, geology, palæontology and anthropology ; the other through the history of civilisations and religions. Both sought to bring out the spiritual content of the great events and great cultures of the past.

[2] i.e. United Nations.

[3] He was not yet known as the author of *The Roots of Heaven*. It is intriguing to note the divergence of views between the novelist and the naturalist-philosopher, the more so that many readers have thought they detected in Romain Gary's Père Tassin a distant portrait of Père Teilhard—but it is so distant, in fact, as to be unrecognisable.

22 November, 1952

[. . .] I am still writing a certain number of short personal notes. I have sent Leroy,[1] for Duhem's *Revue scientifique*, an article on *Hominisation and Speciation*, which will probably upset a good many biologists and anthropologists if it ever appears, but which is, I believe, pretty much to the point, and touches a point about which modern scientists are particularly sensitive. At the same time I have sent a short paper, rather more imaginative, on research (' *En regardant les cyclotrons de Berkeley* ') to Barrat, secretary-general of the ' Intellectuels Catholiques '. And finally, I am turning over in my mind something on ' the end of the world ' and ' the end of the human species ', the idea for which came to me the other day as I was watching the film *Life Begins Tomorrow* —a tedious production for the American public—in which a golden age (i.e. an age of abundance) makes a boringly unattractive appearance ; it was suggested, too, as I was reading a lecture our dear friend Huxley gave at Amsterdam, in which an ' evolutionist humanism ' is presented without reference to a higher pole of aggregation and emergence ; although J. H. insists that the human species is not socially divergent within itself but tends to form ' *a single inter-thinking group* '—which is already a great step forward.

[. . .] Like many others, I shed a tear for Stevenson ;[2] but the masses wanted a hero, a wonder-working saviour, a *deus ex machina*, for Korea ; and in any case ' *a change for the change* '[3] just to see if things would go better. But there are strong indications of the appearance in the wake of the Republican ship of a dangerous school of sharks—capitalists in the worst meaning of

---

[1] Père Leroy, S.J., at present attached to the laboratory of histo-physiology at the Collège de France.

[2] Adlai Stevenson, the unsuccessful Presidential candidate.

[3] Presumably ' a change, for a change ' is intended.

the word—leaping with joy at the thought of the end of the New Deal (no longer, in fact, possible in view of the progress made by the Unions in the twenty years' interval) and playing into the hands of communists abroad. There's little point in harrying the '*reds*' and the '*pinks*' at home, if at the same time you provide justification for their most telling accusations. Foster Dulles's appointment is also disturbing, for this will mean a 'strong line' with Moscow. Unless, of course, Moscow is simply bluffing? But it seems a risky game, quite apart from being altogether too simple and failing to help us along the road we need to follow— the road in which humanity's increase in force would be accompanied within itself by progress in the spirit of non-force. The most reassuring aspect is that Ike knows his job as a soldier too well to play about with war, and that he is utterly honest. He'll keep Taft in hand, I hope.

13 December, 1952

This is an answer to your letter of November 25th. It's not much too early, judging by the number of glittering fir-trees and Santa Clauses blocking the streets, to wish you a happy Christmas and a happy New Year. Happy, both of them, in the sense Our Lord wishes. [. . .] Pray to God for me continually, that I may end in such a way that my end may humbly, but distinctly and worthily, set the seal upon my witness.

(To J. T. de C.)   *New York, 14 December, 1952*

I am still planning ' operation Africa '[1] from a distance. It seems to be taking shape ; and, what is more (*mirabile dictu*), I am writing some articles that seem likely to be accepted. I should add that they are, at least in appearance, technical in scope. The *Revue des*

[1] A projected new assignment in South Africa.

335

questions scientifiques has at last printed ' La Réflexion de l'énergie', and I think the *Revue scientifique* will take ' Hominisation et spéciation '.[1] I haven't yet learnt the reaction of the *Revue des intellectuels catholiques* (Paris) to ' En regardant les cyclotrons de Berkeley '.

You know as much as I do about the political situation in the U.S.A. The present juncture has brought out two anomalies in the constitution. First of all, the inconvenience of the inter-presidential gap (already, however, considerably cut down) when no-one governs ; and secondly the equivocal, and even dangerous, position of the Vice-President, a second-rate stop-gap whom accident may at a moment's notice raise to the highest govern-mental position. I know that many Americans would like to see some remedy found as soon as possible for this second situation. Meanwhile, Ike is becoming more and more likeable and seems to be distinctly anxious to cut loose from Taft (and, let's hope, from McCarthy too).

All this, however, is forgotten for the moment in the ' *Christmas* ' fever. Fir-trees covered in lights are ranged all along Park Avenue ; the big stores have flesh and blood Santa Clauses at their entrances ; and the counters are besieged by customers buying presents for one another. It's a real psychosis in which, as I think I said before, you can't distinguish where shrewd commercial advertising ends and where emotional spirituality begins.

New York, 2 February, 1953

The December number of the *Revue de Paris* came yesterday—thank you. I have already read with great interest Thiébaut's article on the novel, for he raises two important questions simul-taneously : ' art for art's sake ' and ' does art discover anything

---

[1] Appeared in the *Revue scientifique*, Nov-Dec., 1952, and in *La Vision du passé*, ch. 20.

new, or do we do nothing but serve up the same dish with a different sauce?' In science, research is obviously already committed and must become increasingly so, in so far as it manifests its own participation in the evolutionary process of life itself; and it does, as Thiébaut puts it, serve up completely new dishes. This makes me wonder whether it is possible that in the human sphere art represents a stagnant sector (para- or extra-evolutionary) or a sort of inert envelope around humanisation. If man is changing—and progress in inter-thinking shows that he is—then how can art fail to change too, in some process which makes it progressively, if imperceptibly, ultra-human? There we come up against a very deep problem : is art evolutionary, either by nature or by function? On the analogy with science, I am sure that the answer must be Yes, but I cannot quite see how to pick out the element of growth—the additive, the ' *drift* '—beneath the historical rhythms of artistic creation. The ' true ' undoubtedly grows with the passage of time : the ' beautiful ' must necessarily do the same if the world is organically integrated. But where, and how?

At the beginning of March Père Teilhard: who had been greatly interested by Julian Huxley's ' Evolution in Action' and Charles Galton Darwin's (grandson of the great Darwin) 'After a Million Years', was anxious to write a short book on 'the future of the human species' in order to emphasise the characteristic proper to our zoological species, which is to ' converge actively upon itself'. ' I think ', he wrote, ' I may be able to write a hundred pages or so on that subject without coming under fire from the theologians. I am already sketching out my approach, without actually getting anything on paper.' [1] *(To M. T.-C., New York, 1 March, 1953.)*

[1] This plan materialised in ch. 17 of *L'Apparition de l'homme*, (' The special properties of the human species ').

(To J. T. de C.)   *New York, 7 April, 1953*

[. . .] Things continue here much the same. I am not yet out of my period of 'anxieties', an evil of which I can readily find traces in my childhood ;[1] but this doesn't prevent people from congratulating me on my fitness. My friend Dr. Simard is still 'building me up' in every way he can think of, and I believe that I am in fact beginning to come out on the right side. But I shall have had rather a miserable winter in one way and another. I only hope that the Lord may have turned it to good use, in His own way. My work has gone on in spite of everything. I am contemplating a short book (publishable ??) on the future of the human species, to correct or complement certain notions recently brought out by my friend Julian Huxley [2] and by Charles Darwin (grandson of the great man). But I hardly know when I shall get down to writing it.

[. . .] At the end of Holy Week, I went to Long Island to stay the night in the magnificent house of my friend Frick, who wished to show me his latest harvest of palæontological finds. As usual, we visited the park with its magnificent series of conifers, while the hall and the rooms were filled with masses of flowers—mostly azaleas, at the moment—which Mrs. Frick raises in her greenhouses. The tragedy of this splendid place is that, owing to taxation, none of Frick's children will be able to keep things up as they are now. I wonder if Frick will follow his mother's example, who has given her house and pictures (just near the Wenner Gren Foundation, where I am writing) to the city of New York. Will he, that is, make Roslyn into an annexe of the American Museum of Natural History ? I have no idea, of course, but I think it's quite a possibility.

[1] This anxious condition could also be explained by the mental worries undergone in recent years, aggravated by the heart attack.
[2] *Evolution in Action.*

New York, 9 April, 1953

I went last week to spend the night, as I have often done before, with my friend Frick on Long Island. He wanted to show me his new palæontological finds. As usual, the grounds were magnificent, with the magnolias in full flower, and the house was packed with flowers. There I met the youngest son of Theodore Roosevelt (a cousin of Franklin's), a hundred per cent American, who disapproves of all the money his country has given away abroad and wouldn't shrink from the possibility of the United States on their own against the rest of the world. At the same time, he is an extremely nice man, cultivated, and, although he was not liable to be called up during the last war, he obtained permission from his cousin, the President, to go and fight in the New Guinea jungles. A few days before, I had been present (on the platform, with the big shots!) at the presentation of an honorary doctorate to Bidault. Dewey, the governor of the State of New York, made a very pro-French speech. I was only able to talk for a moment to Madame Bidault (we lunched together several times in Paris at de Billy's) and for a little longer with Maritain. He looked very grand in his academic robes—quite grey, but still the same.

(To J. T. de C.) *New York, 5 May, 1953*

No particular news here, except that I am definitely much better—with the result that my journey to Africa is beginning to materialise again in my mind. Diggings—financed by the Wenner Gren Foundation, largely at my instigation—have just been begun at a crucial site north of Pretoria. According to my latest information, the ship I am taking (from here direct to the Cape) leaves on June 29th. In fact it is such a short time since I got back from South Africa that the prospect of the ' *trip* ' doesn't particularly thrill me, apart from the pleasure of re-visiting familiar places. But I am counting on contact with the field material to give me ideas, energy and a rather sounder platform from which to make myself heard in Rome and elsewhere.

Meanwhile, we are having a shocking spring—except today when the sky and temperature have suddenly become perfect. The annoying thing is to realise that I myself am going to meet winter again in July.

I still see very few people. Still, ten days or so ago, I was invited by Lagarde to an all-male luncheon party given for the 'King' of Cambodia (I really couldn't bring myself to call him 'Your Majesty'), where I met Fain (the diplomat) whom I hadn't seen since Pekin, and—better still—Jacques Rueff, the former governor of the Bank of France, with whom I got on very well. I rather understood that Rueff was arranging, for 1954, some sort of conference on human problems, to include physicists (such as Niels Bohr) and biologists : which is just what I am urging Dr. Fejos to do here. I asked him to keep me informed of his plans ; '54 is just the year when I expect to be back in Paris.[1]

---

[1] Père Teilhard writes more than once of his wish to return to Paris : even, and above all, for religious reasons. 'After a certain time it becomes indispensable to go back and breathe the air of Paris.'

July–November, 1953

On July 1st, Père Teilhard embarked for South Africa, entrusted by the Wenner Gren Foundation with the new assignment of assisting in the organisation of anthropological research in the whole of Africa south of the Sahara.

(To J. T. de C.)   *Johannesburg, 26 July, 1953*

[. . .] At this moment I'm sitting and writing to you, not without some surprise, in the very room at the Langham which I left in September 1951, with the same negro newspaper-boys under my windows. It's magnificent weather, of course ; a little cold—there was frost this morning—but cloudless. There has been no rain here for more than two months! The sea-crossing couldn't have been more agreeable in spite of the monotony : blue skies, at least partly blue, every day ; no great heat and no storms—apparently there never are on this route—just the trade winds. The eighteen days went by quickly ; I was able to do a little work and writing on board, as I usually manage to do. But there was nothing at all to look at—some sargasso weed at first, and some flying fish. The most interesting event was to sail by Ascension Island (volcano : two hundred and forty inhabitants who look after the cable service on the military airfield)—green in places—grass, but not a single tree—and one morning to see St. Helena on the horizon.

We feared that we might arrive at the Cape in rough seas, but in fact we found ourselves back in spring weather : red hibiscus flowers in all the gardens, every sort of camelia and aloe. I spent six days in Capetown, where I found an interesting situation from the point of view of my work here : during the last few months, a markedly Neanderthal human cranium had been found on a site which I had visited in 1951 [1] (in the consolidation, full of fossils and tools) ; the discovery calls for new decisions, and for financial backing, in all of which, thanks to the W.G. Foundation, I can be of assistance—for that is the real purpose of my journey to Africa. I am going now to look at the diggings north of Pretoria which were begun in April.

(To J. T. de C.)   *Southern Rhodesia, 2 September, 1953*

[. . .] I left for Livingstone in Northern Rhodesia on August 24th—less than two hours by Comet from Johannesburg—and from there by road for Lusaka, the new capital two hundred and fifty miles north of Livingstone. The purpose of my journey was to visit a number of fissures around Lusaka which contain, cemented in the breccia, some tools of a particularly ancient type. And I believe, with the young and brilliant Desmond Clark (director of the Livingstone Museum), that we have found a strategically important site for the expense of whose development we can call on the W.G. Foundation. It was interesting to inspect, and I learnt a great deal. The journey, too, was extremely picturesque. Apart from the great fauna, which have disappeared except in the reserves, the country can hardly have changed since Livingstone's day—vast rolling expanses covered with bush in which most of the various trees are as tall as the average oak. It's the end of the dry season : a background of tall yellow grasses and bare branches, but quite a few green trees as well. I saw two big

[1] At Hopefield. A find made by Keith Jolly.

rivers : the Kafue, near Lusaka, and right where I am now the majestic and historic Zambesi, with its magnificent falls which I can hear at the moment. These Victoria Falls, though they are in Southern Rhodesia, are only five miles from Livingstone. The day before yesterday Clark took us for a picnic with his family above the falls in a motor-canoe. I even had the good fortune to see crocodiles and hippopotamuses relaxing on the sandbanks or swimming in the water. With the blue sky you always get at this time of the year, it was a delightful excursion. On the whole, and in comparison with the Transvaal, you have the impression of being in entirely new country. Livingstone and Lusaka are still only ' big villages ', with bungalows scattered in a background of bush. Apart from that, all you see is an occasional government building or ultra-modern hotel : at the Lusaka hotel the head waiter was a Parisian! He gets very few French visitors, he told me.

Tomorrow I go back to Johannesburg, again by Comet.

Joh'burg, 6 September, 1953

I am just back from a fortnight in Northern Rhodesia, Livingstone and Lusaka. On this occasion we went by Comet—an hour and forty minutes from Joh'burg to Livingstone, instead of three days by train or car. [. . .] It's a remarkable machine : in spite of the height at which you cruise, thirty thousand feet, you feel much safer than in the old propeller-driven aeroplanes. This time I came close to the heart of Africa, even though it was in its least impressive part—no lakes, no mountains, no huge forests. Even so there is something most impressive in those vast expanses of bush ; the fauna has largely disappeared but the general setting and vegetation has not changed since Livingstone. The waterfall region (Victoria Falls) of the Zambesi is particularly well-preserved (it's a game reserve). Above the falls you

343

can see crocodiles and hippopotamuses in complete freedom. Some time ago the sight would have thrilled me, but now I found it rather a melancholy survival—a world in the course of extinction. What I came to look for, as you know, was a better observation post for studying, at its beginnings, the law of growth in the human 'trajectory'. From that point of view my journey will, I think, have been successful. I have learnt a great deal, and above all I feel that thanks to the support of the W.G. Foundation I shall have helped to establish an exact network of research into human origins, covering all Africa south of the Sahara. A pity, though, that I'm no longer young enough to enter the yellow fever areas : I feel the lack of never having seen the great lake deposits. [. . .]

All this technical side, of course, is not preventing me from reflecting on the living problems presented by the Africa of to-day—far from it. Africa, indeed, seems to me at present, whatever people may say, to function as a zone of reduced pressure (and hence of aspiration for the white and yellow races) in the Noosphere. But above and beyond this continental problem I feel in the very depths of my being the insistence of a question more urgent than ever : the great question of a faith—a Christology—to give the final, supreme burst of energy to the forces of hominisation in us—or, which comes to the same thing, to the forces of adoration.[1]

Père Teilhard's correspondents in France kept him informed of the religious situation. He was pleased to learn from some of his friends of some wise appointments to office in the Jesuit Order. He saw in this ' an excellent symptom ' and without any thought of his own position he wrote ' the Church is as living as ever ; you have only to leave her to grow '.

[1] The more man extends his awareness of his place in the universe, the more his adoration of the Creator will grow in depth and fullness.

(To J. T. de C.)   *Joh'burg, 18 September, 1953*

As far as my own affairs are concerned, things are still going
well; but I am approaching the end of my stay in Africa. On
the 21st I take the 'Blue Train' for Capetown (Mount Nelson
Hotel), and on the 27th—if it pleases the unpredictable Dutch
Transocean line—I embark once again for Buenos Aires. I think
I must have told you that this time my plan was to cross the
Argentine (to see, just for once, the pampas formations and a
section of the Andes) and then to take the comfortable Grace
Line at Valparaiso; this will bring me direct to New York by
Panama, with numerous calls on the west coast of South America.
It's almost as short as, and no more expensive than going right
up the east coast as I did two years ago. Besides, I feel that this
short personal experience of South American geology may help
me a great deal to mature certain ideas on the 'genesis continents'
that I have been nursing for a long time. Of course I would
have liked to see you again too by taking another route; but
for a number of reasons I think it better to put off my visit to
France until the summer of 1954—I'm not without hopes of an
August at Les Moulins. [. . .]

I came back from Livingstone (Victoria Falls), where my last
letter to you was addressed from, as comfortably as I went, by
Comet. The aircraft is pressurised, and extraordinarily steady;
you can breathe as comfortably as in your own room, even
though on our flight we were at least 36,000 feet up when we
reached our cruising height. A vast salty plain, white as snow,
which we saw half-way through the journey, makes me think we
must have cut across a corner of the Kalahari desert. It's not
surprising that you weren't able to find Lusaka in your atlas;
the town—the new capital of Northern Rhodesia—has hardly
yet come into existence. But it already has a big airfield, and a
little way away preparations are being made to dam the gorges

of the Kafue river, a tributary of the Zambesi, to provide electricity for the whole area. What are the hippopotamuses going to say about that?

Since I came back here, I've been to Pretoria (the Geological Service) and then, just recently, to our digs at Makapan, north of Pretoria, of which I've already told you. It was an interesting and rewarding trip even though we left in weather that was already very hot indeed and the next morning had the shock of running into a cold spell—come up, appropriately enough, from the Antarctic—which manifested itself in inky black skies and torrents of rain, the first for six months. To the east of Joh'burg there was thick snow on the mountains: one way and another, it was most unpleasantly cold. The North-Transvaal bush seemed to me rather impoverished after that of Rhodesia: moreover a magnificent aloe bloom, so beautiful at the end of July (imagine the hillsides covered with tritonia flowers, as we used to have them at Sarcenat [1]) had faded and was hardly yet being replaced by the acacia-mimosas. All the same, whatever part of South Africa you visit, it's a magnificent country, and I can't leave it— and the friends I made there—without a pang of regret.

However, I am leaving quite happily for I feel that I have been helping to build something, and that this renewal of contact with the concrete has taught me a great deal and given fresh youth to my mind. I am counting on the voyage to finish some reports and notes for the Wenner Gren Foundation, the Academy, etc. And all this goes towards strengthening the platform that I need so badly if the ' theologians ' are to listen to me.

[1] The Teilhard de Chardin family estate, near Clermont, in Auvergne.

1953-1955

After his return to New York, calling on the way at Rio and Trinidad, Père Teilhard took up residence agáin at 980 Park Avenue and his office at the Foundation.

New York, 8 November, 1953

I have the feeling that my efforts at the Foundation are beginning to bear fruit. For the rest, I hope that ' God will provide '. My future is more or less undecided, apart from a fairly clear notion of going back to Paris for three months or so next June ; I haven't mentioned it yet to the P.R., but I don't anticipate any objection. All that I am quite certain about is that I am anxious to use the last years that remain to me as intensively as possible in ' christifying ' (as I call it) evolution : which calls both for scientific work to establish the ' convergence ' of the universe,[1] and religious work to bring out the universal nature of the historic Christ.[2] Just that—and then to end well—which means to die in giving witness to this ' gospel '.

Pray often, I beg of you, that this may be granted to me. [. . .]

[1] Towards the spirit, through psychogenesis and hominisation.

[2] Père Teilhard is emphasising that the ' universal Christ ' is none other than the Christ who lived in Palestine, the Christ of the gospels, ' God, historically incarnate '. Through Him alone will man be able to realise his unification in love, and achieve his final consummation in God.

347

Another winter now began. At one time Père Teilhard had hoped to take in France in the course of his return from Africa, but he had given up the idea. When his friends asked him whether there was to be no end to his exile, he answered, ' What can be done, as things are ? Rome has not yet, so far as I know, retracted its decision—by no means unfriendly at bottom, but firm—of not wishing to have me " resident " in Paris [. . .] But how long will it go on for ? I constantly have a feeling—you know how I worry—that everything in my life may change at a moment's notice.[1] To end well, as I have often told you, is becoming, so far as I am concerned, my chief prayer and my one great ambition.'
(To M. T.-C., 22 November, 1953.)

The death of his friend, the geologist Emmanuel de Margerie, followed by that of Père Augustin Valensin, who had been his intimate friend and confidant since their novitiate at Aix-en-Provence, affected him greatly.

New York, 5 January, 1954

At the end of December a death that I felt deeply was that of Augustin Valensin at Nice.[2]

It was he who taught me to think. I could tell him everything, and without expressing it often we loved one another deeply. Now, he ' sees '. When will it be my turn ?

---

[1] A premonition of his coming death, no doubt.

[2] Père Valensin, a contemporary of Père Teilhard's, was his most intimate friend in the Society of Jesus. His personality was distinguished by the quality and variety of his gifts ; he was the author of some philosophical dialogues and a penetrating study of his close friend, Maurice Blondel ; after teaching in the Catholic faculties of the University of Lyons, he retired to Nice where he delighted those who attended his lectures at the ' Centre Universitaire Méditerranéen ' by the originality of his literary criticism. Whether he was dealing with Dante, D' Annunzio, Gide or Valéry, he had always some new and penetrating light to throw on his subject. ' An aristocrat of the mind ' he has been called. (A. Blanchet, *Études*, February, 1955.)

I am spending my best hours in gradually writing ' *Les Singularités de l'espèce humaine* '. I don't know how it will turn out, nor how long it will be—some eighty pages of manuscript, I suppose : hardly a book, though there'll be some figures or diagrams. But now that I've made a start, I think I shall finish it—by about Easter ? Its tone is not suited to a literary review. I am trying to make up my mind whether it would be better to bring it out in instalments, in the *Revue des questions scientifiques*, for example, or to take the bull by the horns and try to publish it direct as a short book. I'd prefer the latter. But we'll wait till we've caught our hare. And I want to end with an appendix on ' The Special Properties of the Christian Faith ' ; I don't doubt I'll get it written.

Père Teilhard was always eager to take any opportunity of meet-ing French people as they passed through New York. It was thus that during this last fortnight he twice met Malraux—on the second occasion at Gary's, of the United Nations. He had been surprised to learn that Malraux was deeply interested in his unpublished work.

' *Malraux is still writing about art, but, according to Gary, he is going back to the novel—having grown, from the literary point of view, I hope, and not become " confused " by his mysti-cism, as happened with our dear Aldous Huxley. Malraux came to the U.S.A. with the Museum directors. At the same time as I met him I saw Georges Salles, of the Louvre, again (President of the " Union des Croyants ") and G. M. Rivière of the Trocadéro (Folklore) whom I had lost sight of for years. I am to see them again this evening at Malvina Hofman's.' (To M. T.-C., 24 January, 1954.)*

New York, 28 February, 1954

I had a very kind letter from the P.R., sent from Rome on his return journey from Syria, and giving me permission to spend three months in France. I shall certainly pay a long visit to Lyons [1] and I shall try to strengthen the intimacy of some of my contacts, to make up for the gradual disappearance of my dearest friends. First there was our wonderful Augustin Valensin (a most beautiful death, almost childlike, calling on the sun and God at the same time . . .). Then my other friend, who first taught me to see the truth, Pierre Charles,[2] has also gone : he too must have ended with simplicity and style. So I repeat the prayer that has become *my* prayer, ' May the Lord grant me, not for my own sake but for the sake of the cause I defend (the cause of the " most Great Christ ") *to end well* '.

[. . .] Have you read Jean Lacroix' remarkable article in *Esprit* (January, I think) on modern atheism ? He and I are thinking and saying exactly the same thing ; and yet he cannot have read *Le Cœur du problème*.[3] Nothing is more heartening than such convergence.

I have booked a passage in the *Flandre* for June 4th. [. . .] I am proposing to stay no more than three months, but I rather think that I am starting the precedent of an annual return financed by the Foundation. [. . .] It would, in fact, be useful for the Foundation itself if every year (so long as years remain to me) I renewed contact with people in Europe.

(To J. T. de C.)   *New York, 5 April, 1954*

I am putting the finishing touches to a short new piece on Man, which it might, I think, be interesting to publish A.M.D.G.,[4]

---

[1] The residence of his immediate superior in France.
[2] The Louvain theologian and ' missiologue '.
[3] Subsequently published in *L'Avenir de l'homme*, 1959.
[4] *Ad majorem Dei gloriam*—to the greater glory of God—the motto chosen by St. Ignatius for the Society of Jesus.

but which has a good chance, like the earlier, of never seeing the light, at least in my lifetime.[1]

Just recently I met my English fellow-Jesuit, Fr. D'Arcy, and with him—I mean, at the same ' *party* '—Denis de Rougemont, with whom I got on very well indeed. He lives at Ferney, and has a great regard for the social and commercial talents of our great-uncle.[2] Did you know that after starting his stocking (silk stocking ?) factory, M. de Voltaire graciously sent a pair to the Duchesse de Choiseul, asking her to wear them often and show them off nicely ?

Père Teilhard left for Europe at the beginning of June. His stay in France was tiring and disappointing. He was invited to the ' Centre catholique des Intellectuels français ' to give a purely scientific lecture on Africa and human origins. He readily consented, and a large audience came to hear him.

He appeared again in the hall of the ' Sociétés Savantes '. Tall and upright, as he always was, he spoke with calm assurance and authority. The lecture was over-publicised in the press. The next days brought crowds of visitors and requests for interviews. Père Teilhard found this friendly enthusiasm moving, but also embarrassing and rather overpowering.

He left Paris for New York at the beginning of August. He

[1] The reference is presumably to his *Les Singularités de l'espèce humaine*, which was published posthumously in the *Annales de paléontologie* (vol. XII, 1955) and later included in *L'Apparition de l'homme*, ch. 17.

[2] This branch of the Teilhard de Chardin family is descended directly from a niece of Voltaire's. This was Madame Mignot, née Arouet, a daughter of his sister. Madame Mignot had two daughters : the elder became Madame Denis and the younger, Marie-Élisabeth, married Nicolas de Dompierre de Fontaine. The latter owned Hornoy, an estate near Amiens in Picardy, and this name was in time added to their surname. Among Voltaire's correspondence we find letters addressed to ' *his* dear Picardians '. In 1875 Emmanuel Teilhard de Chardin married Berthe de Dompierre d'Hornoy. They had eleven children, of whom Pierre was the fourth.

may well have thought it was for the last time, for he was quite alive to the constant threat of his heart trouble.

Back in the United States, he found himself sunk in deep depression, which can only be guessed at in his letters. He reacted with his usual energy, which he drew not so much from his temperament as from the vigour of his faith.

29 August, 1954

[. . .] So here I am back again, with a new and rather enigmatic year to face. In order to be ready for any eventuality I have begun by making a week's retreat—which will, I hope, have brought me closer to Him who every day is ' coming closer ' and of whom, if I am to end well, I have every day a greater need.

Above all, I have been trying to sharpen my perception, and to intensify in myself the presence of what I call the ' Christic '. I shall probably devote one of my next essays to this subject. [. . .]

Let me have many of your prayers—I am doing the same for you.

New York, 10 October, 1954

I feel that I am rather marking time at the moment, either because I still have ' anxieties '—which doesn't make for intellectual vitality—or because the subject I have in the end decided to deal with in a paper for the W.G. Foundation (' The antiquity and significance of human culture ') is not really my subject ; so that, to introduce what I really want to say, I am driven to a certain amount of mental acrobatics. Even so, I think that I have managed to strike out something of a new line, which is always heartening.[1]

[. . .] Three days ago, I lunched with Fejos and Julian Huxley,

[1] This was published posthumously : *The Antiquity and Expansion of human Culture*, University of Chicago Press, 1956.

whom I was delighted to see again, friendlier than ever. We are
to meet again for three whole days at the end of the month, at the
Columbia University symposium, in a sort of 'Pontigny' [1] in
the country.

Pray for me to the Lord, that He may allow me to 'keep in
form': I need to so badly if I am to persevere to the end in doing
all I can to bring about the coming of His Kingdom as I see it in
my dreams. I mean the 'implosive' encounter in the human
consciousness of the 'ultra-human' and the 'Christic' impulses—
or, as I often express it, of the Forward and the Upward.[2] I am
more and more convinced—judging from my own infinitesimal
experience—that this process is indeed possible, and is actually in
operation, and that it will psychologically transfigure the world
of tomorrow.

New York, 30 October, 1954

This week brought me an 'extra', in the form of a three-day
symposium-'retreat' in the country to mark the bicentenary of
Columbia University. There were about seventy of us, in a
wonderful countryside, about two hours from New York. The
place has been given to Columbia University by the Harrimans
to try out as a conference centre. It lies in the outlying foothills
of the Catskills, covered just now with fantastic gold and purple
mantling of sycamores. The company was very varied and
representative, ranging from physicists like Niels Bohr to poets
like MacLeish, via naturalist-philosophers like Julian Huxley and

---

[1] The 'decades' at Pontigny, the secularised abbey in Burgundy, had been
started by Paul Desjardins in the period between the two wars. They brought
together, from time to time, eminent French and foreign writers, scientists
and scholars, for informal discussion.

[2] The Forward : the progress of mankind by 'convergence'. The Upward : the spiritual ascent of mankind towards Christ, in whom it will find
its completion and consummation, when, in St. Paul's words, God will be
' all in all '.

theologians like Van Dusen (leader, with Niebuhr, of the new American Protestant movement).

The subject for discussion was the unity of human knowledge. In my section a deep, and vital, ' cleavage plane ' became apparent between the humanists and scientists, which turned ultimately, as I said at the last meeting, on the new Galileo question : Is man still moving biologically upon himself? [1] With Huxley and the majority of the scientists, I, of course, vigorously attacked the immobilist position taken up, alas, by the more Christian-thinking members of the section, such as Gilson, Malik (Lebanese representative at the League of Nations [2]), Battaglia, lay rector of the University of Bologna, and even Van Dusen. Seeing the conflict (which I had long been aware of) brought out into the open and discussed as a living problem, clarified my ideas and confirmed me in my attitude. It has since come back to me from various quarters that my evidence heartened a good many of those who took part. During the conference I initiated a number of interesting contacts. I was greatly taken by Van Dusen, in spite of some traces of Barthian pessimism, and I expect our paths will cross again. I saw much more clearly, too, just where to direct one's effort if the neo-humanism on which, I am convinced, our future salvation depends,[3] is to be given a finally explicit form.

(To J. T. de C.)   *New York, 25 November, 1954*

[. . .] It has been a quiet month here, as far as my own affairs are concerned, apart from three days, from the 27th to the 30th of October, at Arden House for Columbia University's bicentenary Symposium. Arden House is a sumptuous property belonging to the Harrimans (Union Pacific) entirely built—with a road that

---

[1] Printed in the *Revue des questions scientifiques*, Louvain, 20 October, 1949.
[2] The United Nations.
[3] Père Teilhard wished to show, in all his work, that a new humanism can and must be brought into new life by Christian thought.

cost eight million dollars!—before the first war. It stands on the top of a lofty hill overlooking a lake, in a sea of red and golden sycamores (that's how I saw them when I was there for All Saints')—the luxury of a by-gone age : the family are trying to salve their consciences by making it a sort of 'Royaumont' attached to Columbia University. There were seventy of us there, for three days, looked after perfectly : comfortable bedrooms, galleries, spacious apartments. It was a very mixed gathering : physicists like Niels Bohr and von Neumann, biologists like my friend Julian Huxley, psychologists, linguistic experts [. . .] The subject of the Congress was the unity of human knowledge. But it was not by any means a tower of Babel. It was rather a demon-stration—only to be expected—of a deep 'cleavage plane' between 'scientists' and 'humanists' as they call themselves ; the latter, unlike the former, being either unable or unwilling to entertain the idea of a biological ultra-evolution of the human. In my section especially, the difference of opinion was serious if friendly ; and I wound up by recalling the case of Galileo (?). Anyway, it was most interesting and gay and really went with a swing. Columbia is quite a place. At the moment I am busy with reports for the international 'talks' planned by the W.G. Foundation for 1955 and 1956. This serves the useful purpose of making me clarify some of my ideas ; all the same, I would like to have a chance of doing some work in the field, even if not so far away as Africa. However, I have nothing definite in view yet.

New York, 12 December, 1954

I was more than interested yesterday to read in *Time* a long article on the scheme—this time really international (Russia is co-operat-ing)—for a geo-physical year in 1957, to develop a fuller scientific 'awareness' of the globe. As an effort for the spiritual unification of man, it is still terribly superficial,[1] but it is the first step, a finger at least, you might say, on the gear-lever of unification ; and I am deeply moved by this great concerted movement in which for the first time in millions of years, a unanimous gesture—unanimous in orientation—will reach out to the ends of the earth : ' Year 1 of the Noosphere '.

Apart from other things, I have been turning over in my mind this last week the idea of writing a note on the awakening— already beginning to dawn—of new ' senses ' at the heart of the human consciousness : the sense of convergence (towards a thought-out co-consciousness) ; the sense of consistency (indestructibility, ' immortality ' of the co-thought-out thing) ; the sense of confluence (towards a super-ego—not in the ghastly Freudian sense : we need a new word). There I believe we have a phenomenon of real importance, an idea, too, of real importance —viz. that the human psyche comes up against thresholds that it has to cross, that it changes, becomes richer and more trenchant with the passage of time. I would like to pin-point that more exactly yet again.

Years before, Père Teilhard had disclosed these new senses, and put forward a new proof of the ' immortality of the soul ', by showing that spirit is the supreme consistency and that immortality is personal, since the universe is personal in structure :

' Following H. Poincaré, many intelligent people, either in deference to fashionable agnosticism or misled by what they take to be stoicism or sublime unselfishness, think that they can accept without flinching the idea that thought on earth will last only for a

---

[1] No-one has emphasised more strongly than Père Teilhard the necessity of spiritual progress (in the general sense of progress of the spirit : noosphere), understood not merely as a progress in technique but as a *total* progress. The amazing achievements of modern science serve only to underline the need for this ' soul-supplement ', the need, that is, for universal moral progress—which Bergson had already noted—in the new world era we are moving into.

moment, and that we should be ready to give everything for that one moment ; it is " a flash in the night ". We believe that those who think so are deceiving themselves ; they have never worked out the full significance of the phrase " the total death of the universe ". Without realising it, we believe, they flinch from probing the full import of the words they are using. They imagine that some trace will remain of this " flash", something will be retained in some consciousness, in some memory, in some glance. . . . But it is just this hope that we must abandon if we are to give full weight to the idea (probably as absurd as the idea of non-being) of absolute death. No, we cannot admit even that hope—it would still mean everything for the universe just for one moment to have entranced eyes that will never be closed : there would be, all around us, the utter blackness of night, allowing nothing of what we have understood, or made our own, to filter through for anyone. But in that case why bother? Why follow obediently the lead of evolution? Supreme disinterestedness? But there is no virtue in self-sacrifice when no higher interest is at stake. A universe which continued to function, to work, in conscious anticipation of absolute death, would be an absurd world, a monster of the mind, a veritable chimaera. Thus, since the world is before our eyes, " hic et nunc", as a vast activity, developing continually with the assurance of power, there can be no doubt that it is capable of nourishing indefinitely in those who are born of it, a continually more critical, more demanding and more refined appetite for living ; that it contains within itself the guarantee of ultimate success. As soon as the universe admits thought within itself, it can no longer be merely temporary nor can there be limits to its evolution. It must, from its very structure, progress into the absolute. Hence whatever appearance of instability we may find in life, and however impressed we may be by its strict attachment to the spatial dimensions that delimit it and the forces that disintegrate it, one thing above all is certain (because it is as certain as the world itself) : namely, that Spirit always will, as it

always has, make sport of every sort of determinism and chance.
It represents the indestructible portion of the universe.' (L'Esprit
de la terre.)

(To J. T. de C.) New York, *8 January, 1955*

[. . .] No particular news, so far as I am concerned. Most of
my time in December was spent in writing (or in finishing the
writing of) two papers : one for my 'personal archives', the
other for the Foundation's Symposium in June. Did I tell you
that the '*tycoon*' Wenner-Gren has a scheme for establishing
another Foundation (international this time) with an international
committee too, of which I shall be a member ? It's a pity that
I'm beginning to be no longer young enough to take advantage
of the freedom of movement I shall have. Meanwhile I am
trying through a different channel from the one I tried last July
to get the type of visa that I can use for 'commuting' between
France and the United States. Not an easy business. Yesterday
I lunched at Lagarde's, who still seems really well dug in here.
We were to have been tête à tête, but in fact two consuls (Denver and Detroit) who were passing through turned up, which let
loose the sort of conversation in which I had to listen, not without
a certain amount of amusement, to all the latest gossip from the
Quai d'Orsay. The Denver consul told us about the 'uranium
fever' raging in Utah and Colorado : children armed with little
Geiger counters staking out little '*claims*' which they sell for a
few dollars to collectors who, as soon as they have a large enough
area, form a limited company without even bothering to take
any samples or have them analysed. There have been a few
sensational successes, but mostly it's a monumental swindle.

(To the Abbé Breuil)   *New York, 8 January, 1955*

My dear old friend,

I find it hard to forgive myself for not having answered your autumn letter, even when the New Year was coming upon us. Time goes by, and for six months there has been nothing of real importance in my existence. Not that this has prevented me from thinking of you or from having wished you in my heart a happy and fruitful New Year. The shadows are growing longer—and thicker—around us. My one great prayer (and I include in it all whom I love) is to 'end well'.[1] One way or another, I mean my death to 'seal' that for which I have always lived.

I suppose you are still busy all the time with your writing. Happy man, to have a definite task before you. For my part, I am still having an interesting life, but no longer sufficiently rooted 'in the field'. But at least I am rooted in the W.G. Foundation. Fejos calls on me increasingly in the preparation of his symposiums. There is talk, too, of a new 'Foundation', in which I would be one of the '*trustees*'. What leaves me psychologically at rather a loose end at present is having no plan in view for a (constructive) expedition. Everything is going so well in Africa that I have no reason for the moment to go to Joh'burg again.

---

[1] In an earlier letter Père Teilhard had written to his friend : ' I can understand that you should wish for another ten years, and I pray the Lord to grant them to you. But however you look at it, you have already succeeded in incorporating the essence of your vision and work in the definitive current of human thought. That reflection must bring you a great peace.'

(To Count Henri Bégouën [1])   *New York, 9 January, 1955*

My dear friend,

A letter from Max, which came yesterday, told me that you have been ill again, but that you have once again got over it. With the New Year here again I feel that I must send you my best wishes and the assurance of my constant affection. Your life has been a long witness to the truth—a long affirmation of faith, too, in the fundamental greatness of man and of the world. I think that that constancy and that faith may well arouse in you an immense trust in what awaits us beyond the boundary of our life here : trust—complete and inexhaustible—in the great movement of 'being' which has made us and carries us along : that is the only attitude of which we can be sure that it is never deceived and never deceives us. What a wonderful and irreplacable function Christianity performs, in developing this trust until it reaches the point where a 'love' of evolution is psychologically possible! [2]

There is not much to tell you about my own life. I would very much like to be able to go back to Africa.[3] Meanwhile,

[1] On whose property in Ariège some important prehistoric finds were discovered by his sons (the Cave of the Three Brothers and Tuc d'Audoubert : clay bisons). He was Professor of Prehistory at the University of Toulouse, director of prehistoric antiquities of the Midi and curator of the Museum of Natural History at Toulouse.

[2] All Père Teilhard's effort, as scientist and as religious thinker, had been directed towards helping the men of his time to rediscover the idea of the Creation, the work of God, in the evolving universe presented to us by modern science. 'A God who brings to birth, in the heart of things, the successive stages of His work.' This creative activity, he adds, is 'neither less essential, nor less universal, nor, above all, less intimate.' (*Vision du passé*, ch. 5, note 1.)

[3] The 'eternal pilgrim' of science, Père Teilhard was entertaining even more distant objectives. 'One spot which would, for various reasons, tempt me at the moment, namely Formosa (!), has the disadvantage of having sud-

and for want of being able to do enough practical work, I am busy writing as usual. [. . .]

I remain on perfectly friendly terms with my Order.

Devotedly, in deep and constant friendship.

Some time in January, Père Teilhard was invited to take part in a conference at the Sorbonne on present-day problems in palæontology. Fearing that the U.S. Government might, as on the occasion of his last voyage, refuse him a permanent visa (which might prevent his return to America) he was unable to send a definite acceptance to his friend and colleague, Professor Jean Piveteau.

'*Just in case he may be able to use it, I have sent him a written communication: a defence of the idea of orientation (orthogenesis)*[1] *—which does not mean finality—in palæontology : an old idea of mine that still seems to me to be sound.*'

'*That task done : I have gone back to the new draft of the "Christic"; but here I am still finding some difficulty in expressing my view of the subject in such a way as to bring out what is original or re-thought in it, without simply re-casting "Le Milieu divin" or the "Cœur de la matière." In the end : this third draft may perhaps emphasise the treatment of it as energy, at the expense of, but without suppressing, the mysticism of "Le Milieu divin" and the psychology of the "Cœur de la matière". I am still feeling my way.*' (*To M. T.-C., 29 January, 1955.*)

When the Congress met, Père Teilhard had just died.

'*On 12 April last, the International Palæontological Congress, meeting in Paris, had just received an apology for his absence from*

---

denly become "incandescent". But for want of anything better, I am thinking of making another Californian trip this summer.' (To his brother, 22 February, 1955).

[1] Directed transformation. Cf. 'Une Défense de l'orthogenèse', *La Vision du passé*, ch. 21.

its sittings from Pierre Teilhard de Chardin. In the afternoon the delegates were shocked and distressed to learn that Père Teilhard had just died suddenly from an embolism which had struck him down on the evening of Easter Sunday in New York.

'*Teilhard de Chardin was a true scholar, lovingly devoted— with a combination of passion, rigour and technical accomplishment —to investigating the secrets of the earth and of life. His competence was real and far-reaching; his experience vast; his judgment piercing and subtle; his authority weighty. We recall how on more than one occasion during the 1948 International Zoological Congress in Paris, when the delegates assembled from all four corners of the world were discussing some thorny palæontological problem, they would turn respectfully to the great Jesuit: " What does Teilhard think ? "*' (E. Boné, '*Revue des questions scientifiques*', Louvain, 20 January, 1956.)

The same writer sums up Père Teilhard's influence in the world of science:

'*His " presence " in the scientific world, his professional authority, his technical competence allied to his open and generous friendliness, and with it all his transparent and wholehearted faith, could not fail to make a deep impression. He did a great deal to help a whole generation undermined by scientism to listen to the message of faith. There was no untimely proselytising nor indiscreet zeal, but Teilhard, simply by what he was, by the integrity of his scientific effort and the sincerity of his religious belief, lit the flame of hope in the modern world, in academies, universities, laboratories, in the men of today who bear the mark of progress, of developments in organisation, or of the machineage: the hope of reconciling Christian thought with the claims of research and the autonomy of science. . . .*' (Ibid.)

New York, 1 April, 1955

I have just sent back to Masson [1] the page-proofs (passed for press) of my paper for the *Annales de paléontologie*.[2] It has come out well and I don't think its appearance will cause the least disturbance [. . .] Where human truth is concerned, the Christian has a sacred duty to *search* and to communicate what he finds to the *professionals* and on a professional level. [. . .] Bordering on the same field, I have recently sent to the P.R. six pages on *Research, Work and Adoration*. In this I point out that it is impossible for a priest to be in the laboratory (or the factory) without being obliged to reconcile Christian faith in the supernatural and the new 'humanistic' faith in an ultra-human,[3] so that they form a single energising force within him.

In this last essay, Père Teilhard suggested that a special training for priests engaged in scientific research, as for worker-priests,[4] would equip them to penetrate as Christians the thought and human activities of a new age.

He hardly expected to be listened to immediately, 'but once the idea has been launched,' he said, 'it will gather momentum: what we have to do is to broadcast the seed'.

When a heart attack struck him down a few days after he had written those words,[5] this great broadcaster of ideas, who had the

[1] The Paris publisher.
[2] 'Les Singularités de l'espèce humaine'.
[3] The future developments of mankind (nothing in common with Nietzsche's super-man).
[4] These suggestions followed the same lines as the measures later adopted for the worker-priests by the ecclesiastical authorities.
[5] On 10 April. A little while before, when meeting his cousin Jean de Lagarde, he had said, 'I should like to die on the day of the Resurrection.' (Letter from M. de Lagarde to Père Teilhard's brother Joseph, 22 April, 1955.)

'*impatience of a prophet*'[1] *but had pledged himself to patience, was clinging to the firm hope that his effort and example would bear fruit. The '*glorious resonance he dreamed of for all men, vibrating between the adoration of the Upward and the faith of the Forward*', *had made up the harmony of his life. The passion to serve had been his torment. He confessed as much, in the days when he was alone in his solitude, laying the foundations of his thought, in words that have not lost their vigour :*

'The man with a passionate sense of the divine *milieu* cannot bear to find things about him obscure, tepid and empty which should be full and vibrant with God. He is paralysed by the thought of the numberless spirits which are linked to his in the unity of the same world, but are not yet fully kindled by the flame of the divine Presence. He had thought for a time that he had only to stretch out his *own* hand in order to touch God to the measure of his desires. He now sees that the only human embrace capable of worthily enfolding the divine is that of all men opening their arms to call down and welcome the Fire. The only subject ultimately capable of mystical transfiguration is the whole group of mankind forming a single body and a single soul in charity.'

(*Le Milieu divin*, pp. 138–9.)

---

[1] The phrase is Étienne Borne's : 'Such was the genius of Père Teilhard, who, from positive learning and the impatience of a prophet, made one great indivisible whole'. ('Un Grand Penseur religieux', *Le Monde*, 13 April, 1955.)

INDEX

INDEX

Abyssinia, *see* Ethiopia
Académie des Sciences, 304
Afar, the (Ethiopia), 148
Aksu, 185-6
Ala-Shan (Mts.), 79, 82, 89
Albuquerque (New Mexico), 329
America, United States of, and
    Americans, 106, 107, 165,
    167, 199-200, 262, 270-86
    pass., 296-7, 339
Anderson, Dr., 31, 138
Andrews (of the Natural History
    Museum, N.Y.), 125, 165,
    167, 168
Annam, 125
Aouache, the (Ethiopia), 149
Aragonnès, Claude, *see* Teillard-
    Chambon
Arakan-Yoma (Mts.) (Burma),
    236, 237
Araoui (Ethiopia), 147, 148
Arbous-Ula (Mts.), 83, 94-5
Argentina, 316, 345
Ascension Island, 341
Australopithecae, 305-11 *pass.*, 323
Auvergne, 19, 77, 90, 117, 141,
    147, 208, 238, 270, 288, 346

Balla (Ethiopia), 147
Bandoeng, 220, 221, 239
Barbour, Dr. George, 31, 163,
    203, 304-5, 306
Bardac, 223, 241, 249, 288, 331

Batavia, 218, 221, 239
Battaglia, 354
Béchamp, 204
Bégouën, Henri, 360
Bégouën, Max and Simone : let-
    ters from Chardin, 149, 161,
    163, 195, 200, 202, 209, 213,
    232, 238, 239, 240, 256, 262,
    266, 274, 295
Berkeley (California), 244, 328,
    329, 330-2
Berthelot, Admiral, 196
Black, Dr. Davidson (director of
    the Geological Service of the
    Chinese University), 31, 53,
    138, 152, 170, 198, 201-2
Blanc, Alberto, 300
Blue River, 74
Bodet, Torrès (director of
    UNESCO), 303
Bogdo Ula (Mts.), 180, 184
Bohr, Niels, 353, 355
Bolsheviks, *see* Communists
Bombay, 210
Boné, E., 361-2
Borne, É., 364
Boule, Marcellin (of the Natural
    History Museum, Paris), 26,
    83, 138, 242, 287
Bréhat, 267
Brémond, Henri, 21
Breuil, Abbé, 32, 53, 167, 189,
    195, 196, 205, 211, 282, 285,
    287, 292, 309 ; *and see over*

367

Printed in the United States
121670LV00005BA/318/A

9 780548 387139